ISBN 13: 978-1986153270
ISBN 10: 1986153274

Brittney Andrews, Illustrator
Rachel Raimondi, Editor
Catherine Godlewsky, Writer and Editing Assistant
Miranda Dennis and Jessica Evans, Copy Editors
AnnMarie Gervasio and John Druga, Proofreaders
Michael Del Purgatorio, Graphic Designer

Dedication and Appreciation

When I embarked upon my book publishing journey, I set out to inspire the next generation of STEM women, while also shining a spotlight on academic institutions with a proud history of educating STEM women, as well as their STEM alumnae. Because of this, I'm dedicating "Her STEM Career" to STEM women, past, present and future as well as to colleges for women.

Women's colleges were created during a time when it was taboo to educate women, and because many of these colleges included studies in mathematics and science, they increased the number of women in these fields. Today, women's colleges continue to remain relevant and are an effective resource for educating the next generation of STEM women. The stories found within are testament to this phenomenon.

To show my appreciation for these academic institutions (and their forward-thinking founders), I've included a daisy chain, symbolic to many of the women's colleges. As an alumna, I know that without the generosity and support from my alma mater, I never would have earned my undergraduate degree in biology. A similar sentiment is shared by many of my sisters!

I'm also most appreciative to the many individuals involved in the "HerSTEM Career" book project. From the STEM women who graciously shared their stories, to the individuals contributing behind the scenes, ensuring the book became a reality: AnnMarie Gervasio, Brittney Andrews, Catherine Godlewsky, Carolyn Fannon, Gretchen Van Ness, Jessica Evans, John Druga, Kylie Jungles, Lauren Cooper, Michael Del Purgatorio, Miranda Dennis, Priya Paulraj and Rachel Raimondi.

Table of Contents

The Story Behind the Book

Author Diane Propsner is a STEM woman herself. Initially interested in honeybees and their importance as commercial pollinators, she studied biology and graduated from a women's college in Pennsylvania with a Bachelors of Arts degree. Today, her interests have expanded to also include bats and birds. Professionally, Diane spent the majority of her 35-plus year career in the life sciences within recruiting and/or sales roles and benefited from her undergraduate STEM degree. In her current position, she applies her chemistry and microbiology knowledge as a sales representative for a company that provides analytical testing services to various FDA-regulated industries. Diane's experiences with both STEM and with women's colleges inspired her blog, "Advantages of a Women's College," which was the starting place for the book.

> **As Diane expected, the women's colleges were happy to help celebrate women in STEM, and they worked with her to find other women excited about inspiring the next generation of STEM women.**

The idea for this book began in 2015 when Kylie Jungles, a senior biology student at St. Mary's College, contacted Diane about an event Kylie was organizing at her school. Kylie explained that many of her fellow science majors knew they could become doctors or go into the medical field, but that many were unaware of the other opportunities available to them. Thus, Kylie's event would feature STEM women as guest speakers to demonstrate the many ways science can lead to a successful career.

Unfortunately, Diane was unable to attend the event, but she recommended that Kylie write down the speakers' stories and put them together into a booklet. That way, even those who couldn't come to the event would be able to be inspired by the women who made their careers in science.

> **Kylie explained that many of her fellow science majors knew that they could be doctors or go into the medical field, but that many were unaware of the other opportunities available to them.**

As Kylie was busy applying to medical schools, she wasn't able to put together the booklet, but the idea kept coming back to Diane. Why not put together an inspirational book to show women and

girls what they could do with science? Soon, Diane decided to write this book herself, and she would write it about not just science, but all of STEM.

....

Flynn and Diane used the strong solidarity among STEM women from women's colleges to find more stories for this book.

....

Diane began by contacting the women's colleges she had worked with as a blogger to ask if they had any contact information she could use to find successful STEM women who would be willing to share their stories. As Diane expected, the women's colleges were happy to help celebrate women in STEM, and the colleges worked with her to find other women excited about inspiring the next generation of STEM women.

Another great resource for Diane was Flynn Vickowski, a 2014 graduate of Mount Holyoke College. Flynn is an aspiring zoo curator. In between her time studying Andean bears and working with zoos around the word, Flynn found time to share her network of STEM women with Diane. Flynn helped Diane find not only Mount Holyoke alumnae, but also alumnae from other women's colleges. Flynn and Diane used the strong solidarity among STEM women from women's colleges to find more stories for this book. Flynn's story will be included in Book Two.

....

"I wish I had this book as a resource when I was deciding upon my educational and career path back in high school. Although the number of young women pursuing STEM fields has greatly increased over the years, there is still tremendous room for the growth of women in STEM. I feel that so many young women today have a passion for science and other STEM fields, yet they are still unaware of the myriad of career options in these fields."

....

With this assistance, Diane did not have to search far, as so many successful women were happy to donate their time and stories to her project. She began collecting the stories on her own, working on the book as a part-time project, but soon Diane realized that she needed more time to create the book she wanted. When a recruiting project ended, she began to work on the book full time and started to identify individuals who would help make her book the best it could be. (At the end of this chapter you'll meet the book's editor, illustrator, and writer.)

Soon her idea for a small science-oriented booklet from a single event had grown into the book you're reading. Diane found more than 70 women with successful and interesting careers who were excited about sharing their stories, and she began to collaborate with them individually. Each woman wrote her own story and then Diane and her team reviewed the stories, asked questions and helped every story shine.

Kylie, who has stayed up to date with the project, is excited about the book and what it shows about STEM women. She says, "I wish I had this book as a resource when I was deciding upon my educational and career path back in high school. Although the number of young women pursuing STEM fields has greatly increased over the years, there is still tremendous room for the growth of women in STEM. I feel that so many young women today have a passion for science and other STEM fields, yet they are still unaware of the myriad of career options in these fields." Kylie is currently pursuing her dream of becoming a physician at Rush Medical College.

Diane found more than 70 women with successful and interesting careers who were excited about sharing their stories, and she began to collaborate with them individually.

Diane and her team loved collaborating with women whose lives show the excitement of STEM. Working on this project reminded Diane how much fun it is to collaborate with other STEM women, and she hopes that this collaborative effort will show you how welcoming, interesting and satisfying a career in STEM can be.

Meet the, Editor, Illustrator and Writer

"Her STEM Career" is a collaborative endeavor under the leadership of Diane Propsner. In addition to those already mentioned, below you'll meet Rachel Raimondi (Editor), Brittney Andrews (Illustrator), and Catherine Godlewsky (Writer and Editing Assistant).

Rachel Raimondi

Editor

Rachel Raimondi was born and raised in Putnam County, New York. She freelance edits both privately and for two fiction/nonfiction publishers and an academic consulting company. She received her bachelor's degree in English from the State University of New York at New Paltz and her master's degree in publishing from Pace University.

Rachel also enjoys writing. She has published several short stories and a young adult novel. "A Week in the Life of Us" follows a group of girls' first week as high school freshmen, the ups and downs, ins and outs and sometimes even the sideways. She is currently working on a humorous memoir on the trials and tribulations of quitting smoking and two screenplays.

In addition to reading for pleasure (currently working through "A Games of Thrones") and her writing, Rachel also enjoys hiking in national (Acadia!) and state (Fahnestock!) parks and scenic drives all over the United States, most recently through Utah, Arizona, Colorado and New Mexico.

Brittney Andrews

Illustrator

Brittney Andrews graduated from Indiana University Bloomington with a Bachelor of Science in Secondary Education. Today, she is a high school physics and environmental science teacher in Bloomfield, Indiana, who has a passion for STEM, art and dogs.

She brings all three of these aspects together on her Etsy shop, Kit Atlas, where she sells custom magnets that feature her own drawings; each magnet is a unique design, and is completely constructed by Brittney. Often, she draws dogs, inspired by her own two rescue pups Pip and Ollie, but she also specializes in portraits.

Brittney, as an environmental science teacher, is also dedicated to sustainability, so she uses repurposed cardboard to make the backs of her magnets and does not use plastic in her order packaging.

During her free time, she loves hiking outdoors with her husband, Neal, and her dogs. She is also an avid traveler and has a goal of visiting every rainforest in the world.

Using her artistic skills, Brittney created all the portrait sketches included in "Her STEM Career" and she can't wait to see what exciting things the next generation of STEM women will achieve.

Catherine Godlewsky

Writer and Editing Assistant

Catherine Godlewsky is a recent graduate of Centenary University in New Jersey, where she was a part of the Presidential Scholars program and International English Honor Society while earning her Bachelor of Arts. Catherine has been writing and editing since 2013, and she has worked in the fields of academic writing, journalism and business writing.

In addition to writing and editing, Catherine loves to talk about writing. During her undergraduate degree, she worked at Centenary University's writing center as a writing consultant, which means that she tutors undergraduate and graduate students. Catherine enjoyed seeing the students who visit the center improve, and she still participates in writing center pedagogy by attending conferences.

For "Her STEM Career," Catherine wrote Chapter One, "The Story Behind the Book" section, and the introduction to Chapter Two. She also assisted with editing and proofreading the manuscript.

Catherine is enjoying her current writing work, and hopes to further her education by attending graduate school.

Chapter One

You & STEM

STEM & How It Impacts Our Lives

When scientists, educators or business people talk about STEM, they are not talking about the stalk beneath a flower. STEM is an acronym that stands for science, technology, engineering and mathematics (or math). These four parts of STEM all come together to form a network of knowledge that clever people use to solve problems every day, thus improving things on planet earth.

Sometimes, STEM helps us solve big problems, like natural disasters. Often the best STEM solutions to these big problems are to prevent them from happening, as is the case with geographic information systems, often abbreviated as GIS. Geographic information systems are computers that can find, store and analyze information about the earth's surface.

Although geographic information systems might not seem related to big disasters, scientists can use the information stored there to predict earthquakes or volcanoes. The geographic information system can also make really cool maps that show the earth's surface layer by layer as well as place by place. This means that scientists can be aware of what's going on under the earth, while also checking up on pollution hotspots like gas stations or factories.

STEM is an acronym that stands for science, technology, engineering and mathematics (or math).

However, often we forget that STEM is not just for emergencies or disasters, but it also surrounds us every day. Every time you text a friend, you are using an intricate and amazing device that is capable of instant communication, another STEM contribution. All your social media apps and streaming TV services would all be impossible without the hard work of many STEM professionals. When you plug in your cellphone so it can charge, the electricity you are using comes to you courtesy of someone working in STEM.

And STEM is not just found in the ways we communicate with each other. Every time you travel by car, plane or rail, you are using the invention of someone who understood how to use STEM to make our travel faster, easier and more comfortable. Every time you heat up a snack in the microwave, you are not only using a STEM invention to warm your food, but you are also using energy provided to your house by a whole system of STEM inventions. Even ordinary household items are really STEM triumphs in disguise — have you ever thought about how many tries it must have taken to invent plastic wrap?

Some things seem so familiar that you forget to ask how they are made or done. When you turn on a light switch, you just assume that the light will go on, and when you buy lip gloss, you just assume that it will be safe to use. However, electric plants, as we've mentioned, as well as many new, green forms of energy would not be possible without STEM. Your lip gloss, as well as your foundation, mascara, eyeshadow and every other kind of beauty product, from shampoo to nail polish, is made by people working in STEM.

Every time you text a friend, you are using an intricate and amazing device that is capable of instant communication, another STEM contribution. All your social media apps and streaming TV services would all be impossible without the hard work of many STEM professionals. When you plug in your cellphone so it can charge, the electricity you are using comes to you courtesy of someone working in STEM.

When you are ill or hurt, you rely on medicine to help you get better. Everything from bandages, contacts or allergy medicine, to a wheelchair or prosthetic, is made by people in the medical industry, which is a part of STEM. The physicians, nurses, physical therapists, dentists, audiologists, optometrists, pharmacists and other health care professionals who can help you as well as the tools that they use, are all a part of STEM.

Often we forget how important STEM can be because we think of it only as big inventions made by famous people, but really, STEM is any clever and useful idea thought of by anyone.

Try, just for a minute, to imagine how life would be without STEM's important inventions. Think back to early America when indoor plumbing was a luxury, candles were used for indoor light and many relied on horse and carriage for transportation. And more recently, think about when cellphones and the internet were not available. Life would be pretty difficult, wouldn't it? It certainly would not be as easy and enjoyable as it is now.

One of the most amazing things about STEM is that it is all around us. Often we forget how important STEM can be because we think of it only as big inventions made by famous people, but really, STEM is any clever and useful idea thought of by anyone. So, if you have an idea of how to do something better, you are already on your way to working in STEM.

Breaking Down STEM

STEM is becoming more and more interdisciplinary. As the blending of STEM subjects continues, it's sometimes harder to see where each category ends and the next begins.

For example, consider your cellphone, which is a product of advances in STEM. We could say it was built by science because it is scientific experiments that tell us what materials will be safe for us and most effective for the phone. It is a part of technology because it is an advanced design for a useful object, but it is also a part of engineering because this advanced design is the result of the engineers who designed and built it. Lastly, your cellphone is also built by mathematics because of the complicated mathematical equations that allow it to encode and decode messages to or from other phones.

Everything that is a part of either science, technology, engineering or mathematics is connected to all of STEM, as research and a scientific way of thinking is needed for each STEM invention.

Consider the many other ways that we can incorporate technology into our everyday lives, such as computer-controlled smart wearables, or wearable tech. Wearable tech can be anything from a smartwatch to smart ski goggles that tell skiers where they are and how fast they are going. Wearable tech can be used to make our lives safer, as in the smart bicycle helmet that has a GPS, a speaker system, mileage counter and an accident-assistance messaging system built into it. Smart clothing is also advancing and becoming more accessible, including sensors that can be fit into a baby's sock so that a parent or guardian can monitor the child from a smartphone. Smart clothing is also used to help people stay healthy while they have fun, as in a shirt that tracks how many swings a golfer takes, a sports bra that measures your heart rate or a belt that monitors your weight. Just like cellphones, this wearable tech is an application of science, technology, engineering and mathematics, and each piece of wearable tech is an example of many different STEM ideas working together.

Another example of STEM subject blending is 3-D printing. You may have seen a 3-D printer in action, and you were probably fascinated by a machine that could make any shape it was told to. These 3-D printers break down the original shape into tiny slices in the form of a computer-aided

design, a digital image or a model. The printer then builds each slice from the bottom up, creating a perfect new object. The printers can use many different materials, too, from plastics to chocolate. Printing in 3-D is science in its materials; technology in its use as a machine, engineering in its design and mathematics in the codes it interprets to print a shape piece by piece. This printing is even a way to connect technology to things we love to use every day, like clothing. Thus, 3-D printing is a great example of the ways that science, technology, engineering and mathematics come together to create a fascinating and useful product.

Thus, everything that is a part of either science, technology, engineering or mathematics is connected to STEM, as research and a scientific way of thinking is needed for each STEM invention.

Science

Within the category of science, there are several divisions. Physical sciences consist of physics, astronomy, chemistry and geology.

Physics studies every kind of motion or change, as this part of science explores how things affect each other. Physics works on a large scale, like our solar system, as well as on a smaller scale, like a cup of hot chocolate getting colder. People who study physics are called physicists, and they can be found working in research labs, hospitals, power plants, the astronaut corps and many other exciting places. Physicists are constantly making discoveries that can tell us more about how the world works, such as discovering how to make grapheme. Grapheme is the thinnest known compound, and the expectation is that it will be able to help batteries keep their charge longer and could even be used to make a flexible television or phone.

Astronomy studies the universe and the changes that happen in it. This, of course, is a giant task, as it involves the entire cosmos rather than just the earth. Astronomers look at galaxies, stars, moons and every other object in space and try to understand how they work. Because there is so much to know about the solar system, astronomers usually concentrate on one area at a time. For example, one astronomer might spend her time observing the ways that planets work and testing her theories about them, while another might use a computer to map out the inside of a star. In the past, astronomers used powerful telescopes to look into the cosmos, but today they can use special digital cameras to collect their data. Astronomers can often be found working in observatories or laboratories around the world, and of course, they also work for space programs.

Chemistry is the study of matter and energy. Matter is the material that things are made of, and it is composed of tiny atoms. Chemists study the structure of these atoms, how they are arranged with other atoms of the same kind to make elements, and how these elements can be mixed

together. Because everything is made up of atoms, chemists can study anything they want to, and their work is useful in every field. Some chemists, called biochemists, work only with living things, while others, called nuclear chemists, study radioactivity and other ways in which nuclear matter works. Some chemists specialize in food, cosmetics or perfumes and other beauty products. Chemists often work in teams to help provide manufacturers, engineers and other scientists the information they need. While performing experiments, chemists often make important discoveries, like finding the liquid crystal molecule that allows flat-screen displays, like those on a phone, computer or TV, to work.

Geology is the study of how the earth was formed, how it changes and the materials that the earth is made of. Geologists learn about volcanoes, landslides, earthquakes and floods, which they call earth processes. They use what they learn about the earth's history to help understand the way the world is now and what its future might be. Geologists not only investigate rocks and minerals, but also resources like water, oil, coal and natural gases. Geologists are interested in how we can use these resources without harming the earth, and a big part of what geologists study today is the changes happening to the land or climate. Some different ways that geologists work are by collecting and interpreting fossils, being part of a team that helps build roads, bridges and tunnels and spending time traveling the world to complete geological surveys.

Another kind of science is the biological sciences, such as medical and veterinary science, zoology, botany and molecular biology.

Medical and veterinary science is the study of how we can use scientific knowledge to help people and animals stay well. This field includes every kind of people or animal doctor or surgeon, as well as nurses, pharmacists, research scientists, nutritionists, physical therapists, public health workers

Physics studies every kind of motion or change, as this part of science explores how things affect each other.

Astronomy studies the universe and the changes that happen in it.

Botany is the study of plants.

Geology is the study of how the earth was formed, how it changes and the materials that the earth is made of.

Medical and veterinary science is the study of how we can use scientific knowledge to help people and animals stay well.

Zoology is the study of animals and the ways that they behave.

Chemistry is the study of matter and energy.

Molecular biology studies the molecules of living things.

and many other jobs. Everyone who works with medical or veterinary science helps someone every day by learning about how bodies work and what to do if something goes wrong. They can diagnose illnesses and treat injuries, and they work hard to alleviate pain and suffering wherever they see it. Medical and veterinary science professionals work all over the world in hospitals and private practices or even by traveling the world looking for new ways to help.

Zoology is the study of animals and the ways they behave. Zoologists are interested in everything that happens to animals, both the ways that they act, live and reproduce and the ways that they interact with other species, including humans. Often, a zoologist will study a single species (like a Sumatran tiger) or a broader animal group (like big cats) because there isn't time for her to know everything about every animal. Zoologists often use geographical information systems to help them map out animal habitats, track migrations and even predict future habitat ranges. Zoologists work hard to help preserve endangered species by helping animals in the wild as well as studying those in zoos or aquariums.

> **Each kind of science makes important contributions to the way we understand the world around us and the ways that we can make the world better for everyone and everything living in it.**

Botany is the study of plants, which is why botanists are sometimes called plant biologists. Botanists study all living plants, from tiny microorganisms to giant trees, and they also learn about the ways that plants affect and are affected by the environment. Many botanists help protect the environment and study the ways that pollution can harm plant life while others find new kinds of plants and their uses. Some botanists even grow whole plants out of a single cell using a special method called tissue culture, or use their knowledge to help develop new kinds of plants. Botanists can work nearly anywhere, at a garden or herbarium, at a zoo, at a medical plant or research lab or even by exploring the world looking for new plants.

Molecular biology is just what it sounds like — biology is the study of living things, and molecular refers to groups of atoms called molecules, so molecular biology studies the molecules of living things. Molecular biologists often study DNA, which is a set of instructions that tells each cell in an organism what it is supposed to do, and they learn about the patterns that allow cells to perform their function. The discoveries made by molecular biologists are essential to work that is done in many other areas of study, including wildlife conservation, medicine, cosmetics and the food industry. Thus, molecular biologists work everywhere from universities to companies (big and small) to government agencies.

In addition to these kinds of science careers, there are others that incorporate strong communication skills with scientific knowledge, like that of a genetic counselor. A genetic counselor is someone who is trained in human genetics and uses her skills to explain genetic disorders or conditions to the people who have them or those at risk. Genetic counselors often work with families to help find solutions for a child with a genetic condition, and counselors will usually work as part of a team of medical professionals. Genetic counselors may work in clinical settings, laboratories, universities and many other places.

All this information explains only a few of the ways that people can work with science. Each kind of science makes important contributions to the way we understand the world around us and the ways we can make the world better for everyone and everything living in it.

Technology

Technology is often thought of as the product of science, math and engineering, but it is actually different from any of them. Technology studies human-made objects (like cars, laptops or solar panels) rather than natural objects (like rocks, plants or living cells). Technology is also more interested in practical applications for big ideas than some of the other sciences, which is why people who work in technology are all about making things.

One of the most important areas of technology is communication-technology. This kind of technology helps us to exchange or store information quickly and accurately and is the reason we have phones, computers, emails, text messages, social media and websites. Because there are so many ways we can make communication easier, there are many different jobs that fall under the communication-technology category.

> **Technology studies human-made objects
> (like cars, laptops or solar panels) rather than
> natural objects (like rocks, plants or living cells).**

A computer programmer contributes to communication technology by writing the code that computers need to work. Computer programmers work with many different computer languages to write codes for things like an app on your phone or a complicated computer operating system. Computer programmers also test the code that they write and correct any errors that may show up as well as create code libraries to help make writing code easier.

Computer programmers often work closely with software developers (also referred to as software engineers), who use their creativity to think of new things to do with a computer or device. Software developers work to understand the things that people need to do with their computers and think of ways that they can develop new software codes or update old software codes to make that possible. For example, have you ever updated your computer, phone or game to a newer version? If so, you have benefited from the ideas and skills of a software developer.

Technology is simply anything that applies science, engineering or mathematics, but it also is a separate way of looking at the world. Technology takes what we learn in other parts of STEM and applies it to everyday life to make the world easier and more fun to live in.

Software testers are essential to the process of developing software, as they troubleshoot and find bugs within new or existing kinds of software. Software testers are essentially trying to outsmart a software program by running tests to find its weaknesses. Once software testers have found the faults within the software, they can point out solutions to the problems. Software testers will often meet with software engineers to discuss the problems they find. Software testers need to document and report every glitch, so they need to have almost perfect concentration and attention to detail. Because every industry needs software that works properly (including banking, social media, finance and health care), software testers are found working for nearly any large or small company, or even the government.

Another job in communication technology is a computer network architect. Computer network architects design and build both local area networks (which link devices that are close to each other, like all the computers in a school or workplace) and wide area networks (which link devices that are not close to each other, like the whole internet). Computer network architects also build intranets, which are like small internets only open to specific people, like employees of the same company. Computer network architects are also responsible for making sure that existing networks and intranets continue to work properly, and for researching technology that could help the networks of the future.

Computer network architects often work with information security analysts, who are the people in charge of making sure that all the information exchanged through networks or stored on computer systems remains safe. Information security analysts use protective software and careful testing to make sure that information is safe from hackers. Information security analysts are always doing more research into the ways that information is at risk and they look for new ways to protect it.

Yet another way to work with communication technology is to become a computer information and research scientist, who thinks of new ways to use existing computer technology or ways to improve it. Computer information and research scientists often think about computers in relation to other fields, such as medicine or business, as they can help people who work in these fields to do their jobs better. In order to improve the ways we use computers, computer information and research scientists work with both hardware (the things you can touch, like a memory stick) and software (a code that tells the hardware what to do) and even invent new computer languages.

Medical technology is used to help humans and animals live healthier and happier lives. People who go into medical technology often have a background in one of the sciences, such as chemistry or biology, but many of the people who help make medical devices are engineers, or even have a degree in medical device engineering.

Improvements in medical technology include things like improved testing for diseases, more comfortable hospital beds or wheelchairs, operating tools that can allow surgeons to be more accurate and help operations be safer, or an X-ray or CT scan machine. Creating the technology required for the medical field requires careful collaboration between medical professionals and technology creators or engineers, which is why medical technology is a great example of how all the different parts of STEM work together to improve our lives.

Construction technology helps us build better things more quickly and efficiently. Some kind of construction technology is used to create every kind of building from skyscrapers and treehouses, to eco-friendly homes that have no impact on the environment. People who work in construction technology may be involved with actually building the structures or they may work on the machines buildings are made with. They may even think of new ways to use materials to build things, such as a new kind of Styrofoam panel that can be used to insulate houses from winds up to 140 miles per hour, is termite resistant and is more eco-friendly than other kinds of insulation.

Communication technology helps us to exchange or store information quickly and accurately.

Medical technology is used to help humans and animals live healthier and happier lives.

Construction technology helps us build better things more quickly and efficiently.

Entertainment technology consists of all the products or services that make fun more fun.

People who work in construction technology also work with computer programs that can visualize buildings in a 3-D model before they are even constructed. They can even use a similar system called Building Information Modeling that collects and stores information about buildings under construction, which can keep all the engineers and designers working on a building up to date on its progress.

Entertainment technology consists of all the products or services that make fun more fun. Some examples of entertainment technology include video games, special effects in movies or games, digital cameras, flat-screen TVs, speakers or even electric guitars or pianos. Everything that your favorite artist uses to record a song and everything that your favorite youtuber uses to upload a video is the result of someone working in entertainment technology. Many people who work in the movie industry, from those who design and build lighting and sound equipment, to those who create CGI effects or work in a recording studio, are also a part of entertainment technology.

One of the most important parts of entertainment technology today is removing barriers to artists' creativity, whether they are musicians using an app to record song ideas, gamers using a new online streaming service, or someone making her debut in the entertainment business. People who work in entertainment technology use science, engineering and mathematics to make life more fun for everyone.

A big part of the technology field today is artificial intelligence (AI). AI is technology that is specially programmed to do things that ordinarily only a human could do, such as learning, reasoning, problem-solving and understanding languages. The people who work in AI seek to develop machines that can do things like play games, answer questions and respond to new situations. There are so many applications of AI that it is almost impossible to see how it will be used in the future, but the people who work in AI know that it has the potential to make our lives easier and more productive than ever before.

Technology is simply anything that applies science, engineering or mathematics, but it also is a separate way of looking at the world. Technology takes what we learn in other parts of STEM and applies it to everyday life to make the world easier and more fun to live in.

Engineering

Engineering uses science and math to solve problems, and engineers are the link between an idea and an invention people can use. Much of what an engineer does involves finding simple and effective ways to make complicated ideas useful. Engineers also are responsible for evaluating which designs are good ones, testing designs and ideas, modifying designs so that they will work better and building the designs themselves. Thus, engineers work in nearly every field and there are more than 200 kinds of engineering.

One kind of engineering is chemical engineering. Chemical engineers work with raw materials, or chemicals, and turn them into things that we use every day. Chemical engineers can make anything from the chemical solutions that we use to clean our homes or clothes, to the dyes we use in our food and drinks, to the medicine we need to be healthy. Chemical engineers also work in the fashion industry by making clothing dyes that will not fade or bleed into other clothes in the wash. Chemical engineers also make the synthetic materials out of which our clothes are made, including nylon, rayon or polyester. They also help develop other materials, like the plastics used in manufacturing. Chemical engineers are responsible for making sure that the products they make do not have a negative effect on the environment, and so many of them are involved in researching and finding solutions for pollution. Chemical engineers usually work in laboratories or offices, but they can also travel to different factories, plants or refineries.

Environmental engineers combine their engineering knowledge with biology and chemistry to find solutions to environmental problems. Often, environmental engineers will work with chemical engineers or soil scientists to find ways to stop and clean up pollution in rivers, lakes, oceans, the soil, the air or anywhere else in the environment. Environmental engineers may do things such as

Chemical engineers work with raw materials, or chemicals, and turn them into things that we use every day.

Environmental engineers combine their engineering knowledge with biology and chemistry to find solutions to environmental problems.

Robotics engineers often use electricity in the way electrical engineers will, but their main focus is on creating robots.

Electrical engineers study anything that uses electricity or power.

Mechanical engineers work to design, build and test machines.

Manufacturing engineers design and operate the systems of production.

Civil engineers design, build, test, oversee and help operate construction projects.

check mercury levels in fish, find ways to clean up oil spills or find new ways to use wind or solar power. Many environmental engineers work within the public health sector, which means they try to make the world a healthier place for everyone. Environmental engineers help invent ways to purify drinking water and live sustainably. Many environmental engineers work as consultants for companies that want to become more sustainable or to decrease their impact on the environment, but they also can work for the government or do research.

Electrical engineers study anything that uses electricity or power. They make sure that we have electricity to power our homes and factories as well as work with all kinds of electronic devices. They can do anything from designing a giant power plant or electrical distribution grid to designing household appliances like a coffee maker or a toaster. Electrical engineers also make circuit cards, which are the electrical brain of a machine or robot. For example, when you send a text, the keys you press are the input that the circuit card processes into a coded message to send to another phone. Because there are so many different kinds of things that use electricity, there are many different kinds of electrical engineers. Some electrical engineers specialize only in computers, while others specialize in the way that electricity is used as a power source. Many electrical engineers also work to help people without electricity by designing things like hand-cranked radios. Electrical engineers can work anywhere from a mine or industrial plant to an office or a lab; they can be found anywhere electricity is used.

Much of what an engineer does involves finding simple and effective ways to make complicated ideas useful. Engineers also are responsible for evaluating which designs are good ones, testing designs and ideas, modifying designs so that they will work better and building the designs themselves.

Robotics engineers often use electricity in the same way as electrical engineers, but their main focus is on creating robots. Robotics engineers design and build robots. These engineers are always looking to invent new robots that can make our lives easier and safer. Robotics engineers design robots that do everything from boring factory work to entering a collapsed building to look for survivors. Thus, robotics engineers need to test their robots to ensure that they are doing the best job possible. They use machine learning, cognitive science and AI to improve robots. Robotics engineers can be found in labs, offices, factories, classrooms and many other places where robots are used or invented.

Mechanical engineers work to design, build and test machines. These engineers identify problems and discover what kind of machine they can build to solve the problem. They build everything from car engines to factory assembly lines to battery-operated toys, and they often use computers

to help them do this. By using advanced computer programs, mechanical engineers can design their machines and even test whether they are likely to work before spending the time and resources necessary to build the machine. Mechanical engineers also design sensors, controllers and remotes that interact with machines. Mechanical engineers often work with a team of other engineers to build a product, and they can work almost anywhere. Many mechanical engineers work in manufacturing, while others do research to discover better ways to make machines.

Manufacturing engineers often work with mechanical engineers, as manufacturing engineers design and operate the systems of production. These systems may include engines, robots, computers and all other kinds of equipment, and manufacturing engineers make sure that these systems are running safely and as efficiently as possible. Thus, a manufacturing engineer will encounter many different kinds of systems, depending on what is being manufactured. For example, she might be working for a company that makes cars, where she would be responsible for making sure that the robotic assembly line is running smoothly and safely. Or, she might find ways to use computer technology to work with chemicals dangerous to humans. Manufacturing engineers can be found working in factories, offices and many other places throughout the manufacturing industry.

Civil engineers design, build, test, oversee and help operate construction projects. Civil engineers often work on large projects, like roads, bridges or airports, and they usually work with a team of builders, other engineers, architects and many others. Civil engineers are often responsible for making sure that construction projects comply with government safety regulations, that they do not have a negative impact on the environment, and that they will not become unsafe over time or after exposure to the elements. For example, some civil engineers (known as water engineers) focus only on the infrastructure required to get clean water to everyone who needs it. Water engineers

Energy engineers work to bring us the energy we need from natural resources as well as sustainable energy sources.

Aerospace engineers are special engineers who make it possible for humans and human-made objects to fly.

Materials engineers explore the uses of the materials available to us as well as look for and develop new materials.

Plastics engineers study the ways that polymers and plastics are made and help build things out of plastic.

Systems engineers use their understanding of engineering to help customers or clients find the best solutions to their individual problems or needs by overseeing an entire project.

Food engineers take raw produce and turn it into the foods you find in a grocery store.

also make sure that sewage and waste water is safely disposed of, and they prepare the infrastructure that guard against floods. Civil engineers can work in offices, at construction sites or many other places. Often, civil engineers will work for the government or for large corporations. Civil engineers sometimes get to travel from project to project, and they love seeing the world through their work.

A food engineer is someone who takes raw produce and turns it into the foods you find in a grocery store. Food engineers come up with new ways to process and package food and are responsible for making sure that the food we buy is safe to eat as well as healthy and nourishing. Food engineers are always inventing new ways to help preserve food, but they also think about the technology needed to cook and transport food. Thus, they invent things like a pizza oven that uses less energy, or a portable freezer that can be used in ice cream trucks. Food engineers also look for ways to solve problems with food supply around the world and help combat world hunger. Many food engineers studied food sciences, life sciences or agriculture in school in order to prepare them for their work.

. . . .

Engineers work in every field because they use a scientific way of thinking to build simple solutions to complicated problems.

. . . .

Aerospace engineers make it possible for humans and human-made objects to fly. They design airplanes, spacecraft, drones, satellites and missiles using the science of flight (called aeronautics) as well as mathematics and engineering. Aerospace engineers design, build and test equipment like airplanes, helicopters and supersonic jets, and thus they are essential to the ways that we travel. But the work of aerospace engineers is also used by the federal government for mail and shipping services as well as for national defense. Aerospace engineers also make satellites, which are the machines that orbit the earth and do everything from providing GPS systems, to helping predict weather patterns, to sending TV signals to providing phone service. Many aerospace engineers spend their time building and improving all kinds of aircraft, while many others research new ways to make things that fly.

Materials engineers explore the uses of the materials available to us as well as look for and develop new materials. These engineers work with metals, ceramics, plastics, composites and nanomaterials, and often they will invent new combinations of these materials or even entirely new materials based on the requirements for a certain project. Materials engineers also test materials to determine whether they are safe to use, which is especially important for new materials. Materials engineers often work in teams with scientists and other engineers to make sure that the material they create or test will be right for a project. They often work in labs, but they also work in offices, factories and many other places.

Similar to materials engineers, plastics engineers study the ways that polymers and plastics are made and help build things out of plastic. So far, plastics engineers have discovered and learned how to use about 21,000 different kinds of plastic. Because plastic is a material that is strong and lasts a long time, many of the things we use every day are at least partly made from plastic, including our phones, our shoes, our sports equipment, our cars, our cups and plates and the packaging that we use for nearly every object that we buy. Many kinds of plastic are used in construction as well, because anything from a slide on a playground to the pipes that bring water to or from your home can be made of plastic. Plastics are also used in the health care field to make everything from bottles that hold medicine to implants. Plastics engineers also spend a lot of time researching and testing plastics to discover which ones are safe for us to use. Plastics engineers can work in nearly any industry, including technology, textiles, cosmetics or manufacturing, and they often work closely with chemical engineers.

Energy engineers (sometimes called energy systems engineers) work to bring us the energy we need from natural resources as well as sustainable energy sources. Energy engineers are responsible for making sure that energy is distributed efficiently and safely, and they will design machines and systems to make that happen. Energy engineers are often interested in sustainable energy sources, and they might be found managing a solar power plant, inventing a new wind turbine and running tests to find out how our use of energy affects the environment. These engineers might work on their own, or they may work with teams of other engineers and scientists to improve the way we use energy. Energy engineers work in laboratories and offices as well as on the sites of energy plants or natural resources.

Another kind of engineer is a systems engineer. Systems engineers use their understanding of engineering to help customers or clients find the best solutions to their individual problems or needs by overseeing an entire project. Systems engineers work with clients throughout the development of new products and make sure that all the different kinds of engineering come together to create a unified and useful product. They will listen to what a client needs and help design a solution for that need. For example, if a problem requires something made of plastic with an electric motor that will be able to fly, a systems engineer will make sure that the work of the plastics engineer, electrical engineer and aerospace engineer is right for the product. Systems engineers may also be responsible for investigating alternative solutions, testing a product and making sure a product is meeting the allowed cost and time requirements. Systems engineers work with every other kind of engineer as well as with individual clients and marketing teams. The engineers need not only to understand all the engineering that goes into a product, but they also need to be able to coordinate all the different kinds of engineering to make the solution possible.

This is only a small sampling of the different types of engineers. There are many more kinds of engineers because there are many more kinds of problems that need solutions. Engineers work in every field because they use a scientific way of thinking to build simple solutions to complicated problems.

Mathematics

You are probably familiar with math as a subject in school, but you may not realize that there are many jobs that are centered around mathematics. Nearly every STEM job uses some kind of mathematics, and STEM certainly could not exist without math. No matter how much data scientists gather, it would be almost useless without the equations that interpret it. For example, chemists, engineers, biologists and computer programmers all rely on mathematics to do their jobs. Thus, mathematics is an essential part of all STEM. However, math is important by itself, too.

One interesting math-centered job is cryptography. Cryptographers study, invent and solve ciphers or codes by using complicated mathematical equations, and they often work with information security analysts to make sure that information stays a secret. Cryptographers work with different levels of encryption because not every piece of information is of the same value. For example, an important government secret would require a more complicated code to keep it safer than your social media account would. Cryptographers write the codes for every kind of information that needs to be secured and work in many different fields, including banking, online stores, insurance companies and internet providers.

> **Nearly every STEM job uses some kind of mathematics, and STEM certainly could not exist without math. No matter how much data scientists gather, it would be almost useless without the equations that interpret it.**

Actuaries use mathematics to analyze the risks and uncertainties of events, and measure the costs of these events occurring. Most actuaries work for insurance companies, where being able to predict the likelihood that someone will become ill within the next year, or that a natural disaster will occur is essential for knowing how much money the company will need to fix these problems. Actuaries are also responsible for designing and testing different insurance plans. They often put their calculations into chart form to make them easier to understand. Many other actuaries work for companies that want to predict whether a project or product will succeed or fail. Actuaries work in many different kinds of companies because their ability to give a better mathematical guess at the future can help businesses make better decisions.

Statisticians collect numbers to help solve problems. They look at a question, determine what kind of information is needed to answer it, and then find a way to get that information. Often, statisticians find their information by using surveys, questionnaires or experiments. Once they have the information they need, statisticians use special software and equations to analyze this data so that it provides an answer to their original question. Then, statisticians will carefully test the validity

of their answer to see if there is anything that their surveys, questionnaires or experiments missed. Next, they chart or report the answer to those who need it. Statisticians can work in nearly any field, including marketing, sports, psychology, education or health care.

Market research analysts are similar to statisticians in that they collect numbers to answer questions, but their efforts are focused on the ways that numbers are used in sales. Market research analysts gather data about customers and products that help businesses know what kind of products people need and how much they are willing to pay for them. Market research analysts measure the effectiveness of past products and even predict the future buying habits of consumers based on the ways they have acted in the past. Like statisticians, market research analysts use special software and equations to help turn the complex data they gather into charts or reports that are easy to understand. Market research analysts work for nearly every company, including finance companies, manufacturing companies and wholesale trade companies.

Financial analysts are similar to market research analysts, but rather than examining the buying habits of consumers, they look at investments, stocks and bonds to help individuals and companies know what to do with their money. Much of our information about the economy comes from the work of financial analysts, who examine the present and past economic trends to help predict the future. Financial analysts work with companies and with individuals to help them create an investment plan so that their money will be safe for the future. Some financial analysts are called buy-side financial analysts, meaning that they work with individuals or companies that have money

Market research analysts collect numbers to answer questions and their efforts are focused on the ways that numbers are used in sales.

Accountants and auditors help individuals and companies keep track of their finances, pay their taxes and prepare their tax returns.

Operations research analysts work for individual companies and organizations and use mathematics to help those companies make decisions.

Statisticians collect numbers to help solve problems.

Cryptographers study, invent and solve ciphers or codes by using complicated mathematical equations.

Financial analysts look at investments, stocks and bonds to help individuals and companies know what to do with their money.

Actuaries use mathematics to analyze the risks and uncertainties of events, and measure the costs of these events occurring.

to invest. Other financial analysts are called sell-side financial analysts, meaning that they work with financial agencies that sell stocks or bonds or those who are looking for investors. Financial analysts usually focus on one specific area of finance, which may be geographical (such as North America or Eastern Europe), or industrial (such as cosmetic products) or even on the exchange market between different countries. Financial analysts often work for credit card companies, large corporations, banks, insurance companies or on their own as consultants.

. . . .

People who work in a mathematics career love using numbers to solve problems. They understand the importance that numbers play in things like business, finance and even the internet.

. . . .

Operations research analysts work for individual companies or organizations and use mathematics to help those companies make decisions. Operations research analysts are in charge of collecting all the information they can about their company, including sales records, customer feedback and market information. They may also gather information from company employees and are involved in every aspect of the company. After collecting their data, operations research analysts then think about the information they collected and determine what kinds of problems it might show or solve. They also look for the best possible way to analyze their data and then chart or present this information to their company. Operations research analysts may work for any company, including those in health care, finance, insurance or manufacturing.

Accountants and auditors know all about financial record keeping. They help individuals and companies keep track of their finances, pay their taxes and prepare their tax returns. Accountants and auditors need to know a lot about the government's rules about money and taxes, and they need to be able to explain these complicated systems to the businesses or individuals being helped. They also look for ways that individuals or companies can use their money more effectively and will often suggest ways to save money. Accountants and auditors may also work in company payroll, which means that they make sure every employee gets paid the correct amount on time. Accountants and auditors often work for accounting, tax or payroll companies, but they also may work for finance or insurance companies, or work on their own with individual clients.

People who work in a mathematics career love using numbers to solve problems. They understand the importance that numbers play in things like business, finance and even the internet. These are only a few examples of the ways that math permeates STEM; there are many other ways that mathematics can be applied to everyday life.

Why Study STEM?

While there are many reasons to study STEM, popular reasons include an interest in a subject (like cosmetics) or wanting to make something better or easier to use (like making a better cellphone).

And because there are so many different ways to work in STEM, there is a place in STEM for everyone. No matter what field you are interested in, there is a way to apply STEM to make that field better. For example, even writers use STEM! Laptops, tablets, voice recorders, video recorders, even ballpoint pens — without the work of STEM scientists, writing could not operate the way it does today.

No two STEM careers look the same, but the people who work in STEM usually share several key characteristics.

One of the most important things they share is curiosity. People who work in STEM are the kind of people who are always asking "how," "why" and "why not." They want to know how everything works, why it works the way it does, and whether they can think of a way to do it better.

Another quality that STEM professionals share is a love of collaboration. Because there is so much to know about the world and no one person can know all of it, STEM professionals are always sharing the knowledge that they gather and using the knowledge that has been shared with them. Wherever STEM professionals' curiosity drives them, they always work with and for other people.

Many people think of collaboration as being in a room with lots of other people trying to solve a problem, and sometimes that is what collaboration is. But, in other cases, collaboration is about sharing ideas with people who you don't even know. STEM women excel at both kinds of collaboration, which helps them achieve even more amazing things than they could by themselves.

Do you like asking questions or solving puzzles? Do you like sharing your ideas with other people or learning from them? Are you interested in a subject or do you want to make the world better? If so, you already excel at the things that STEM professionals like best about their jobs, and you will probably like working in STEM. Remember that any field can be made better by STEM, so there is a place in STEM for everyone. Working in STEM offers you a chance to answer for yourself some of the biggest questions in the universe as well as learn about the answers other people have found. You can find ways to make the world better and learn more about your favorite things all at the same time. And what could be more rewarding and enjoyable than this combination?

Chapter Two

Girls Who Discovered STEM

Introduction

Now that you have an idea of what STEM is and some of the ways people can study or work with STEM, it's time for you to read some examples of how STEM works in real life. You will learn about the different kinds of studying needed for a career in STEM as well as get a firsthand account into what some successful STEM careers look like.

. . . .

**By learning about what these inspiring women are doing now,
you can learn about what you can do in the future.**

. . . .

The following stories were contributed by women who have gone into a STEM field. Each one of them tells a different story, but they are all united in their love of their work and the great contributions that they make to the world around them. They work in every field, ranging from medicine, astronomy and biology, to teaching, writing and art. They work for various employers in industry, academia and government. Their work environments also vary and include laboratories, offices, classrooms or in the field, and many of them even work on their own as entrepreneurs or consultants. Wherever they work, you will see that they are always looking for new ways to make advances in their chosen field.

These women have contributed to the STEM fields in unique and amazing ways. Some of them work with science to heal patients, solve crimes, help the environment or make products such as makeup or even fuel. Others work in technology to develop and test software or hardware, keep information safe or build new kinds of technology that can help us with things we do every day,

like cook a meal, talk to our friends or watch a movie. Some work as engineers to design and build the products that comprise our world, like computers, bridges or green energy fuel cells. Others work with math to make sure that people and businesses understand their finances, apply complicated codes to keep hackers from stealing information or use physics to study light. Whatever areas of STEM these women work in, they show how much they can achieve and how much there still is left to learn and to do.

....

These women work with science to heal patients, solve crimes, help the environment, make products from makeup to cars to fuel, and do many other things.

....

Their different paths to and in STEM are even more inspirational because no two girls took the same path to the successful careers they have today. Even though sometimes the path to a certain job is clear (for example, if you want to become an analytical chemist, you need to study chemistry), often the ways that these women became experts in their field may surprise you. They show that there is a place in STEM for everyone, and all you have to do is find it.

As you read, you will learn about many different STEM careers. Each of these careers happened naturally as girls learned about what they were interested in. Many of them began to be curious about the world of STEM at a very young age, while others did not discover their love of STEM until college, or even later.

....

Whatever areas of STEM these women work in, they show how much they can achieve and how much there still is left to learn and to do.

....

However these women came to STEM, it is encouraging to think that you can learn from their paths while forging your own.

While you learn about the contributions these women have made to STEM, remember that you can do things like this, too. By learning about what these inspiring women are doing now, you can learn about what you can do in the future.

Alayna Westcom

Pathologist

*I may be Miss Vermont 2015, but I'm also an autopsy technician
with dreams of going to medical school to become a pathologist.*

I wish I could say that others have always supported my career goals, but this is not the case. Over the years, I've heard comments about my appearance and gender too many times to count. "You're too pretty to be a scientist!" has been a frequent one, with a close second being, "Are you sure you want to be in that field? It's not really a career for young women." I think my favorite comment will always be, "You do not look like a scientist," as though we're all supposed to look the same. Last time I checked, everybody looks different, so there's no reason why we have to conform. When I was told these things at such a young age, it made me question what I wanted to do. If everyone else thought that I couldn't do it, what made me think that I could?

But I'm determined because pathology is an important field of medicine for me. I have lost family members to diseases and cancer, and knowing what the cause of death is can help to plan for preventative care, genetic research and many other health care options.

"My career path involves working with dead people. That sounds spooky, but really, there's so much more to it."

Growing up, I couldn't do anything without my parents finding out, so there was always pressure to do well. I grew up in a small town with less than 1,500 people. My town has one small school, a gas station and no restaurants. We have only volunteer fire services. So when I say small, I mean small.

I went to the same school as my dad and even had some of the same teachers as he did. I fell in love with science when I was 10. My school offered hands-on education that brought science to life and I always participated in the school science fair. Some years I took home nothing, but sometimes I was awarded first place. Each year, we were asked to choose a topic that was interesting to us and something that could be beneficial to many groups of people, so I did experiments ranging from trying to relight a match with gas produced by aquatic plants, to making a Braille clock. My favorite part was learning how to explain my experiments to others in a way that they understood and intrigued them to learn more.

I was in the sixth grade when I decided I wanted to pursue a STEM career. I have always wanted to be a doctor, but I wasn't sure what specialty. Over the years, I began to develop an interest in human disease and pathology, and that's how I decided on my end goal. It wasn't until after I fell in love with science that I started getting comments about my career choice and love for STEM.

Back in small-town Vermont, I realized that if a career in STEM was what I really wanted, I'd have to work twice as hard to prove to everyone else that I could do it. When I say work, I mean I worked. I loaded up on all the Advanced Placement science and math courses I could take and the effort paid off. I applied to and was accepted at two colleges. One was a co-ed university and the other was all-women. I decided on attending the all-women school, in part because of the varying levels of support I had received over the years. I thought it would help me with my career in STEM, since everyone else had probably experienced something similar. I decided on forensic science as my major with the thought that I would go on to medical school.

Becoming Miss Vermont has always been a dream of mine. Miss Vermont is the state local to Miss America, and comes with the responsibility to be a role model to young women around the state, while being awarded scholarship money for higher education. To become Miss Vermont, there is a competition with areas judged by professionals of every kind. Some areas of competition include interview, on-stage questions, lifestyle and fitness, talent and evening wear. My talent was a science demonstration, the first ever on the Miss Vermont stage, and later, the first ever on the Miss America stage.

One of the most important parts of competing and becoming Miss Vermont is community service through a personal platform; this is something each contestant is passionate about and will work with and toward during the year. My platform was entitled Success through STEM: Science, Technology, Engineering and Mathematics. On April 25, 2015, having competed for the title of Miss Vermont for seven years (and competed for Miss Vermont's Outstanding Teen for two years), I was crowned Miss Vermont.

· ·

I was in the sixth grade when I decided I wanted to pursue a STEM career.

· ·

Once crowned Miss Vermont in September 2015, I competed to become Miss America 2016. Although I did not win, the experience will last a lifetime. My work as Miss Vermont 2015 took me to every city and town in the state of Vermont, all 251 of them! The main focus of my year was teaching STEM education to students of all ages. Through hands-on experience and thoughtful conversations, I was able to teach thousands of students how important STEM education is to everyday life. Being Miss Vermont gave me the ability to interact with students I would not otherwise been able to talk to; it gave me the capacity to use my voice for women in STEM.

My career path involves working with dead people. That sounds spooky, but really, there's so much more to it. I work alongside medical examiners (forensic pathologists) and anatomical pathologists to determine the cause of death of people in my community and state. I assist in collecting blood samples, evidence if need be, and with eviscerating the body, which means I help to remove all the organs for further inspection. The role of the pathologist is to carefully examine each organ, artery and glands to determine what the cause of death might have been.

My professional goal is to be a pathologist. For now, being an autopsy technician and assisting helps to make sure I am choosing the right career path. It feels good to know that I'm helping to provide answers to families, now as well as in the future.

My Favorite Things

In the summer, I love to garden. Each year I add a new vegetable to change things up. I also love to pickle and can everything that I grow in my garden.

The color pink, but my power color is blue.

Anything written by Harlan Coben, he is seriously the best!

Chocolate whoopie pies.

My science teachers that made learning fun and made me want to pay attention and continue my education.

Monkeys.

Education

B.S.,
Bay Path University,
Class of 2013,
Major: Forensic Science

Post Baccalaureate
Certificate,
University of Vermont,
Class of 2015,
Medical Laboratory
Science

On a personal note, another goal of mine is to make sure young women know that gender and appearance do not have to dictate what they can do for a career. Throughout my life, I have heard so many comments about my gender, appearance and attractiveness and how those factors should dictate what I want out of life. Luckily, during my education, and while working to help educate students about the importance of STEM, I discovered a bit of wisdom that has really made a difference for me. Do not ever feel like you are inadequate based on what someone else says. Know that you are capable of completing any goal and attaining any career, including all STEM careers, as long as you are willing to focus on what you want, and be persistent. •

Alexis M. Scott

Cyber Security Engineering Manager

Even though I have always been good with numbers,
I have often felt invisible with my peers.

In school, I was always the smart one, even though girls weren't supposed to be smart. We were supposed to be cute, and we definitely weren't supposed to do well in math and science. What I enjoyed and what I excelled at did not fit the norm of what my peers were doing, so it made me feel like people didn't see me. It is something that has stuck with me throughout my educational experiences.

In elementary and high school, I often felt like I blended into the background. There weren't many other girls like me — girls who were interested in and good at math and science. Because school came easy for me, I often felt like my accomplishments and my intelligence weren't of any importance to other people, never mind the fact that I was one of the only girls in my class who enjoyed math and science subjects.

About Me

I was born in Dallas, Texas and have three brothers (I am the only girl and the oldest).

I read often and have many favorite books (too many to list).

My favorite color depends upon the season.

In June 2017, I launched a book called "Embracing STEM Smarts." This book is full of stories from young women who have followed their passion in STEM.

> " I work with an assortment of different people to make sure systems are secured sufficiently and that the systems can obtain a variety of security certifications."

Even when I worked on my master's degree in mathematics, there were very few women in my department who were getting higher-level degrees in the same subject. In fact, in my first few jobs as an engineer, I was either the only one or one of two. And don't even factor in if they were women of color. In that regard, I was the only one. That can be very intimidating at times.

In elementary and high school, I often felt like I blended into the background. There weren't many other girls like me — girls who were interested in and good at math and science.

However, as I have grown into my business position and my educator position, I have become more comfortable in my roles. It appears that my invisibility has started to fade as people around me took notice of what I was doing. Now, I no longer resent that feeling of not being seen, but instead I use it and embrace it. In both my engineering job and the education profession, people want to hear what I have to say.

I am an engineering manager for a defense company with a team of 11 engineers. I also own my own educational services center where I manage between eight and 10 tutors.

Early in my career, I wondered what I would do with a math degree. I currently hold both a bachelor's degree of science and a master's degree of science in mathematics. A

mathematics degree will allow you to do a multitude of things. Mathematics gave me the ability to figure things out and to think things through. That is primarily what a mathematics problem, or proof, is. What steps do you need to take to get to the answer? There are always a number of ways to get to the end of a problem, but one thing I love about math is that the answer is objective.

Originally, I wanted to be a CPA — a certified public accountant. In addition to my math degree, I obtained a minor in business. After I attended graduate school, my thought process changed. Being a CPA didn't sound like the job for me, so I took a position in the laboratory of one of the country's most prestigious STEM schools. For four years, I threw myself into learning and became proficient in computer programming and analyzing radar data.

I looked at computer programming like solving a puzzle. Once I figured out one language, I had the key to all the other computer languages. So before I went into system security engineering, I was a computer programmer and analyst. After I truly mastered that, the next step for me was to secure these programs. I wasn't sure how to do that or what tools or steps would be necessary to get a secure system.

> **I looked at computer programming like solving a puzzle. Once I figured out one language, I had the key to all the other computer languages.**

I work with an assortment of different people to make sure systems are secured sufficiently and that the systems can obtain a variety of security certifications. For a job in system security engineering (also known as cyber security), you need to have a degree in math, computer science or engineering.

When I started in this field in 2005, there was no such thing as cyber security. At that time, the field was known as information assurance. Today, information assurance is often referred to as cyber security and is defined as the practice of assuring information and managing risks related to the use, processing, storage and transmission of information or data, and the systems and processes used for those purposes. The main triad of information assurance is CIA, which stands for confidentiality, integrity and availability. At its basis is confidentiality, which prevents people from gaining access to information. Integrity alerts people to changes in information. Availability makes sure information is available when it should be available.

My Favorite Things

Pastries (cakes and cookies) for dessert.

I really enjoy reading, music and science fiction.

Celebrating my birthday.

All the many teachers who influenced me to be the person I am today and encouraged me to continue in my studies in math.

Vacationing in Las Vegas or any island in the Caribbean.

Dogs.

Education

B.S.,
Spelman College,
Class of 1993,
Major: Mathematics

M.S.,
University of
North Texas,
Class of 1995,
Mathematics

I make sure systems are in place so that the triad is implemented in the best ways possible to provide the most minimal risk to a company. Most companies in the world use some form of cyber security. The primary industry that uses cyber security is the defense industry. Cyber security is also used in the banking industry as well as in retail and educational settings.

Around 3 p.m., I leave full-time job number one in cyber security engineering and go to full-time job number two as an educator and entrepreneur. I have been working in education for more than 20 years. I started my own tutoring services business in 2011.

To be honest, I love teaching math. I started tutoring math in college in 1989 and continued tutoring during both undergraduate and graduate school. In addition to tutoring, I started teaching my own class as an assistant to a professor. That is when the teaching bug really hit. I enjoyed being in front of the classroom talking about math and working with the students. Somehow, I developed the gift of making math relatable and getting students to grasp the concepts.

After graduate school, I started my first job as an engineer. Even though I enjoyed what I was doing, there was something missing. I realized it was because I wasn't teaching. So I began looking for part-time teaching positions. This meant I would work at my full-time engineering job during the day and teach college math courses in the evening and weekends. It was great. I continued this trend for 14 years.

As an educator, I give tutoring sessions in a variety of subjects, most notably math and the sciences. My goal for all of my subjects is to bring students confidence in the materials. Many students come in the center frustrated with homework or a test, and my team and I make sure they have the adequate foundation to succeed.

There are so many things that can be accomplished via STEM careers that the possibilities are endless. When you master mathematics, you increase your career options, and this is one of the reasons I'm so passionate about teaching mathematics. Mathematics is for everyone! •

Allison Dalbec Buchheit

Analytical Chemist

I became interested in STEM-related careers because of my father.

He was a textile engineer at a local company in Spartanburg, South Carolina, near where I grew up. Early on and throughout my life, he has always been my advocate for science. We shared a special bond over all things science, but in particular, the school science fair. We always looked forward to the fair and would spend hours discussing what idea or project we were going to try next. I was always thankful to have my father with me as we conducted experiments, built models and learned about science.

Today, I work in the energy industry in a field called bio-fuels. My job as an analytical chemist is to develop test methods for alternative fuels and energy sources. Just as we need tests to see if you have the flu, new test methods need to be developed for new fuels that are being developed. As the demand for energy increases, we have to make sure our energy supplies are sustainable and environmentally friendly.

My employer uses plants to make energy. I work with algae (tiny sea plants) that have been genetically changed to make ethanol. Ethanol is a fuel that can be used for energy and is in your car's gasoline. In

About Me

My birthplace is Spartanburg, South Carolina and I have two siblings.

My favorite book is "The Rhythm of Life."

I love cookies and cream ice cream.

"As the demand for energy increases, we have to make sure our energy supplies are sustainable and environmentally friendly."

my job, I'm asked to analyze for metals like iron, copper and cobalt, using a machine called ICP-OES (inductively coupled plasma optical emission spectroscopy…say that five times fast). One of the aspects of my job is that I have to figure out how to test for these metals in seawater and in algae, at very small amounts. I find this job so rewarding because the work I'm doing contributes to a greener planet and an alternative fuel resource.

A typical day in my job usually starts with checking emails to see if there are any needs for additional test methods. Then I make sure all my stocks of chemicals are sufficient. I prepare all my chemicals for the day and record what tests and experiments I would like to do to further develop a test method for my work. After that, I prepare my instrument for analysis for the day. I put my lab coat and my protective clothing on, because in analytical chemistry, you can work with some hazardous materials. My samples are prepared for analysis and put into the instrument I'll be using for the day. Once the instrument is done analyzing, I review and record the data, sharing it with my colleagues. Then I decide what needs to happen the next time I conduct the experiment.

I work in the energy industry in a field called bio-fuels. My job as an analytical chemist is to develop test methods for alternative fuels and energy sources.

An analytical chemist can work in a wide range of industries such as fuels, cosmetics/skin care, the FBI, NASA, marine research, pharmaceutical, medical device, nutraceutical, food or even the pet food industry. I have worked as an analytical

chemist for academic schools, manufacturing companies and research companies. Sometimes an analytical chemist is involved in method development. This is where chemists come up with the actual test to determine what is in a material.

In order for you to be an analytical chemist, you will need to have strong math skills and a strong understanding of chemistry and physics. You also will need steady hands for handling small materials or plumbing small objects. Are you a problem solver? You will definitely need that once your instrument breaks. You will find yourself asking questions such as, "Why did my instrument just turn off? Why is my chemical not going into the machine to analyze?" When you ask yourself these types of "why" questions, you're actually conducting a root-cause investigation. Other key skills that are beneficial for being an analytical chemist are having skills to write reports and scientific writing. A big skill needed for an analytical chemist is public speaking in front of crowds. You need to be able to share and tell the world all these great test methods you came up with.

....

I had parents who encouraged me to just be me. That meant that no one in my family thought it was weird that I was interested in science and math.

....

In middle school, the boys in my class were all really interested in science and math, but the girls were mainly focused on literature and languages. Luckily for me, I had parents who encouraged me to just be me. That meant that no one in my family thought it was weird that I was interested in science and math. Because of my support system at home, I decided that since I knew I was good in math and science, I was just going to be myself and be good at what I did best.

Each year at the science fair, I won first place. I had a fellow classmate who always got upset with me because I won. Maybe he didn't like losing to a girl, or maybe he realized that my projects were better than his and he was competitive in nature. In my final year of middle school, my science-fair project went on to the regional competition where I placed third in the region. My project investigated varying amounts of sunlight and fertilizer in order to grow the tallest plants over a period of four weeks. I was so excited to go to the regional competition, and that experience helped instill in me the knowledge that with hard work and confidence in my ideas, I could go far.

In high school, I took all honors-science classes to learn as much as I could about science. I began to start thinking about careers with science in more depth, and

Education

B.S.,
Converse College,
Class of 2005,
Major: Chemistry

M.S.,
University of South Carolina,
Class of 2007,
Analytical Chemistry

considered becoming a doctor. I knew becoming a doctor was a possible career path for girls, and my parents and teachers always told me that doctors make a lot of money.

During high school, I participated in the National Youth Forum, which was a camp focused on shadowing careers in the medical industry. It was a two-week camp based out of Georgetown University. We toured medical schools, hospitals and the National Institute of Health (NIH). While at the NIH, I shadowed a man for the day who was doing research on different drug therapies for nicotine addiction. I thought I could easily see myself having a career like that one day. I still toyed with being a doctor, since it seemed like an established career path for girls, but my true desires were on conducting research and science experiments.

Once at Converse College, degrees in math, physics, chemistry and biology were all offered and all of them appealed to me. I enjoyed being in the lab, which made me lean toward the sciences. I had taken biology in high school, but didn't love all the memorization that it required. I thoroughly enjoyed physics and chemistry, especially using the periodic table and math to work problems out. When I realized that chemistry incorporated elements of math and physics in the curriculum, it felt like the right fit for me as a major.

Regardless of the industry or role you decide on, analytical chemistry is a team-oriented career that's fun and challenging. A rewarding aspect of the job is collaborating with fellow coworkers to get the right test method. It's also exciting to work with and contribute to the latest technology; other analytical chemists can use my test methods in their own research. What I find most challenging about being an analytical chemist is when you find yourself in the middle of developing your test method, and your instrument breaks. While this is frustrating, I've learned patience and flexibility.

STEM opens the door to so many career opportunities, and there are a lot of career options if you choose to be an analytical chemist. Analytical chemistry is used in many different fields, from ensuring products are safe, to helping NASA investigate the universe, and even to helping find new fuel sources. With this many options, you'll always be assured a job! •

Amanda Lee Salb

Wildlife Veterinarian

Upon reflection, in addition to my parents, I'm most appreciative of my kindergarten teacher Mrs. Jan Hastings. She took an inquisitive, slightly disruptive child and taught me classroom manners without dampening my personality, all while nurturing my curiosity.

As a little girl, I was always outside catching frogs and insects, or wading in the pond with a net. I loved to climb trees around my home so that I could get a better view of the wild fauna. I have always been drawn to the natural world and science. In elementary school, I spent time memorizing field guides for birds and mammals. By high school, I had a prize-winning insect collection. I didn't think any of this was strange or unusual for a girl; I was just being me, embracing and exploring the world around me. When I wasn't doing that, I probably had my nose in a book.

My adventure continues as I work for a wildlife nongovernmental organization located in a small country in southern-central Africa, Malawi. My employer provides veterinary medical care for wildlife

About Me

I was born in Springdale, Arkansas and have three siblings — two sisters, one brother (and all three are the best!).

When asked what's my favorite holiday, I reply, "Anytime that I'm hanging out with my siblings."

> "As head veterinarian, I'm involved in developing a new program that will be instrumental in improving the welfare of wildlife across Malawi by rescuing wildlife in trouble, implementing animal confiscations and providing education to the public."

in need. Sometimes you can bring injured wild animals to a wildlife hospital, just like a dog or cat, and set them free again when they are well. But some free-ranging wild animals are too big to be brought into a wildlife hospital, like elephants and rhinos. If they have medical problems, it is often best to treat them right there in the wilderness where they live. That's my job — a wild-animal doctor.

As a wildlife veterinarian, I love being able to work outside, get dirty and appreciate the weird and wonderful fauna, big and small. Science and medicine has given us enough answers to be able to help these wild animals, while still sparking those countless questions that keep me thinking, learning and discovering every single day. I love the opportunities my job gives me to understand, experience and enjoy the natural world. That's worth any of the challenges that pop up from time to time.

I came to Malawi in 2013 to work for a wildlife sanctuary that serves as a rescue and rehabilitation center. Initially, I was in Malawi to work as a monkey vet, but it's led to so much more. Today, I run a wildlife emergency response program. The program is a joint partnership between my employer and a government wildlife agency. In addition, I also oversee the veterinary activities at a wildlife center. I'm the head veterinarian, managing various projects and programs.

The wildlife emergency response program was developed in response to the need to have an in-country veterinarian available to assist wildlife that were victims of poaching injuries, especially snare wounds. Some of the wildlife found includes endangered species like black rhinos and flagship species like African elephants. I've treated all sorts of animals in the wildlife sanctuary, ranging from yellow baboons, lions and African pygmy hedgehogs.

As head veterinarian, I'm involved in developing a new program that will be instrumental in improving the welfare of wildlife across Malawi by rescuing wildlife in trouble, implementing animal confiscations and providing education to the public.

In my job, I don't really have an office. I live in Lilongwe, the capital of Malawi, and am based out of the wildlife sanctuary, but I'm either at the clinic or on the grounds of the sanctuary. I can spend a lot of time in the field, but it depends on what is needed and the time of year. During the rainy season, some parts of many parks are inaccessible. The fact that it's variable is one of the aspects of the job I enjoy.

Even though I had training and experience in exotic-animal medicine in the United States, working with wildlife in the field is something else entirely. I took a training course on the capture of African wildlife in Zimbabwe in 2013. It's actually the same course that they show on the Animal Planet show "Wild Capture School."

It may sound fun and exciting, and it is, but it is also a lot of hard work. I need to be flexible and imaginative; wild animals rarely want to follow my plans and often have their own plans, to which I must adjust. Being organized is necessary so that I can capture an animal, deliver the treatment efficiently, and then get out of there quickly so the animal experiences as little stress as possible. Having a sense of adventure helps as well.

. . . .

As a wildlife veterinarian, I love being able to work outside, get dirty and appreciate the weird and wonderful fauna, big and small.

. . . .

Before becoming a wildlife veterinarian, my parents supported my interest in animals, and I spent a lot of time outside with my dad and my grandfather. I think that my family encouraging us kids to pursue whatever we were interested in gave us the freedom to feel comfortable finding our passions; that support has led me here.

Of course, back in the '80s and '90s, if you were vaguely good at science in school, everyone would say you should be a doctor. My grandfather was a physician, so honestly, I just went with that idea since I was a people-pleasing kid. It wasn't until I actually shadowed my grandfather in his office that I decided being a physician was not what I wanted.

I don't remember feeling a lot of pressure to pick a career, though. A lot of my science-major friends were similar. Actually, we were second-tier students, so maybe

My Favorite Things

Favorite books include, "The Lord of the Rings Trilogy" and "A Primate's Memoir."

My favorite color is purple, but I also like pinks and blues a lot as well.

For dessert, I prefer red velvet cake, but anything sweet will do.

Vacationing near a beach is the best!

Favorite animals include rock hyrax, vervet monkeys and elephants.

Education

B.A.,
Mount Holyoke College,
Class of 1999,
Major: Biological Sciences

M.Sc.,
University of Calgary,
Class of 2011,
Medical Science
(Wildlife Epidemiology)

D.V.M.,
Louisiana State University,
Class of 2004

that says something. The tops of our class knew exactly what they were about and went for it with gusto. A lot of my vet-school classmates knew that they wanted to be veterinarians pretty much since they were embryos, which boggled my mind. It goes to show you that you do not have to have your stuff together in college to make it in life.

I went to school for eight years in order to become a veterinarian — four years for a bachelor's degree and four years for my Doctor of Veterinary Medicine. As a biological sciences major at Mount Holyoke College, I filled most of the prerequisite classes for veterinary school just by taking the science classes required for my major. Many of the classes required for admission to veterinary schools are STEM classes.

In college, I thought about veterinary medicine, but heard it was really competitive and only top students got in. I eked out a 3.0 after my first semester at college and wasn't overly optimistic. Over the next few years, I took biology classes and thought about pursuing graduate research, and did a summer internship in a genetics lab. I quickly found out that spending all day in a lab was not for me. My college friends and I used to sit around the dorm and talk about possible careers; we called it "the plan of the week."

It wasn't until November of my senior year at MHC that I finally decided that I should go to vet school. It just made sense. When I applied, I knew I was interested in wildlife medicine. And the more experience I had with wildlife and exotics at school, the more I knew that I wanted to pursue this path.

Now that I'm on my path, I'm not sure about future plans, because plans have a way of making themselves sometimes. I used to try to plan and have goals, but oddly, it wasn't nearly as exciting or satisfying as going along with the flow. Once I realized that I cherished freedom more than security, I could be happy with a little less structure! •

Angela Gupta

Physician-Scientist

*From an early age, science, and in particular, medicine,
has played an important part in my life. My younger sister
Alisha is both mentally and physically disabled.*

Witnessing the effects that a severe ailment has had on someone close to me, I have had firsthand experience with the personal impact that a physician can have on a patient and their family. Despite not being able to cure Alisha's complex illness, I was amazed at the empathy her physicians showed. Her doctors were there for her day and night, putting our family's anxiety and frustrations at ease. Alisha's doctors showed me that physicians can bring change into people's lives, with or without the use of a prescription.

As my interest in medicine grew as a kid, science and math became my favorite subjects. I found every opportunity to learn about STEM careers. In sixth grade, we gave presentations on what we wanted to be when we grew up. I was so excited and spent hours researching every detail about what a pediatric neurologist does. Instead of going to regular summer camp, I would ask my parents to enroll me in STEM programs. I loved spending my summer designing and building roller coasters, programming Lego robots and learning CPR.

About Me

I was born in Cleveland, Ohio and have one sibling.

My parents have been my best teachers! They led by example every day by showing me how to be caring, compassionate, dedicated and hard working.

My favorite holiday is Diwali and I love ice cream.

"I never expected to attend college at 13 or start an eight year-long M.D.-Ph.D. program."

My teachers and the administrative staff at my school were incredibly supportive as my interests in science and math continued to grow. I took high school math classes in middle school. I spent afternoons at the local free clinic shadowing doctors. Despite this, something was still not clicking for me. I was bored in class. My peers were not as motivated and driven. I was being picked on and labeled as a "nerd." I was seeking something more from my education; I wanted to take classes that would challenge me, and be surrounded by a supportive group of peers.

After talking to my guidance counselor, my family and I found out about the Program for the Exceptionally Gifted (PEG) at Mary Baldwin College for Women, which allows 12-16-year-old girls to skip high school and start college early. I was apprehensive about going to college at 13 years old, but after exploring the program and talking to students and professors, I knew it would be the best fit for me.

My first day at my alma mater will always be ingrained in my mind because it was one of my happiest days. For the first time in my life, I felt like I finally fit in with my peers. During the next four years in the PEG, I flourished both personally and academically. Finally, the coursework I was taking was challenging and interesting! I was surrounded by amazing, bright, multitalented young women who inspired me to work harder. There was a huge shift in environment for me because the students I had been with previously focused more on clothes, hair, makeup and boyfriends. Being smart, kind and hard-working was what was valued in the PEG in the women's college environment.

I chose biology as my major, intending to pursue a premed track, with the intention of going to medical school. Even though I was interested in medicine, I sought opportunities to be involved in research projects as an undergraduate, which completely changed my outlook on my career choice. Exploring topics and potentially making new discoveries that could contribute to the treatment of human disease was

Reading the Harry Potter series.

The color purple.

Hiking.

Vacationing in Europe.

Dogs.

really exciting for me. Going to a small, private women's college allowed me to be in the driver's seat of my research project. I was able to be involved in the growth and development of my project and work directly with my faculty adviser. The summer of my junior year, when it came time to apply to medical school, I couldn't imagine my future career without research. After more exploring, I came across M.D.-Ph.D. programs and learned about the career path of a physician-scientist. It didn't take long for me to decide that this was perfect for me.

However, applying and attending graduate school at 17 years old was not easy. Although I felt like my qualifications were comparable to my older peers, my maturity, academic ability and commitment was always a question for others. I often had to work extra hard to prove myself, but I enjoyed the challenge. These circumstances taught me the importance of being well prepared, poised and well-spoken.

What interests me the most about being a physician-scientist is the potential it has to positively impact people's lives.

Currently, I am a sixth-year M.D.-Ph.D. student in the middle of completing my doctoral thesis. My aim is to become a physician-scientist. A physician-scientist is a person who works both as a doctor to treat patients, and as a research scientist to help better understand human disease. The goal of a physician-scientist is to go beyond the role of a doctor, to not only help patients, but also generate new medical knowledge.

Every day I am amazed and feel lucky to be able to work at the interface of research and medicine. To me, it is exciting to investigate and study unfamiliar topics. What interests me the most about being a physician-scientist is the potential it has to positively impact people's lives. What's better than being able to not only help individuals directly as a doctor, but to also contribute to the long-term development of new therapies as a researcher? It's like one profession is incomplete without the other; working as a physician gives me motivation to find new therapies as a researcher, and the discoveries I make as a researcher can in turn help me treat my patients.

Many careers allow you to help people. I chose the career of a physician-scientist because it is challenging, inspiring and gratifying. I have to balance my creativity with

Education

B.S.,
**Mary Baldwin
College for Women,**
Class of 2012,
Program for the
Exceptionally Gifted,
Major: Biology

M.D.-Ph.D.,
**Virginia Commonwealth
University School of
Medicine/Medical
College of Virginia,**
Anticipated
Class of 2020,
Biochemistry and
Molecular Biology

rationality, attention to detail with a broader awareness and ambition with patience. These skills, along with good time management, strong leadership abilities and perseverance are crucial to succeed.

A typical day as a physician-scientist is hard to describe, mainly because each day is so different. Typically, physician-scientists work in research centers or academic institutions. They split time between working in the clinic/hospital and running their research labs.

Because there are so many areas of research that are relevant to medicine, many undergraduate majors within the sciences can help prepare you for a career as a physician-scientist. Biology, biochemistry and chemistry majors are a good start, but if you are interested in medical devices/technology, majoring in engineering may also be a great choice. After graduating college, there is more than one way to pursue the career of a physician-scientist. M.D.-Ph.D. programs provide the most rigorous and specialized training, but take the most time.

Looking forward, it's difficult for me to say exactly what I will be doing in 20 years. I've learned from my past experiences that life takes unexpected turns, and plans don't always work out as intended. I never expected to attend college at 13 or start an eight-year-long M.D.-Ph.D. program. I do know I will be doing research and practicing medicine as a physician-scientist, but besides that, I am keeping my options open. Right now, there are so many different fields that interest me, and the great thing is that the opportunities with an M.D.-Ph.D. degree are endless!

Choosing a career path is not about picking what you are best at. Just because science is really hard for you doesn't mean you can't be a scientist. If you just choose something you are passionate about, your motivation will drive you to work hard and make you the best in that field. Even today I often struggle with learning new things in the research lab, but it is exciting and rewarding to work through that.

A great source of strength and motivation for me has been the amazing group of female peers that I am surrounded by. My friend circle includes aspiring doctors, artists, graphic designers, engineers, scientists and dancers. Even though their careers are so different than mine, seeing them so passionate about achieving their own goals gives me the drive to work harder! •

Anna Cooks

Electrical Design Quality Manager

*Imagine if you walked into your bedroom and flicked on the light switch,
but nothing happened. Or if you went to power on your tablet and all you saw
was a blank screen even though it had been charging all night. Or worse, what
if you were going to take a shower and there was no hot water?*

All these experiences would be inconvenient and frustrating. What would you do? Would you try to solve the problem? Great engineers are problem solvers. They know how to identify a problem, investigate possible solutions and determine which solution is the best. They also know how to communicate their ideas, work with other people and follow through until the problem is solved.

I became interested in STEM in middle school. I attended various summer programs, camps, lectures and participated in activities related to math, science and technology. The more I learned, the more my interest grew. My parents were supportive of these opportunities and encouraged me to explore them to discover what I liked best. Math and science classes were always my favorite, but what I really

About Me

I was born in
Milwaukee, Wisconsin
and have three siblings.

I love to travel and
my favorite vacation
destination is Zanzibar.

My Favorite Things

The color purple.

Apple cobbler.

Christmas.

My teachers; I've had
so many wonderful
teachers along the
way that I can't
pick a favorite.

This also applies to
books, too many
favorites to list.

loved were hands-on experiences. My dad bought complicated puzzles and erector sets that I loved to solve and build — I never backed down from the challenge! My parents watched me diligently solve every puzzle, no matter how long it took; they noticed how intrigued I was and encouraged me to pursue a career in engineering.

My high school physics class was a defining moment in my life — it is where I was introduced to the study of electromagnetics. Electrons, protons and positive and negative charges were mysterious and fascinating, and I wanted to learn more. That's when I knew electrical engineering was for me. I researched it as a career and never looked back — it was exactly what I knew I would become.

I chose the Spelman College Dual Degree Engineering Program (DDEP) to begin my journey in engineering. It was a perfect fit for my goals and interests. Yes, I loved science and math, but I also enjoyed literature, writing and music. The Spelman College DDEP gave me the best of both worlds. I wanted a well-rounded education so I would eventually become a professional who had many experiences to rely on. I did not want to miss any chance to learn something new. I loved learning, and still do. When I graduated, I earned solid educations in both liberal arts as well as STEM. The environment at Spelman College was tailored specifically for me as an eager and intelligent young black woman. It was at Spelman that I truly felt at home.

....

My high school physics class was a defining moment in my life — it is where I was introduced to the study of electromagnetics.

....

My academic courses were not easy. I studied…a lot. Much of my free time was devoted to coursework. My determination to be successful gave me the incentive to stay the course and finish strong. My support systems at Spelman and at home were critical to my pursuit. Spelman brought out the confidence that my family placed in me. I needed that inner strength to achieve my goals. The encouragement I could count on from my family was just a phone call away. If there was no one readily available, I learned to encourage myself, seek help, ask questions and always do my very best.

After college, I embraced my career as an electrical engineer. I reminded myself that I was prepared for the challenges I faced. I told myself, "I am a critical thinker and a creative problem solver….I am an engineer and I solve problems every day." I knew

"Every day I help keep the lights on in Georgia and I love it. Power is essential to life, and I am proud to be a part of that."

I was smart and capable, never letting anyone convince me otherwise. I believed in myself and my abilities. This belief and knowing has unfolded into the most remarkable of careers. I truly am blessed.

Currently, I am a team leader in the quality department of an electrical engineering organization in the power industry. Every day I help my team follow processes and procedures that ensure we deliver error-free solutions to the power plants we support. My quality team verifies the engineering solutions we give to our customers work, meet standards and are safe. It's exciting to be the last stop before a project becomes a reality. It is even more exciting to know that my skills guarantee the very best of the best is produced.

Every day, I help keep the lights on in Georgia and I love it. Power is essential to life, and I am proud to be a part of that. So, each time I turn a light switch on, charge my cellphone and tablet or use hot water, I am reminded of how awesome it is to see my hard work and talent making a difference in everyday life! •

Education

Dual Degree
Engineering Program

B.S.,
Spelman College,
Class of 1996,
Major: Mathematics

B.S.,
Georgia Tech,
Class of 1997,
Major: Electrical
Engineering

M.B.A.,
**Georgia State
University,**
Class of 2009,
Organizational
Management

Anuja De Silva

Materials Scientist

If you've ever eyed the newest iPhone and wondered how it changed from the last version, working as a materials scientist might be your perfect STEM career.

The unveiling of the latest phone or tablet device is an eagerly anticipated event by most teenagers. You will be amazed at the latest designs, how sleek and thin they can get and how fast they process data.

Before the marketing and advertising teams get together to tout it as the next big thing, there are thousands of scientists and engineers who are working behind the scenes to uncover the next technology. Making computer chips that are smaller and faster is a billion-dollar industry that supports big data analytics in every field.

As a materials scientist, I work in the research and development team at a major multinational technology company's systems and technology research group. Finding new problems and looking for ways to extend the computer chips to the next generation fuels my daily research goals. As we continue

About Me

I was born in Colombo, Sri Lanka and have one sister.

A favorite pastime of mine is traveling and includes a memorable family trip with my husband and kids to Italy.

I also enjoy visiting and vacationing in New York City.

to shrink down the size of the transistors, the designs need to get more innovative. My background in chemistry and materials science is the starting point for having a technical job in research.

Since my days as a graduate student, electronic materials and nanotechnology have been the focus of my career. I develop new types of soft materials like polymers or plastics, and hard materials like metals that are needed to make computer chips. To keep shrinking the size of electronics, materials scientists work to produce materials that have new useful properties in the small scale. Making an electronic device at about the size of 1/1000th of a human hair requires a lot of innovation. It is truly exciting to see how things behave when they are scaled down in size. Not only do you need a lot of patience, but you also need special equipment to work on such a small scale. There are many areas within the field of making a computer chip. My job has been a constant learning process.

> ### I develop new types of soft materials like polymers or plastics, and hard materials like metals that are needed to make computer chips.

When I started in this field, I was amazed at how many different types of specialties are needed to make just one working computer chip. Electrical engineers and physicists help to design more efficient transistors. Chemists, materials scientists and chemical and mechanical engineers are needed to find new materials and methods to fabricate these devices in hardware.

You can get your start with an associate or bachelor's degree at the technician or junior engineer level, but an advanced degree (master's or doctoral) will be required to gain expertise in a specific area.

A typical day for me is about eight to 10 working hours. Part of the day is spent in meetings discussing results, understanding the conclusion of previous experiments and discussing future work. This means that I work closely with a team. I enjoy the collaborative work environment and learning from experts in different fields. My favorite part of the day is coming up with new ideas to solve problems as well as gaining new knowledge about materials.

When we come up with a new idea, filing a patent and making a legal claim to our invention is one aspect on how we are judged within the company. To learn that

"Finding new problems and looking for ways to extend the computer chips to the next generation fuels my daily research goals."

we're the first people to find something new is truly an exciting feeling. Our research goals are driven by the challenge to solve the problem in a new way that benefits the company with a better and cheaper way to do things. Keeping up on what other research teams are doing in both competitor companies and academia is another aspect of my job.

I have always loved math and science and hence invested a lot of time and energy on these subjects. Even when certain concepts are difficult to understand, I break them down to pieces that I can digest. Even today, when I'm faced with a challenge, I try to solve it one step at a time and engage with mentors who can help me.

. . . .

STEM subjects are the cornerstone to the understanding of and application of how things work and new inventions. STEM subjects also offer career paths that are interesting as well as rewarding.

. . . .

I grew up in Sri Lanka, a developing country with a British colonial influence. My parents, who are accountants, worked in finance and valued math skills and encouraged scientific study. Studying science as a career helped me forge my own path without taking the easy way out by following in their footsteps.

Though I have always been acutely aware of biases against girls, I have never let it affect my passion for science. I have had enough role models of working moms who

Education

B.A.,
Mount Holyoke College,
Class of 2003,
Major: Chemistry

Ph.D.,
Cornell University,
Class of 2008,
Chemistry (focus on materials and polymer chemistry)

were doctors and engineers to inspire my STEM career path. Knowing that the path has been paved before by other women before me affirmed that I was capable of excelling in this field. That's how I ended up applying to Mount Holyoke College in Massachusetts to study chemistry. And not just because it was a women's college. It was a school dedicated to the progress of STEM, and it truly embodied the mission that women can change the world. I had mentors everywhere during my time at Mount Holyoke, ranging from senior students who shared internship information, to professors who encouraged me to take classes I was nervous about, to friends who helped me through overnight study sessions. Being surrounded by women who aimed high only made me more determined to be an expert in my field. The next step toward my goal was graduate school at Cornell University. I continued gaining expertise in my area by following up with a postdoctoral position, and eventually joined the semiconductor industry as a scientist.

In scientific research it is common to work for several years without getting the desired result. Many of us find lots of things that don't work until we find the one that does. For every experiment that results in a discovery, there are hundreds of ones that don't work. These results are equally important in advancing science. But we don't usually hear about these failures so it can be discouraging when you're starting out. After this experience in graduate school, I'm aware of the dedication needed for results that can revolutionize the world. So I keep myself motivated on the learning you do on things that don't work as I march toward the goal.

STEM subjects are the cornerstone to the understanding of and application of how things work and new inventions. STEM subjects also offer career paths that are interesting as well as rewarding. For me, it was applying my interest in chemistry within the semiconductor industry. •

Bree Vculek

Agricultural Biotechnologist

*I grew up in a small, close-knit, agricultural community
in North Dakota. At that time, I felt underprivileged.*

I had this feeling that I was missing out on something bigger, something greater, something more. My parents farm for a living by producing onions, corn and soybeans. As a middle school student in a class of 49 students, my "small community" frustrations included having only three sports to choose from, there was no such thing as competitive gymnastics and I spent my weekends jumping on hay bales instead of shopping at the mall. I have always had a competitive drive, and it seemed like I was slipping behind my perception of society by the minute. I felt isolated and closed off from the rest of the world.

Growing up in such a close-knit community, I knew all my classmates by name. I knew where they lived and what their parents did for work. Living in the country, I enjoyed a large backyard and a big garden with continuous exposure to commercial agriculture.

About Me

I was born in Lisbon (middle-of-nowhere), North Dakota.

My one and only sister, Larissa, is my best friend!

I've always thought that failure provides me with wonderful guidance, because it continuously teaches me to have perseverance, confidence and love what I do.

"I graduated with an emphasis on crop improvement and regulatory science."

Scholastic life was pretty good until fifth-grade math, which was a massacre. Up until that point, school had been pretty much smooth sailing. Math hit me like a brick. I was in danger of failing. I had never even imagined a B, much less an F. I remember thinking: "This is over. I'm done. There is no going forward. I am a failure. I'll never do anything worth doing."

But then my mom took me to a tutor, which I wholeheartedly despised. I still hesitate to admit that naming shapes helped improve my long division, but the prolonged practice with the material helped me to skate by with a B. This experience, although extremely debilitating to my psyche and to my confidence, sparked a fire within my heart that screamed, hard things were possible and I was capable! I was an overcomer.

Although I did not end up a mathematician, today, my schooling and career in research incorporate a great deal of mathematical models and skills. Maybe math was not my thing, but I did fall in love with science in middle school. I loved to see and to literally breathe the essence of life. I had so many questions about how things worked and how everything is somehow accomplished in nature without hurry.

High school expanded my horizons slightly. I tried "crazy" things like playing clarinet, painting ceramics and taking television production classes. I enjoyed the spontaneity and the ability to allow my creativity to soar, but the logistics and structure of physics, chemistry and biology completely captivated my attention. I also participated in 4-H, volleyball, gymnastics and competitive horseback riding throughout my high school career.

After much contemplation, I ended all activities after my junior year so that I could focus on taking a few college classes via interactive TV, and apply for college. This was a sacrifice I was willing to make. It was one that many of my classmates, teachers, coaches and family were not willing to understand or support. That was challenging for me. I cried about making the potentially wrong decision many times. I wanted to do what was best for my future, and I let my conscience and my passion decide. This was the first strong opposition I felt in my life, and it was such a growing point.

But things worked out in the end and I found myself interested in a career in the sciences.

My dream job is to be a research and development scientist in an agricultural biotechnology company. Agriculture encompasses the production of textile and consumable goods, and biotechnology is a collection of tools and techniques that are used together to improve and enhance agricultural products. I'm like a plant doctor who prevents problems from happening to the production of healthy organisms.

The improvement of agricultural crops is essential as our population continues to grow at rapid rates, and our available and suitable land for plant production is decreasing just as rapidly. It is important that we take necessary action to produce as much nutritious food that we can with a limited amount of land and resources, such as water and fertilizer.

What I love most about my work in agricultural biotechnology is the ability to dramatically improve the lives of producers, consumers and the environment. When a crop is producing more with less, the farmers are making more money, which helps with local, national and global economics.

. . . .

What I love most about my work in agricultural biotechnology is the ability to dramatically improve the lives of producers, consumers and the environment.

. . . .

I went to St. Catherine University in St. Paul, Minnesota, which has a foundations of biology curriculum required for a biology major. Foundations were essentially general biology, but broken into three different courses: evolution, cellular/molecular biology and ecology. These courses, along with a rigorous chemistry course load, definitely gave me a run for my money. I embraced the challenge, and I liked the material. It wasn't until the third foundational class with an emphasis in ecology that I really fell in love. We talked a lot about environmental issues, ecosystem ecology and agroecology.

I remember adoring the familiarity of agriculture, but being horrified by the harmful implications current practices had on our natural ecosystems. My heart was being torn in two: one way for the defense of modern agriculture, and the other for my compassion and concern for our natural ecosystems. I took a required class in plant biology and was one of 30 students who didn't absolutely dread the class. I really enjoyed discovering the idea of nutrient limitation and seeking innovative ideas to increase crop production. This interest and excitement led me to pursue my master's

My Favorite Things

July, for two reasons, first it's my birth month and also the month of my favorite holiday, the Fourth of July.

My favorite animal is my horse, Rico.

I love vacationing in Cabo San Lucas, Mexico.

The evidence-based nutrition book, "How Not to Die" by Michael Greger, M.D.

The color of chlorophyll, green.

90% cacao dark chocolate.

Dr. Jill Welter. She taught me how to think deeply and mechanistically, that is a lesson that will cultivate and bloom for the rest of my life.

Education

B.A.,
St. Catherine
University,
Class of 2015,
Major: Biology

M.S.,
Texas A&M University,
Class of 2017,
Biotechnology

degree in biotechnology and a certificate in business at Texas A&M University. I graduated with an emphasis on crop improvement and regulatory science.

I would love to continue my educational pursuits and earn a Ph.D. in molecular and environmental plant sciences (or some equivalent) and contribute to the agricultural biotechnology industry in research and development of edible food crops.

I am naturally a serious and intense person. That personality trait coupled with a ground-driven-Midwestern-farm-raised work ethic, the thirst for success and a slight (at times, debilitating) case of perfectionism, has led to a lot of late nights studying (and agonizing over the future) and Saturdays in the library, and very little time for "fun things."

I would work overtime until my eyes were no longer able to stay open. I would skip lunch. I was obsessed with schoolwork and research. It defined my life. When I graduated college, my research adviser and favorite professor gave me a pair of party glasses and a sweet note about her pride and joy in my success.

She signed it, "And don't forget to have fun." I think that having fun is subjective for everyone, so at the time, I kind of laughed and thought it was cute, but didn't take it too seriously. I think she has a good message, and I really appreciate, respect and honor such advice. It's important to do what you do with passion, but to have fun and to laugh often. Today, my favorite pastimes include horseback riding around the farm, mud running through fields with my four-wheeler, chasing waterfalls, drinking smoothies, distance running, yoga and laughing with those I love.

Take a break from studying to go sledding or treat yourself to a pedicure. Life is meant to be lived and to be lived with joy!

I never recognized how the exposure to agricultural production and the biological sciences were literally ingrained in me since day one. Amazingly, I would eventually grow to adore and appreciate each and every small community "inconvenience," as it shaped who I am as a human and as a scientist today. •

Caitlyn Holland

Software Tester

While I had a real passion and interest in math, my time in middle school was really hard. In addition to being teased and picked on, I also suffered from a mental illness.

Suffering from depression in middle school was challenging and painful. My depression didn't always stem from being picked on. Sometimes I just felt like everything was so much bigger than I was and I couldn't possibly handle everything that was being thrown at me. I felt so overwhelmed with emotion and it seemed like I couldn't get control back. I felt like no one could ever understand what I was going through, but I was wrong. My parents have always been my major support system, but I didn't let them know early enough that I was struggling because I thought they wouldn't understand. Once I was finally able to reach out and tell them I needed help, they helped me understand that I was experiencing a mental illness and it wasn't something I could control. They got me the help I needed and things improved dramatically!

About Me

I was born in Beacon, New York and was an only child growing up, but now I have a wonderful sister-in-law.

My favorite holiday is Christmas as I love baking Christmas cookies!

"While I enjoy being a tester right now, I plan to be a manager and maybe even a director in the future."

The good news is that while this was going on, I enjoyed working on word problems and algebra problems in middle school. What I've always liked about math is that the answer to the problem isn't based on a biased opinion. It wasn't like writing a paper. A grade on a math test is straightforward; you either solved the problem and found the right answer or you didn't. I didn't know what I could do with a major in math, but I knew that is what I enjoyed learning about, and so that is what I always wanted to go to college for.

Even though I always knew I liked math, it wasn't the easiest thing to admit to other kids in school. In middle school, I was teased because I was smart. I got made fun of by kids who didn't do as well as me.

Being smart is nothing shameful, but it was hard to remind myself of that sometimes. I was lucky in middle school because I don't think I was teased as badly as some of my other classmates. The reason that I wasn't picked on as often for being smart was because I sat next to one of the "popular" kids. Instead of bullying me, this kid asked for help. I helped him with class worksheets and he would always stand up to the kids who made fun of me. In high school I went on to different math classes and we lost touch, but I still remember that his bravery helped me get through middle school. He never made me feel badly about myself. This kind of bravery is hard to find.

In high school, I was in honors classes, and so that atmosphere of being picked on for being smart faded away. Feeling less stressed, I also felt better about myself. I was surrounded by people who were like me. Being in honors classes really helped me grow more confident in the fact that it was not only okay to be smart, but it was something I should be proud of. In high school, I continued to excel in all my math classes, and so I knew that wherever I went to college, I would want to major in mathematics.

Unlike most kids, I knew what I wanted to major in, but I didn't know where I wanted to go. Choosing the college to go to was more challenging for me than deciding what to do with the rest of my life. It seemed like there were countless options and so many places to pick from, and then one day I stumbled across Meredith College at a college fair. After going on a tour of Meredith College, I knew that that was where I was meant to be.

My college experience was truly remarkable. I learned so much in the classroom and also grew as a person. The professors at Meredith really help you succeed.

My senior year at Meredith, I became ill during my final spring semester. I had pancreatitis and had to be hospitalized for five weeks. Normally missing that much of a semester would be really hard to catch up on, but because I was determined to graduate on time, and because I had such a wonderful support system at Meredith, I was able to make up all the work that I had missed when I was in the hospital. My professors worked with me after I recovered to help me get caught up on everything. Without my professors taking time out of their schedule to help me, I don't think I could have graduated on time.

. . . .

Even though I always knew I liked math, it wasn't the easiest thing to admit to other kids in school.

. . . .

Today, I am a development tester, and I work in the technology industry for an analytics software company. Analytics software is a computer program that companies can use to make business decisions. Analytics gives companies information based on their past trends which can help them make better business decisions for the future.

As a development tester, my job is to ensure the software that is produced by the programmers is working like the company using the software expects. Some companies also call my role quality assurance. I use the software as a customer would to make sure that it produces results and it's easy to understand. I like to describe my job as trying to break things and pushing the software to its limits to make a good product a great product. When I have found an issue, I get to tell someone else that they need to find the solution to fix it. I am the advocate for the customer before the product gets delivered to them.

In order to be any type of software tester, you should have critical thinking skills. It is also important to be confident in yourself and in your work. As a tester, you need to have the confidence to speak up in meetings if you feel like decisions are being made that could impact the customer experience in a negative way. You are the voice for the customer and you need to always keep that in mind when discussing implementation

My Favorite Things

The Harry Potter series.

The color purple.

Tiramisu is my most favorite dessert.

Swimming.

Mr. Seamen, my fourth-grade teacher, because he helped me learn to enjoy reading.

Capri, Italy is my favorite vacation destination.

Dolphins.

Education

**B.S.,
Meredith College,**
Class of 2014,
Double Major:
Mathematics and
Computer Science

Leadership Certificate
Program,
Cornell University,
Anticipated Class
of 2018

of new features or pieces of software into the product. Having confidence to speak out is not just a skill that would make you a great tester, but it is something that would help you in any career that you choose to pursue.

I work in the customer-intelligence department of my company. This department focuses on helping companies get information about their customers so that they can personalize the advertisements that they show to each customer. An example of customer-intelligence software at work is if you are shopping online for clothes and you look at a specific sweater from a retail store, but decide not to buy the sweater. Later on that day, you receive an email from this same store offering you free shipping on that exact sweater. You may be more inclined to buy this sweater now that they have offered you some sort of a discount. This specific advertising is the main focus of customer-intelligence software.

In order to be any type of software tester, you should have critical thinking skills. It is also important to be confident in yourself and in your work. As a tester, you need to have the confidence to speak up in meetings if you feel like decisions are being made that could impact the customer experience in a negative way.

There isn't just one major that you can choose in college that is specific for software testing. A major in mathematics would provide you with the critical thinking skills you need as a tester. Mathematics would also give you some introduction to computer languages so that you have some basic knowledge on coding. A major in computer science would also provide you with critical thinking skills and even more in-depth programming skills to become a tester.

While I enjoy being a tester right now, I plan to be a manager and maybe even a director in the future. I am currently enrolled in a leadership certificate program at Cornell where I am taking graduate classes about leadership. I hope to become a test manager and be a leader in my company. I have been selected to be a part of my company's leadership development program. During this year-long program, I get to attend different workshops and training events that give me insight into what being a leader at my company would be like. I hope that I will be able to inspire young women within my division. My ultimate life goal is to be a role model for other female employees and empower them to achieve their big dreams in life! •

Catherine Burke Volle

Academic Scientist

It wasn't until college that I really began to enjoy science as a subject.

Since I had decided to become a veterinarian by the time I entered high school, I made sure to take all the science classes I could. I enjoyed them, but the pressure to get good grades made the classes less about what I was learning and more about how I could improve my scores on tests and homework assignments. Math, however, was something that had to be endured. My interest decreased sharply after I finished algebra. My attitude in school was one of grim determination; I had to make sure I did well so that I could get into a good college and continue on my path to becoming a vet.

You see, I've always loved animals, dogs in particular. In fact, I learned to stand by grasping the fur of my family's chocolate Labrador retriever. I figured out pretty quickly that by holding onto her fur, I could pull myself up. Later, she was in charge of pulling me in a wagon or sled. This helped develop my sense of independent exploration. At the time it seemed logical to find a career that would let me take care of dogs all the time. However, I had no idea what vets did or how one became a vet.

"I think that I will always work for women's STEM education."

Luckily, because we had four dogs, my family knew several practicing veterinarians in the area. These professionals were willing to answer my questions about what it would take to become a vet. I learned that I needed to get good grades and study lots of science and math. I found science interesting, but I wasn't so sure about math. During high school I finally had the opportunity to shadow a vet. I observed patient visits and surgeries. Being able to see a vet in practice helped strengthen my resolve to go to vet school.

When I was choosing colleges, I knew I wanted a small college with a good science curriculum. I ended up choosing Mount Holyoke College because they had been training women to succeed in sciences for a long time. When I went on a campus visit, the tour guide was oddly proud of a giant pile of dirt. This would eventually become the new science center. Looking back, I also chose the college for the community it built on campus. That community eventually became a huge part of why I succeeded in college. I majored in biology, but took most of my classes with the other students headed to medical or veterinary school.

I was devastated when I learned I would have to take two years of chemistry to even be considered for vet school. Chemistry was my least favorite science in high school. But that first chemistry class in college changed my life. I had never before seen someone so excited about a subject as my professor. He delighted in what he was teaching, and his enthusiasm was infectious. I discovered that I liked chemistry, and I liked how it fit together with what I was learning in my biology classes.

In my junior year of college, I decided to try independent research. I was sure I would hate it, but I heard vet schools were more interested in students who had research experience. I asked a professor to join her research lab which worked on DNA repair. But instead of doing that, I started research investigating the predatory bacteria Bdellovibrio bacteriovorus. Bdello eats other bacteria but doesn't eat eukaryotic cells. My project was to investigate how Bdello recognizes something as food. I started slow; just trying to grow the bacteria was a challenge at first. But eventually I began to make serious progress on my project. I could isolate molecules in the outer membranes of Bdello and its food and use chemical and physical techniques to search for differences. This work helped my professor get funding for the research, and part of that funding was a job for me once I graduated.

I decided not to go to vet school right after college. I was feeling burnt out after working so hard throughout high school and college. I was also beginning to have doubts about being a vet. I spent a summer during college with my grandparents in Texas working as a veterinary technician. I finally got the hands-on experience I had wanted. I loved it, but I called my parents crying more often than not. It was hard to see animals come to the clinic in pain.

During my two years working at Mount Holyoke after graduation, I became a scientist. My mentor was on sabbatical at Harvard for my first year, so I conducted research and kept the lab running. This was great training for later on in my career. I made significant progress on my project and developed several others. I went to my first scientific conference and presented my data to an international audience.

Currently, I'm an academic scientist, which means I teach students, both in the classroom and in the research laboratory. More importantly, my occupation is about mentoring young women in science. I work at a small women's college where I mentor students as a professor, adviser and as a scientific researcher.

In my second year, I had enough data to start writing my first paper, which was accepted and published. I was also developing a new passion — supporting women in STEM. As I began interacting more with the wider scientific community, I became more aware of the challenges faced by women and other underrepresented groups. I realized I was incredibly fortunate to have such a wonderful mentor. I wanted to do for others what she had done for me. I decided to become a professor. Vet school applications were abandoned. Instead, I applied for Ph.D. programs, eventually selecting a program at Brown University.

Currently, I'm an academic scientist, which means I teach students, both in the classroom and in the research laboratory. More importantly, my occupation is about mentoring young women in science. I work at a small women's college where I mentor students as a professor, adviser and as a scientific researcher. Throughout my career, I have spent a lot of time in a research laboratory. It's where I learned to think critically and analyze data, and made contributions to scientific enterprise. Now, I teach my students to do those same things.

Academic scientists work in a variety of higher educational settings. Some work in large universities and are expected to publish many scientific papers per year. Other academic scientists work in a college setting where their main focus is on teaching.

My Favorite Things

Vacation spots that include the ocean.

The color blue.

Reading "Wyrd Sisters" by Terry Pratchett.

Peanut butter chocolate cake.

Fermenting! I like using microbes to make food and even teach a class. I make my own cheese, yogurt, bread, sauerkraut and brew kombucha.

Dogs.

Education

B.A.,
Mount Holyoke College,
Class of 2006,
Major: Biological Sciences

Ph.D.,
Brown University,
Class of 2013,
Molecular and Cellular Biology and Biochemistry

They still produce scientific work, but it is secondary to teaching students. These scientists have all received similar training.

Work in a research lab can be independent. Usually researchers have their own project and the majority of their time is spent performing experiments related to that project. Research isn't always done alone; many times a scientist's work will be one part of a larger project; collaborating with others is crucial to everyone's success. Scientists need to be creative, thorough and skeptical so that they can design experiments that will provide them concrete information about the problem they investigate. They need to be able to integrate information from many different sources relating to the topic they study. They also need to be able to clearly and concisely communicate their findings to the wider scientific community and the general public.

> **Women in STEM need mentors and advocates, and they need to be told that they are capable of succeeding in these male-dominated careers.**

In an academic setting, this work takes on an extra dimension. I am responsible for beginning the training of the next generation of scientists. As the head of my research lab, I make sure that my students are getting the proper training to work independently and that they develop the technical and nontechnical skills that will serve them once they leave my lab. These skills include certain laboratory techniques as well as scientific communication and leadership.

Because I am head of the lab, I don't do as much research myself. During the summer and occasionally during the semesters, I'm in the lab doing research, but mostly I am supervising research students, preparing for and teaching classes and advising students. A typical day for me involves teaching one or two classes. I teach both introductory classes and advanced-level seminars. I also meet with students, either to discuss class work, research or to advise them as they decide on a future career.

I think that I will always work for women's STEM education. Women in STEM need mentors and advocates, and they need to be told that they are capable of succeeding in these male-dominated careers. Men, too, need to understand how their actions can affect the STEM environment and how they can be better advocates for and partners with women in STEM. I realized that alone, I can't change the status quo for women in STEM. But if I train many smart, capable women, and they train smart, capable women, together we can make STEM more accessible for everyone. •

Charlotte Brown

Clinical Research Coordinator

In elementary school I always tested high in English, reading and social studies. It was easier to get good grades in those subjects, but they didn't thrill me like science.

Science has always captivated me. I decided to take the STEM path of interest because it was the path that sparked the greatest passion for me. The easier path for me would have been to stick with studying English and liberal arts. But instead of doing that, I followed my heart, knowing I could master science, and I'm glad I did. My decision to challenge myself helped me realize I could do what I love. For me, that meant following my passion into a STEM field.

I'm a clinical research coordinator (CRC) and work for a comprehensive cancer center. In this role, I work with physicians and other clinical professionals to conduct clinical trials for pharmaceutical firms. Clinical trials are conducted before a drug is available and are part of the Food and Drug Administration (FDA) development and approval process. This process is lengthy as well as rigorous; the purpose is to establish drug efficacy and safety. All potential drugs, regardless of their therapeutic area, are required to go through this process.

About Me

I was born in Fruitport, Michigan and have two younger sisters.

My favorite time of the year is the fall when the air is just getting crisp and I can eat pumpkin everything.

However, if I were to have to pick a favorite holiday, I would say Christmas, it's such a magical time.

I work in the field of bone marrow transplant, which typically involves patients who have blood cancer. Potential cancer drugs are available to eligible cancer patients interested in participating in a clinical research trial. Once a patient is enrolled in a clinical trial, this is where I come in.

I love what I do because my role provides me with a unique opportunity to combine clinical research with a medical practice.

As a CRC , I must be organized, as our team is often working on multiple, complex clinical trials at the same time. We are the "protocol experts," which means we must know what sort of patients are eligible to go on a trial and when all the information needs to be gathered. This can include blood tests, pathological test (tests that can confirm a cancer diagnosis or remission), when study participants receive the new drug and what to look for so the pharmaceutical company can report its results to the FDA, that decides if a drug can be approved or not. There are a lot of rules to follow to protect patients' health and safety in the medical field, and then there are even more in the field of clinical research. We must know all of them and make sure they are being followed.

. . . .

I love what I do because it is always changing! We are learning and changing the face of cancer treatments. And when some of these new chemotherapy drugs come out, I know I helped with that approval. Without my STEM education, being in this position would not be possible.

. . . .

Every patient enrolled in one of our clinical studies is asked to sign a "data collection" consent form. Their consent permits us to follow up with the patient and continue to collect data on them. This data is critical because it helps us better understand the science of transplant, resulting in the creation of new treatments. Since data collection is an important component of a clinical trial, I also must be detail-oriented as well as accurate when capturing data points.

In my role, I also meet and talk with the doctors and nurses every day about our patients. We walk down to the clinic, where the patients come in to see the doctors and nurses, and make sure that all the information is collected. I also get to meet with pharmaceutical companies on their new studies. Sometimes they even fly us out to conferences to meet with other people doing the same research around the country (or the world!) and to learn about their new therapies.

"In my job today, I'm always expanding my science knowledge. Plus, working in a collaborative field is extremely rewarding."

Having an undergraduate degree in biology has helped me understand the drugs better. Classes like anatomy, physiology and biochemistry are what I have relied on most. CRCs have at least a bachelor's degree. Traditionally, CRCs were all nurses, so I work with a lot of people who have their bachelor's degree in nursing. Some of my peers also have their master's degrees in public health or a similar concentration, although a master's degree is not required for most positions.

I love what I do because it is always changing! We are learning and changing the face of cancer treatments. And when some of these new chemotherapy drugs come out, I know I helped with that approval. Without my STEM education, being in this position would not be possible.

. . . .

During my four years as an undergraduate, I worked and learned from an amazing group of professors and staff. I collaborated with some of the smartest young women I have ever known.

. . . .

The human body is fascinating, and there is so much we still do not know about it. When I was a little girl, I thought I wanted to be a doctor. That idea stuck with me, even as I applied to colleges. I can't remember a time that I wasn't interested in science and math. Math has always made sense to me because it's exact; there is no ambiguity about what is right or wrong. Science, particularly biology, is the study of life. I sent applications to several schools and was accepted at some prestigious and large universities.

My Favorite Things

Great books, especially "The Great Gatsby" by F. Scott Fitzgerald.

The color blue.

Dark chocolate anything.

In my free time, I love to bake! I also love to read and to practice yoga.

The science faculty, and most all the faculty at Saint Mary's have had such a profound impact on the person I am today. They taught me so much about science and fostered a sense of family among our peers. They have all been important to my learning and growing in different, but important ways.

I love vacationing in Northern Michigan, especially Traverse City.

Narwhals. They are pretty cool animals.

Education

B.S.,
Saint Mary's College,
Class of 2013,
Major: Biology

M.P.H.,
**George Washington
University, Milken
Institute School
of Public Health,**
Anticipated Class
of 2018

Ultimately, I settled on Saint Mary's College in Notre Dame, Indiana. The class sizes were small, and I knew I could make an impact there. What I didn't know is how great of an impact Saint Mary's would have on me. During my four years as an undergraduate, I worked and learned from an amazing group of professors and staff. I collaborated with some of the smartest young women I have ever known. We pushed ourselves and each other to do better and be our best students and selves. While studying at Saint Mary's, I discovered my love for research. I majored in biology and minored in both chemistry and math, which set me on the path for my STEM career.

In my job today, I'm always expanding my science knowledge. Plus, working in a collaborative field is extremely rewarding. I have found that it is not in competition with my peers and coworkers that I have learned the most or that the best work has been done, but when we all work together; it's a cliché for a reason. Empowering each other is so very powerful. By doing so, we can do the most good working together. •

Christina Churchill

Technical Sales Specialist

My mom has always been a huge influence on my love and appreciation for STEM-related subjects. She was a computer programmer for more than 20 years.

Having her as a role model was one of the reasons I never questioned being a young girl interested in STEM. My parents never parented through gender roles. I lived in a post-gender debate household. My dad taught me to fish and shoot a gun and no one ever dared to think I shouldn't love math.

I feel like I was luckier than most because I was never made to feel that my passion and success in STEM were abnormal. I was always great at math, science and logic. As a young child, I took apart toys and put them together again. My first memory of knowing that I had an aptitude for STEM was in first grade. Halfway through the school year, I started taking second-grade math. Every day after lunch, my teacher would walk me to the second-grade classroom. After several months, my parents and teachers decided I could handle all the second-grade lessons and moved me to second grade full time. For the rest of my school career, I was always the youngest in my class. This didn't make a huge difference until high school and college, but it never truly bothered me. I would never change skipping a grade. I was intelligent and I deserved the challenge. I carry that mindset with me to this day.

About Me

I was born in Raleigh, North Carolina and have one sibling.

My all-time favorite dessert is triple chocolate pound cake, made by my awesome mom.

And I LOVE cats! I have two — Noah and Charlie.

> "Working with clients is rewarding. I love being able to help solve real business problems with technology solutions."

My eighth-grade logic class was truly inspiring. While word problems are more interesting than plain arithmetic, logical reasoning really got me fired up. I absolutely love logic truth tables and logical fallacies. My logic class helped me realize that STEM can change the world because of the innovative reasoning you learn from studying mathematical and scientific principles.

. . . .
My eighth-grade logic class was truly inspiring.
. . . .

At my high school, there were two mathematics tracks: trigonometry/statistics and precalculus/calculus. I was one of three girls who chose the precalculus/calculus track. There were 12 boys in the class. That's 20 percent female. Twenty percent. Why had so many girls already decided calculus was a skill they would never need? We were only in 11th grade. Who was telling them this? I didn't concern myself much with it at the time, but looking back, the statistic genuinely bothers me. I excelled in the classes and many times found myself at the whiteboard explaining calculus problems to the class.

In high school, I decided I wanted to major in engineering. I landed on computer engineering, a decision inspired by my mom's career in computer programming. I had always planned to go to North Carolina State University. I was successful in fulfilling that dream, but not in the way I imagined. My junior year of high school, I was invited to the Junior Women's Leadership Conference at Meredith College, a small women's college a mere mile down the road from NC State. It was that day that I learned about the Engineering Dual Degree Program (EDDP) between Meredith College and NC State. The EDDP is a five-year program between the two colleges that allows you to earn a degree from Meredith in mathematics or chemistry and

a degree from NC State in engineering. Meredith College was a lot like my high school: intimate. I found a program that allowed me to continue learning how I learn best — in small settings — and it allowed me to earn a degree from the university I had always dreamed of attending. The idea of attending two schools and earning two degrees was frightening. It was challenging. I reminded myself the lesson from elementary school: I am intelligent and I deserve to be challenged. In the spring of my senior year, I committed to the EDDP.

I majored in mathematics and computer engineering and decided to apply my technical skills and knowledge in the field of sales, launching my career as a client technical sales specialist. I'm employed by a large cloud computing company. We sell software and hardware solutions that meet our clients' business needs. I specifically work with clients in health care, state and local government, education and life sciences.

Working with clients is rewarding. I love being able to help solve real business problems with technology solutions. I work with many clients who all have their own unique business needs and ideas. Some days I work from home and some days I work in a client's office. Other days I might end up working out of the airport lobby for a good portion of the day.

· ·

I majored in mathematics and computer engineering and decided to apply my technical skills and knowledge in the field of sales, launching my career as a client technical sales specialist.

· ·

It's very important that I understand their business needs. Technology changes quickly, so you must have a love for learning to succeed in this role. New innovations are added to our solutions and it is your responsibility to understand the new product abilities. You also need to have great verbal and written communication skills paired with an outgoing personality.

These skills help you form a relationship with your client. Empathy is a skill that will also help you better connect to your client. Presentation skills are critical as well. You will be working with many different team members over the course of a sales deal and product implementation, so it is important to be great at collaboration. Self-motivation is necessary to accomplish sales and business objectives. You also need to understand business requirements and be able to translate them into technology solutions.

My Favorite Things

Reading "You Are a Badass: How to Stop Doubting Your Greatness and Start Living an Awesome Life" by Jen Sincero.

The color gold.

Playing basketball.

Memorial Day Weekend is my favorite holiday.

Dr. Jennifer Hontz, one of my mathematics professors at Meredith College. She is absolutely brilliant and never afraid to be real with her students. Dr. Hontz gave me her unfiltered thoughts and advice and is always pushing me to be my best.

Lake Gaston, North Carolina is the best vacation spot!

Education

Dual Degree
Engineering Program

B.S.,
**Meredith College and
North Carolina
State University,**
Class of 2016,
Majors: Mathematics
and Computer
Engineering

This role requires a bachelor's degree in any of the following: computer engineering, computer science, information technology, computer networking, data science or other similar degrees.

Meredith College supported my dreams more than I could ever have imagined. I was surrounded every day by strong, intelligent and passionate women. I developed personal relationships with my professors that allowed me to flourish inside and outside the classroom. A defining moment came during my junior year.

My junior year in college was HARD. Up until this point in life, I always excelled. My identity was rooted in success and good grades. In one week, I failed two tests. I was breaking down and wanted to quit. I spent a lot of that week crying. I cried in a restaurant while out to dinner with my boyfriend. I called my mom crying as I sat in the school parking deck, dreading stepping into class. I even cried in my professor's office. But once again I reminded myself that I am intelligent and deserve a challenge. I learned that it is okay not to be perfect. Grades and GPA aren't equivalent to intelligence and passion.

Being at the beginning of my career, I haven't made solid future plans yet. Luckily, I have a variety of career paths I can follow. I could make the transition to business sales or pursue management. The area that interests me most right now is product-offering management. This role oversees product roadmaps, taking client and industry feedback to develop new features and functionality of the product. I will most likely go back to school to earn my master's in business administration. I believe having an M.B.A. will take me further.

Sometimes I'm asked how I use my STEM education on the job. I'm not using specific equations or theorems, but rather the ability to learn and reason. I also carry the soft skills that I developed, such as time management, teamwork and leadership. My technical background allows me to easily learn new product capabilities and my soft skills help me connect to my clients.

I am continually inspired to succeed so I can support my family. My parents made so many sacrifices for me to get where I am today. I do all that I can to give back to them and make them proud. I also have a younger sister who is in high school, so I try to be the best role model I can be for her.

For now, I'm looking forward to being part of improving the world by understanding and using technology. And, of course, continually advocating for women in STEM! •

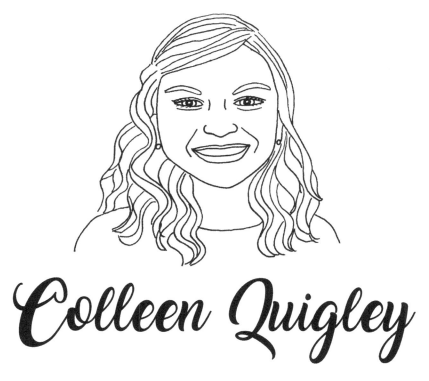

Colleen Quigley

Physical Therapist

*Being injured in a soccer game years ago began pointing
me toward the career I was meant to pursue.*

While playing soccer in eighth grade, I tore my ACL. The ACL is an important ligament in the knee. This injury required me to experience physical therapy (PT) for the first time as well as a reconstructive surgery. I guess you can say that my initial exposure to PT was fairly typical.

When I was in grade school, my dream of being a health care provider manifested itself in a desire to be a physician. I was fascinated by how the human body was put together and worked, so much so that my mom took me to a hobby shop and bought me a "visible woman," a human model for me to build. The skin was made of a clear plastic covering so that the internal organs and skeleton could be seen. In my mind, being a physician was the logical choice for someone who loved science and, more specifically, the human body.

It was not until my eighth-grade year that I realized there were more options than just the typical physician role.

I was born in Fort Wayne, Indiana and have two sisters.

I've been blessed with many great teachers along the way; one of my more recent great teachers is Dr. Reena Lamichane-Khadka. She teaches microbiology at my alma mater. I was able to complete a cooperative research project with her regarding methicillin-resistant Staphylococcus aureus (MRSA), a common bacteria that often causes hospital-acquired infections. I learned so much from that experience about conducting research, maintaining professional relationships and presenting yourself and the work you have done in a way that demonstrates balanced humility and pride.

"It's a good feeling knowing that things always have a way of working out, even when everything appears to be falling apart."

My injury was my first exposure to PT, but it didn't deter my career choice of becoming a physician. PT is often thought of as something athletes do after they get injured, or somewhere a person goes after they have had an orthopedic surgery. When I first learned about PT, this was my impression, too.

Two years later, I tore my ACL again, right after returning to soccer. That time, I elected to take the conservative approach, avoiding surgery, and just doing therapy to help strengthen surrounding structures so I could go forward without an ACL. That was when I finally realized how much PT could offer. My second time through, I began paying attention to the other people in the clinic when I was there, noticing how varied their reasons were for being at therapy and how creative the therapists had to be to help patients of all ages and mechanisms of injury get better. I noticed how therapists noted improvements and built relationships with their patients, spending quality time with them at each appointment. When I came back and shadowed my therapist later, it cemented my desire to pursue physical therapy as a career.

It was not until my eighth-grade year that I realized there were more options than just the typical physician role.

Moving forward with a clear picture of the career I was reaching for, choosing to major in biology was a logical choice. At school, the desire to pursue PT only grew. I took a class about medical ethics where we delved into dilemmas that plague those in the medical field. It gave me a great opportunity to think about the things I believe

"The Immortal Life of Henrietta Lacks" by Rebecca Skloot, the Harry Potter series and "Milk and Honey" by Rupi Kaur (to name a few).

Cherry Pie.

The color purple.

I love to read, watch too much Netflix and sketch and paint.

Thanksgiving.

Vacationing in the Smoky Mountains.

I have always been fascinated by wolves and by elephants.

regarding the rights all people have in terms of health care, and to ask myself how I would handle difficult situations as a PT. It was a great chance for me to look beyond the science and begin to consider the many other facets involved in the career I had chosen to pursue.

As I began researching the career, I found out that PT is much more than just sports rehab. While rehab is a big part of it, PTs also play an important role in other settings, including wound care, neurological rehab (necessary for a person who has experienced a stroke or a traumatic brain injury) and cardiopulmonary rehab (helping people to gain cardiovascular endurance). Right now, I am still in school working toward figuring out which setting I feel most drawn to, but I expect I will not stay in the same setting for my whole career.

Before entering a PT program, a bachelor's degree is required as well as the shadowing of different settings, and completion of specific prerequisite courses such as anatomy, physiology, physics and psychology. Many programs also require exercise physiology courses. I completed my prerequisites during my biology major with a minor in psychology. You can have any major, as long as you have completed the prerequisite courses. PT school is now a doctorate program, taking three years to complete, which includes the time spent in clinical-education rotations.

· ·

In my journey toward PT school, I have learned that it is okay to not have your whole life plan figured out in grade school or high school when people start asking you what you want to be when you "grow up."

· ·

Depending on where a physical therapist practices, whether it is in an inpatient setting, outpatient setting, nursing home or home-health setting, days may look very different. In general, physical therapists will see a number of patients and work on whatever deficits they may be presented with, such as limited range of motion, weakness or impaired balance. Movement is at the forefront of our treatment of patients. Through prescribing therapeutic exercises, the goal is to return patients to their normal level of function, or if not, to improve their functioning. A therapist will work with a patient on various exercises, employing other techniques, such as soft tissue manipulation or external modalities, while they are in the clinic. Patients will also receive a home-exercise program to work on when they are not in the clinic in order to make more lasting changes.

Education

B.S.,
Saint Mary's College,
Class of 2015,
Major: Biology

D.P.T.,
Indiana University,
Anticipated Class
of 2018,
Physical Therapy

During my time at Saint Mary's College, I had the opportunity to volunteer at a medical location of my choice. I spent time at a local nursing home, where I was able to shadow and help the PT department as needed. It was a great chance for me to get some experience interacting with those receiving PT in an environment I had not really been exposed to yet. The experience encouraged my desire to attend PT school. Along the way, I received a great deal of help from my preprofessional studies adviser who helped me make sure I was hitting all the courses required both for my major and for my future entry into PT school. I could not have gotten to where I am now without the help from her and my openness to changing my mind.

In my journey toward PT school, I have learned that it is okay to not have your whole life plan figured out in grade school or high school when people start asking you what you want to be when you "grow up."

I did not know what I wanted, but I was open to different opportunities and options. At first I thought I wanted to be a physician, and then changed my mind. Getting injured was not fun, but it led me to a career I am excited about every day, even when school is hard and officially being a PT feels far away. It's a good feeling knowing that things always have a way of working out, even when everything appears to be falling apart; if not for my injury ending my time playing soccer, I may not have found my dream career path. •

Deborah L. Eunpu

Genetic Counselor

In 11th grade, when other students were writing their term papers in English on Hawthorne or Shakespeare, I convinced my teacher that I had to write about "The Double Helix", and I proceeded to write my first article about genetics.

I knew I loved science from early on. I was fortunate to go to a summer science camp in middle school. As a high school student, I knew as soon as I took biology that that is what I wanted to do. I had a terrific teacher who encouraged me to reach beyond what I thought was possible. You will know if genetics is for you because it arrives as a passionate interest you cannot deny.

Once I decided that I wanted a career in genetics, specifically genetic counseling, my biggest hurdle was not having anyone who could guide me in my planning. The profession was so new, there were few people in the field and there were few positions. As a profession, genetic counseling came into being in the 1970s. As I reflect, I realize that my summer experiences were instrumental in helping me decide what I wanted to do with my life.

About Me

I was born in Troy, New York and have three brothers, all younger than I am.

Right now, my favorite books are French cookbooks: "Essential Pepin" by Jaques Pepin and "Mastering the Art of French Cooking" by Julia Child.

"I have always felt that I was a helper to families whose children often have complicated, difficult and sometimes fatal diagnoses."

I attended a college where I could excel in my own way, and I knew my personality was a perfect fit for the emerging field of genetic counseling because I have always been a pioneer. I've always been the one who is willing to try new things, and challenges don't deter me. Genetic counseling is more accepted now, but it's still a growing and changing field, so flexibility and a willingness to be open to change remains important.

I majored in biological sciences at Smith College and graduated in 1974. I learned a lot about how I wanted to work in the field. I was fascinated by what I learned in biology, but my strengths were less in the hands-on lab experiments and more in a clinical setting where I could use my social and caring skills. I thought about going to medical school, but ultimately decided on the newly created master's degree program in human genetics and genetic counseling. As soon as I found information about the graduate program in genetics, I knew it was for me. Within two months, I observed in a genetics clinic, applied and was accepted to the program on the condition that I finish the required statistics course. I earned a Master of Science in genetic counseling from Sarah Lawrence College in 1977.

Genetic counseling is a communication process. A genetic counselor works with families to provide information and support to individuals, couples and/or families who have either a risk for an inherited disorder or a family member diagnosed with a condition for which there is an underlying genetic basis.

A genetic counselor in clinical genetics works in a hospital or outpatient facility most of the time. Genetic counselors in pediatric genetics often work as a member of a team that includes nurses, physicians, social workers, medical assistants, laboratory technicians and other specialists.

Days are divided between preparing for clinic and reviewing records, and meeting with the family for their evaluation and counseling, then writing up the notes for the visit and following up with the family by phone or through future visits.

Pediatric genetics has allowed me to use my biology background, genetics specialized training, and my education and counseling skills. In pediatric genetics, the genetic counselor's role is varied and encompasses medical, social, psychologic and genetic topics to help answer a family's most common questions: "What is my child's diagnosis? Why did it happen? Can it happen again?"

· ·

Genetic counseling is a communication process. The genetic counselor works with families to provide information and support to individuals, couples and/or families who have either a risk for an inherited disorder or a family member diagnosed with a condition for which there is an underlying genetic basis.

· ·

In genetics, the "patient" is the family, and genetic counselors spend time with each family first, getting to know them and their concerns and questions. After determining what the family wants, the genetic counselor obtains a thorough medical history for the patient to be evaluated and constructs a detailed family tree, or pedigree. Typically, genetic counselors in the pediatric setting will work with a physician trained in medical genetics. Together, they examine the patient to determine what the diagnosis might be. Testing is common, and often it is the genetic counselor who will explain what the testing entails. After tests are completed, the genetic counselor's job as educator and counselor starts. We explain results to the family in a language they can understand to help the them understand the diagnosis, what they can expect over time, the genetic contribution to the diagnosis, its chance of happening again and options for future pregnancies and children. In many cases, the genetic counselor may also assist the family in identifying supportive educational, medical and social services as they learn to care for their child's needs.

The work with families whose children have inherited disorders, birth defects or cognitive differences is always challenging and rewarding. I have always felt that I was a helper to families whose children often have complicated, difficult and sometimes fatal diagnoses. This is the part I have always loved most, helping families find their way on an often unwanted and unexpected journey. The other aspect of my work that

My Favorite Things

The color blue.

Dark chocolate.

Cooking, gardening and singing.

Thanksgiving.

Peggy Jarman, my biology teacher in high school, because she always went the extra distance to make our learning relevant, and she knew how to help me grow my interest in biology.

Vacationing in a cottage on a lake in northern Maine.

My dog.

Education

B.A.,
Smith College,
Class of 1974,
Major: Biological
Sciences

M.S.,
**Sarah Lawrence
College,**
Class of 1977,
Human Genetics and
Genetic Counseling

I have always enjoyed is the daily learning. In a relatively new field still experiencing many new developments in diagnosis and treatment, there is always an opportunity to learn. After many years in this field, I am still not bored, and I love the challenge of continuously learning as I work.

Most of the 4,000 genetic counselors in the United States have a master's degree in human genetics or genetic counseling from one of the approximately 40 graduate programs in the United States or Canada. In the United States and Canada, certification and/or a license are required.

Genetic counseling is a field in which there are many directions one can go after the basic training. Genetic counselors work in clinical settings, laboratories, research, academic/teaching universities and community-based agencies. I have mostly worked in clinical settings, specifically in pediatric genetics. Over the years, my clinical positions have been at a major pediatric hospital associated with a medical school, a community hospital pediatric department and an outpatient specialty pediatric clinic. I have also taught genetic counseling at a university, and most recently I have been managing an online website that provides information about labs and clinics that provide genetics testing and clinical services. Although I have had many different roles, I will focus on my work as a clinical genetic counselor in a pediatric setting.

My career in clinical genetics has been exciting and expansive. Involved from the inception of the field, I've been able to create clinical and academic programs to further the growth and development of the profession over my career. I've also taken on leadership roles in all professional organizations, including founding member and past president of the National Society of Genetic Counselors, founding editor of the Journal of Genetic Counseling and past president of the Mid-Atlantic Regional Genetics Network.

Today, I work as a manager of the first website established as a resource that lists labs and clinics that provide tests and genetics services. I'm not seeing patients now, but that's okay. I get to work on the broader level, making sure clinicians can find the information they need for their patients. I still love learning about new developments in genetics, and I am not disappointed to continue learning daily.

I honestly think I have the best career in the world and who knows; maybe a career in clinical genetics is right for you! •

Debra Peattie

Science Executive

I've always liked exploring how things work.

I grew up in Texas, where summers were so hot that it was common to hear people say, "It's so hot, you can fry an egg on the sidewalk." One especially warm summer day, I started thinking about that and wondered if the saying was true. I was 8 years old and loved trying to answer questions about nature. So I did what any curious kid would do. I went into the kitchen, got an egg from the refrigerator and headed outside. I cracked the egg open on our front sidewalk and waited to see what happened. It didn't cook as quickly as it would have on the stove, but slowly and surely, the egg turned from raw and runny to cooked and gelatinous. My experiment was a success, and I was hooked on exploring what else I could discover about the world around me.

My 10th-grade chemistry class sealed the deal for me — I had a fabulous chemistry teacher, Mrs. Sellers, and I discovered that I loved thinking about molecules. I enjoyed physics and biology in 11th and 12th grade, even though I found physics hard. But I truly loved chemistry.

About Me

I was born in Dallas, Texas and have one sibling.

My favorite animals are my pets; currently a mixed terrier rescue named Shawn.

I'm always interested in vacationing anywhere that's near water, away from lots of people and close to excellent restaurants.

"*My role as a pharmaceutical executive allows me to earn a good living and make a positive contribution to society while pursuing my love of science.*"

A key challenge for me throughout my middle school and high school years in Texas was that I was a girl interested in science. When I wanted to take shop instead of home economics, which was a school class that girls used to take to "teach" them how to do "womanly" things such as cook and sew, my high school counselor told me shop wasn't an option because I might cut off my finger. Right. So, we compromised on drafting, where I guess I was safe from stabbing myself with a pencil. In 11th grade, my (female) physics teacher nominated me for a summer internship at a science research program sponsored by a local university. I completed the application and interview process, but both summer positions were awarded to boys. Only after I had completed college and had been admitted to Harvard for graduate school, did that summer program choose to identify me as an "applicant alumna." Thankfully, society has changed a lot since I was a young girl in Texas. Your challenges will be different than mine. We now have Title IX, which became law in 1972, and has encouraged generations of girls like you to go after and achieve what you want. We have had decades of people advocating for equal rights, equal pay and equal treatment, and you can build on that while achieving your goals and helping others achieve theirs.

I chose Hollins University because it wasn't in Texas and because I was ready for a change. The small liberal arts college in Roanoke, Virginia has a beautiful campus, and there was a brand-new science center in which I could envision myself happily working day after day. In addition, the chemistry department strongly supported students and offered constant encouragement and resources.

When I applied to graduate school, the entire chemistry department supported my applications. One professor took it upon himself to write each graduate school

directly to say that my lower-than-average GMAT scores shouldn't affect my chances of admission because my low standardized test scores (hate those tests!) reflected little about my ability to tackle and solve real scientific challenges. This level of support coupled with my coursework and lab research at Hollins translated into numerous graduate-school options for me. I applied to six of the top graduate programs in biochemistry in the country and was admitted to each of them. I chose Harvard University and obtained my Ph.D. in biochemistry and molecular biology in 1980.

The pharmaceutical industry originated in the mid to late 1800s when apothecary shops began producing and dispensing natural remedies. Around this time, dye and chemical companies began discovering medical applications for their products. Until the early 1980s, almost all therapeutic drugs were small molecule compounds that could be isolated from natural sources or synthesized in the lab. Small molecule drugs are taken by mouth — aspirin or ibuprofen would be good examples. Today, pharmaceuticals are of two key types: small molecule drugs that are taken by mouth and protein drugs that are injected because they would be broken down in your intestines like food if you took them by mouth. Insulin, used to treat diabetes, is a good example of an injectable protein drug.

In my current role as a pharmaceutical executive, I focus on recognizing unmet therapeutic needs for patients, identifying early stage scientific discoveries that could lead to medicines to address those needs, and then working to develop those new medicines. It is a long and expensive process; it takes anywhere from 12 to 15 years and almost $3 billion to develop a new drug.

> **In my current role as a pharmaceutical executive, I focus on recognizing unmet therapeutic needs for patients, identifying early stage scientific discoveries that could lead to medicines to address those needs, and then working to develop those new medicines.**

I like my work for several reasons. I love science, value the opportunity to think about it every day and enjoy being surrounded by smart, motivated people. It's rewarding to be involved in discovering ways to treat disease, and I like the financial benefits and professional security that the pharmaceutical industry offers. As with any profession, however, there are aspects of my work that I like to minimize, such as the time spent in meetings or the time it can take to move new ideas through the internal approval process.

Education

B.A.,
Hollins University,
Class of 1975,
Major: Chemistry

Ph.D.,
Harvard University,
Class of 1980,
Biochemistry and
Molecular Biology

M.B.A.,
**Harvard Business
School,**
Class of 1996

The pharmaceutical industry offers a range of professional opportunities. If you like scientific research, you could work in a lab doing hands-on research, for which you would need an undergraduate degree related to biology or chemistry, and you would do well to have an advanced degree (such as an M.S., Ph.D. or M.D.). If you like science or medicine but would prefer something other than bench or clinical work, the pharmaceutical industry offers numerous ways to leverage your skills in areas such as statistics, clinical-trial design, marketing, sales or business development, and you might be able to pursue these opportunities in various parts of the world given the global presence that many pharmaceutical companies have. An M.B.A. would be useful, but not required, to pursue the marketing, sales or business development avenues in the pharmaceutical industry.

My role as a pharmaceutical executive allows me to earn a good living and make a positive contribution to society while pursuing my love of science. I use my STEM education every day, whether it's to evaluate a new scientific collaboration or to learn about an area of medicine that could benefit from a new therapy. I also use my STEM education in solving day-to-day challenges, such as figuring out how to thaw my frozen water pipe (raise the temperature in the cold basement room where the pipe is in the ceiling), how to remove pine tree sap from my car (use rubbing alcohol to dissolve the sap) or how to stop my home fire alarms from going off when there's no fire (vacuum them because they've gotten dusty and the dust is disrupting the light beam detector in the same way smoke particles would).

My career path has been rich and rewarding, offering me the ability to focus on translating early-stage science into commercial products. I've been a researcher and professor at a major university, a scientific and business founder at start-up companies and a health care venture capitalist. I've also worked at a mid-sized pharmaceutical company with one marketed drug and fewer than 10,000 employees worldwide, and I'm now working at a large pharmaceutical company with multiple marketed drugs and almost 100,000 employees worldwide. In addition, I'm still involved in undergraduate science education. For more than 25 years, I have been a mentor in the biochemical sciences at Harvard University, working with undergraduate students to explore ways to leverage their interests in science after they graduate. A STEM education offers numerous avenues for your future.

Like anything worth doing, a STEM education will be multifaceted. Based on my experience, it will be fun, frustrating, challenging, rewarding, humbling and enabling. •

Devon Chenette

Tissue Regeneration Scientist

Have you ever fallen in gym class and scraped your knee? It happens to all of us. You put a bandage on and in a few days, it's totally fine. You may not have wondered how your body just repaired itself, but I'm totally fascinated by it! I'm a tissue regeneration scientist.

I have always been interested in understanding how things worked. Basic functions that your body does every day, like breathing, are extremely complex processes that scientists are still studying.

When I was younger, I would always ask questions to better understand the world. Despite my natural curiosity, it took until college for me to realize that biology was my passion.

In middle school, I gravitated toward STEM. I appreciated and understood the methodical and logical aspect of these topics. I even joined the robotics team, partially to balance out my athletic extracurricular activities like field hockey and tae kwon do. As a student-athlete, I was particularly attentive during biology class. The complexities that make up the human body fascinated me, even at a middle-school level.

About Me

I was born in Rochester, New York and have one older sister.

My all-time favorite book is "Jurassic Park" by Michael Crichton.

While I was drawn to STEM, I kept my options open for high school. I started looking into an alternative academic path and simultaneously applied to both high school programs and college through Mary Baldwin College for Women's Program for the Exceptionally Gifted, PEG. PEG presents a unique opportunity that gives young women the chance to challenge themselves and gain accelerated education in a supportive environment. In doing so, PEG fosters the minds of intelligent women and helps shape their future careers.

When I was younger, I would always ask questions to better understand the world. Despite my natural curiosity, it took until college for me to realize that biology was my passion.

When I needed to make a choice on what to do, I choose to defer acceptance to PEG and attend a magnet high school focused on math and science. During my freshman year of high school, I continued to play field hockey while studying a wide array of topics. Just as in middle school, I was still drawn to human biology. At the end of the year, I needed to revisit my decision to defer acceptance to PEG. I made the slightly terrifying decision to leave high school behind and go to college at 15 years old.

I was nervous and excited to take a college-level biology class. My first experience handling DNA, a genetic code that makes up living things, amazed me. I knew I wanted to learn more and focus my education in this area. At the beginning of my sophomore year, I declared myself a biology major and chemistry minor without any doubts.

After deciding my major, I took as many biology classes as possible, maybe even a few too many. I studied everything from freshwater biology, which included fieldwork at local rivers, to anatomy and physiology that focused on the human body and the way each organ works. In my junior year, I applied to summer research programs, and accepted a fellowship at a large university. This was my first true laboratory experience and I felt challenged in a way that was empowering. While I only stayed in this laboratory for three months, I left feeling certain that I wanted to attend graduate school and earn my Ph.D. in medical research. Immediately following college graduation, I began a Ph.D. program at the NYU School of Medicine, Sackler Institute for Graduate Biomedical Studies.

While the transition from a small college town in Virginia to New York City at the age of 19 took some adjustment, I believed in my education and myself. I knew

"I made the slightly terrifying decision to leave high school behind and go to college at 15 years old."

that I had the training and potential to successfully complete my Ph.D. During my first year of graduate school, I worked in three laboratories before deciding where to complete my Ph.D. research. Two of the three laboratories I worked in were cancer research groups. The third was focused on tissue regeneration. It was something new that I had no experience with, but was so fascinated by. I truly enjoyed the work and the research team. Those factors, combined with my drive and determination, made the perfect recipe for success.

I currently conduct medical research at a major university's school of medicine. Here, I use the experimental techniques and mental processing I have acquired to study neuronal regeneration. My long-term goal is to run my own laboratory as a principal investigator. This would allow me the opportunity to direct medical research and train the next generation of young tissue-regeneration scientists.

. . . .
I currently conduct medical research at a major university's school of medicine.
. . . .

Moments of discovery make the struggles of being a tissue regeneration scientist well worth it. Research does not happen on a regular schedule and not all experiments will give the expected results. To be successful, research scientists must be self-motivated and independent thinkers. I am constantly asking new questions and developing experimental approaches to answer them. The work I do in the laboratory is only limited by my imagination, followed by finding the right resources. I am in an environment that combines creativity and methodical thinking to answer unknown questions.

My Favorite Things

The color cobalt blue.

Cookies and cream ice cream.

Teaching my rescue puppy new tricks.

Thanksgiving.

My college thesis adviser, Dr. Pentz, because he found the perfect balance between pushing me outside of my comfort zone and encouraging me in a way that enabled me to feel empowered.

Walt Disney World in Orlando, Florida.

All dogs.

Education

B.S.,
**Mary Baldwin College
for Women,**
Class of 2010,
Program for the
Exceptionally Gifted,
Major: Biology

Ph.D.,
**NYU School of
Medicine, Sackler
Institute of Graduate
Biomedical Sciences,**
Class of 2016,
Cellular and
Molecular Biology

As a research team, we ask specific questions in the form of a hypothesis. We then conduct experiments to collect data that either answers our question or helps us create a new theory. The whole process is one big puzzle. Our experiments help us fill in the pieces. Our goal is to understand the human body's ability to regenerate tissue and use this understanding to create new therapies for those in need.

Completing experiments and analyzing data ultimately results in making a discovery. This moment is nothing short of incredible. For me, this happened for the first time as a graduate student working on my Ph.D. I was trying to understand the function of a specific protein in the cells that repair skeletal muscle injury, known as stem cells. I spent years studying this protein, and one day the data came together and created a clear image of how it controlled regeneration. This discovery helped start my career and confirmed my love for biomedical research.

In addition to having the right attitude, a career in medical research requires highly-developed technical skills. These skills are learned over time and with practice. A final key factor is patience. Good science takes time. In this field, there are no quick rewards or answers. Each experiment builds on the one before it, in a cycle that continues until a discovery is made.

After working in skeletal muscle regeneration for six years, I completed my Ph.D. following the publication of my scientific medical research. By sharing my data and discovery, I'm contributing to the greater good of human medicine. Following this success, I've had the opportunity to meet with multiple pharmaceutical companies, nonprofit organizations and other laboratories interested in building on our work. I hope that my graduate research as a tissue regeneration scientist will contribute to helping people in need of new therapies.

While this may make my journey seem like a natural progression of events, that is certainly not the case. Like medical research, my path has been full of ups and downs. From middle school through college, I have not always been a straight-A student. However, I have never been afraid to work hard and ask for help. I know that education can take me anywhere and knowledge is greater than the sum of my fears! •

Donna L. Vogel

Biomedical Program Director

I wasn't a very social child. Instead I was constantly reading.
If you called me a bookworm, you'd be right.

My first love was astronomy, then chemistry and biology much later. My parents were very supportive of my interests. I have always known I wanted to be a scientist. The idea first occurred to me when I was small, maybe 5 years old. All along, I loved math. In fourth and fifth grade, I was taking seventh and eighth-grade algebra and geometry. That didn't make me any more likable among my classmates. As time passed, I became more and more intrigued by the human body. As my interest in the human body grew, I also started coming out of my shell. I even had a boyfriend. Despite my focus on science and math, I enjoyed arts and literature as well — I wrote poetry and did a lot of acting. I'm convinced that my theater experience has helped me in my professional life with speaking at science conferences about research and orally presenting cases of medical patients. And I was never much of an athlete, but there was no escaping sports. Somehow, I ended up as captain of the varsity girls' soccer team, on account of sheer brute strength and attitude.

About Me

I was born in Buffalo, New York and have one sibling.

The best teacher I ever had was my fifth-grade teacher, Mrs. Cummins. I most enjoyed being part of a group that went to her home once a week to write poetry.

"*I have been lucky in that no one ever told me I couldn't do this or that. My parents and teachers encouraged me to become a scientist.*"

My school was small (40 in my graduating class), and the college counselor knew everyone well. I didn't have a very clear idea about colleges, and fortunately, I got good advice. My counselor thought that Bryn Mawr would be exactly the right place for me. I took her word for it. My class numbered fewer than 300, and we were all high achievers. It was a leveling experience — suddenly it seemed like everyone had been the editor of the high school newspaper. I was vaguely interested in premed, although not in treating patients for a living. At that time, the biology department was old-fashioned, but the chemistry department was more up to date, so I majored in chemistry. I concentrated in physical chemistry, which has a lot of calculus.

After college, I was in a combined M.D.-Ph.D. program. It took six years to complete and was followed by three years of medical training. I really wanted to do research, so I pursued more training at the largest federal health research agency as a postdoctoral fellow. I trained as an endocrinologist. Endocrinology is a field of medicine that concerns hormones. Hormones are essential for development and normal health. Disorders of hormones, such as diabetes and thyroid disease, are common. After my training, I mostly stopped seeing patients. Like most researchers, I was motivated by the excitement of discovering something that had not been known before. Expanding human knowledge has a powerful attraction. Medical research even more so, because your discoveries have the potential of directly helping people.

To be a researcher, you need curiosity, persistence, honesty and the ability to be critical about your own work. You have to understand the results and figure out whether the results are believable. You need to be able to learn from what others have done, but also to understand what hasn't been done yet. Professional skills are also important. You need to be able to get along with different kinds of people, to work in and lead teams,

to communicate by speaking and writing about your research and to understand the purpose of the place you're working in, or may want to work in the future.

After working as a researcher for about six years, I moved into a position called program officer, where I managed a grant program. I loved this job because providing money through a grant program can make a major impact on the field. My particular program was reproductive medicine and was similar to the research I had done as a fellow. The scientists supported by the program worked on male and female reproductive development. The difficult part of the job was being a small piece of a large government agency. Sometimes political concerns that had little or nothing to do with the value of the science would limit what we could do. After 13 years, I moved within the agency to lead an office advising postdoctoral fellows such as I had been.

···

Like most researchers, I was motivated by the excitement of discovering something that had not been known before. Expanding human knowledge has a powerful attraction. Medical research even more so, because your discoveries have the potential of directly helping people.

···

After five years, I left the government and worked briefly at a foundation managing grants again. Then I found my dream job. For eight years, I was director of the professional development office at a major research university in Baltimore. I got to do what I loved most all the time. Some of it was individual advising, and a lot of it was teaching. I never stopped loving the work, but the commute became too much. I was taking two trains and a bus to get to work, so I retired. Even after leaving that job, though, I continue to give talks and workshops, and advise people about careers in science. I have made it my mission to inform students, trainees and their advisers about what I like to call diverse careers. Even now, there are a lot people who don't know about these jobs and how to get them.

Much of my time these days is spent volunteering. Some of it is a lot like my work, and some of it is nothing like my work. For example, I am the career development representative for Bryn Mawr in the Washington, D.C., area. I put on events and give career advice to recent and not-so-recent graduates of my college. That's just like my work, except they are not all in STEM. I also work with the Association for Women in Science and some other professional societies. Though I didn't start out as a people person, I have become one.

My Favorite Things

Isaac Asimov's book, "The Foundation Trilogy."

Gardening.

Thanksgiving.

Without a doubt, Rehoboth Beach, Delaware is my favorite vacation spot.

My favorite animal is a cat.

The color purple.

Eating Heath Bar ice cream.

Education

A.B.,
Bryn Mawr College,
Class of 1971, Major:
Chemistry

M.D.-Ph.D.,
**Albert Einstein
College of Medicine,**
Class of 1977,
Medicine,
Developmental
Biology

Most people in biomedical research major in biology or chemistry. But I have seen many trainees and researchers who have other majors, not surprisingly physics or math, but also anthropology, philosophy, foreign languages and more. Professors and other faculty usually have a doctoral degree, either a medical degree (M.D.) or a research doctorate (Ph.D. and others). In public health and biomedical engineering, a master's degree may be the qualifying degree. Research teams provide technical and other positions in which holders of bachelor's and master's degrees can make a real contribution in support of a faculty member or other independent investigator.

Today, I use my scientific background to understand the work of the people I advise, and help them express themselves more clearly. Incidentally, I also use my knowledge in an unusual way. I am a volunteer reader for Learning Ally, a nonprofit that provides digital books to students with vision and learning disabilities. They like having me because I can pronounce the hard words in the science and medical books, and I love doing it because I like to perform.

I have been lucky in that no one ever told me I couldn't do this or that. My parents and teachers encouraged me to become a scientist. I still call myself a scientist, even though I have not done an experiment since 1987. Why do I say that? Because you never stop being a scientist. It's a way of thinking, a way of looking at the world. Some people think that if you are not peering at test tubes or yelling "Throw the third switch," you are not a "real" scientist. I disagree. If you can look critically — that is, with an eye toward whether what you hear or read can be believed — at the world around you, and draw conclusions based on valid evidence, you are a scientist. Our world needs STEM-educated writers, educators, health care professionals and entrepreneurs. Learn what is out there, figure out what you love and apply your best skills to a career that combines your passion, your gifts and your values. •

Elizabeth "Beth" Winslow

Pharmacist

For me, it was difficult to decide between a career in the arts or health care, and I soon found myself in a stressful dilemma.

To complicate things, since I never liked seeing blood, I worried that it would not be possible to have a health care career. Looking back, I now realize that I was simply considering all my options. Today, I'm excited about my future as a health care professional (although I never overcame my aversion to blood).

In middle school, I liked my science classes and thought the human body was incredibly interesting, but I was also interested in art. I loved going to art museums, where I was curious about how the artist chose the medium that was used.

With parents in the health care field, I was exposed to the field throughout my childhood, but I didn't know if I wanted to follow in their footsteps. I always enjoyed visiting my parents at work. My father is a paramedic. The way I always imagined it was that my dad went to pick up someone who needed help and would take care of them on the way to the hospital, where my mother would take over as a nurse in the ER.

About Me

I was born in Chesapeake, Virginia and have four younger siblings.

My favorite color is pink and I love cheesecake.

"*The pharmacy profession is all about making the daily lives of our patients better.*"

Needless to say, sometimes I felt conflicted about what I wanted to do with my life since art and health care both appealed to me. Going into high school, I was so nervous because I didn't know what I wanted to do with the rest of my life. It seemed like all my friends already knew. So I decided that I'd have to become a doctor, since that was the only career I knew of in the health care field other than a paramedic or a nurse (while in the back of my mind, I kept thinking the aversion I had to blood could be problematic).

My sophomore year in high school, I took chemistry and something clicked. I knew I wanted chemistry to be involved in my career somehow. Looking back, this was the turning point in my decision to pursue a STEM career that didn't involve being a doctor. I still had no idea what I wanted, though.

During my junior and senior years in high school, I decided to take a two-year art course. A portion of the course involved art history. We took a class on restoring art and I was amazed to discover that even art involves chemistry! Chemists take old paintings and sample the paint to find out how it was made when the painting was created. I thought I'd found my future career as a chemist in art restoration. At least, that's what I thought at the time.

About a year before this, a close family friend was diagnosed with Lou Gehrig's disease, or amyotrophic lateral sclerosis (ALS). This diagnosis made me think about a career in health care yet again. It was a constant shift back and forth between art and health care all through high school. I knew I wanted to be involved with Lou Gehrig's disease in some way, but I didn't know if I wanted it to completely be my life. I toyed with the idea of research and trying to find the cause and cure for ALS, but I performed a

survey experiment in high school around ALS, and I discovered research was not for me. When I entered college, I still wasn't sure what I wanted to pursue.

I decided to go to Hollins University because I felt most at home there. It was far enough away from home for me to grow on my own. Hollins was comfortable and welcoming from the start. It has small class sizes and close relationships with professors. When choosing my major, I went in with plans to do a double major in chemistry and art history because I wanted to pursue art restoration.

....

Currently, I'm a compounding pharmacy intern at a local compounding pharmacy as I study to become a pharmacist.

....

After my first semester at Hollins, I discovered that health care was what I wanted to do with my life. I knew I did not want to be a doctor. But I was still focused on how I could help ALS patients. At that time, there was only one medication on the market that was used to treat ALS symptoms. I thought to myself, "There must be more out there that can treat this disease."

When deciding on my major, I reached out to a few professors and my parents to talk out my thought process. My mother knew a pharmacist from my hometown, and through him, I had my first experience in pharmacy. He hired me to work in the pharmacy during the summer and over school breaks. After my first summer working in the pharmacy, I knew it was the health care pathway that I wanted to pursue. When I returned to school for my sophomore year, I began to take biology classes to start fulfilling the prerequisites for pharmacy school.

That spring, when it came time to declare my major, I had to choose between biology, chemistry or mathematics. I had 2 1/2 years left at Hollins and had to be realistic in what I could complete in that time. I was equally torn between those three possible degrees, but biology made the most sense for my choice to pursue pharmacy.

Currently, I'm a compounding pharmacy intern at a local compounding pharmacy as I study to become a pharmacist.

The pharmacy profession is all about making the daily lives of our patients better. The pharmacist is the most accessible health care provider, which means it is usually easier to see a pharmacist than it is to see a doctor.

Education

B.S.,
Hollins University,
Class of 2015,
Major: Biology

Pharm.D.,
**Virginia
Commonwealth
University,**
Anticipated Class
of 2019

Pharmacy is the monitoring, protection, research and development of prescription and nonprescription medication. Pharmacists can be found in the pharmacy, the hospital, in a science lab, in the classroom, on Capitol Hill and working with doctors in their offices. We can be found just about anywhere.

The best part of my job is the connection that I make with my patients. What I do at work directly helps them live better lives. To be in the pharmacy profession requires that you are good at doing lots of varied tasks, have a good memory, have compassion for others and are willing to listen to patients so that you can fully understand how best to help them.

Most aspiring pharmacists/pharmacy students have an undergraduate major in chemistry, biology, biochemistry or a health science-related major. After college, you go to pharmacy school to get a doctorate degree in pharmacy, called a Pharm.D., to become a practicing pharmacist.

A typical day for me in pharmacy school includes classes for about three to five hours. I participate in different pharmacy organizations and study a lot. I know it will be worth it in the end. Practicing pharmacists spend their day checking prescriptions, taking new prescription orders from doctors and talking to patients about their medications. Pharmacists also give people vaccinations.

On a daily basis, I am inspired by my colleagues and my patients. My colleagues remind me every day why I chose this profession, through their kindness to patients and interactions with everyone around them. My patients inspire me through their strength and patience. Medication does not always work the first time, and it can be frustrating.

Looking toward my future, I have about two years of pharmacy school left. I still have a lot of options open.

Mark Twain said, "The two most important days in your life are the day you are born and the day you find out why." I did not know that I wanted to be in pharmacy until college. In pharmacy school, I still do not know what kind of pharmacy field that I want to pursue, and that is okay, too! •

Emma Regan

Applied Physicist

I have a few friends who knew they wanted to be scientists since they were tall enough to look into a telescope or old enough to make a model rocket. Not me.

I was always a curious and creative kid, but I spent a lot of time doing other things, including painting, building with blocks, cooking for my stuffed animals and catching bugs. My parents are not scientists or engineers, so I didn't know what scientists did or what they were like. All I knew is that I loved to learn, play and explore.

In eighth grade, I was chosen for an independent project where I was asked to pause and consider what I found really fascinating. At the time, this was green architecture. I wanted to build energy-efficient homes to reduce our impact on the environment. I took a trip to a greenhouse-building competition for college students, and I learned that even college students could use science and technology to build beautiful, energy-efficient homes. These students were already ready to create, test, discover and contribute to the world. I wanted to do the same. My dad helped me design and build a model green home. It was the first time I was told to run wild with an idea; in retrospect, there was no reason to wait until I was told.

About Me

I was born in Washington, D.C. and have one sibling.

While I don't have a favorite book (simply because there are many great ones out there), I do have a favorite teacher: Ted Ducas. He was my college physics professor. Dr. Ducas is encouraging, challenging and hilarious.

When I got to high school, our school had a robotics club, but it was mostly boys, which made me a little nervous, so I joined an all-girls robotics team. I had no knowledge that would help me build or program the robot, but I was excited to learn. Along with my team, we designed, built and programmed robots to play a game against other robots. Working with the team helped me develop a lot of skills I still use today. There were only a handful of girls at the competitions and even fewer all-girls teams, but we showed everyone that girls can build amazing robots, too. The competitions were a blast — strategizing with other teams, borrowing parts that had broken in the previous match and running to fix our robot before the next match began.

During my junior year of high school, I was so excited about biology that I skipped physics to take an extra biology class. When I finally took physics, I realized I loved it — even more than biology. I started to think about biology in terms of physics.

The most important part of my robotics experience was meeting students and mentors who supported my curiosity. Our coach became a key figure in my development as a person and a scientist. In addition to advising the robotics teams, he encouraged us to learn and explore the world. We launched a weather balloon with electronics and chased it all over the state, we tried to design a super lightweight rocket and we had hours of fun exploring and building in the robotics lab. I credit much of my sense of adventure to him.

I turned to my robotics coach when I realized I was interested in biology. A few years earlier, my grandma passed away from cancer. I couldn't understand why doctors didn't cure her. My grandpa, her husband, was a doctor and sent me a college-level textbook on cancer biology. It was way over my head, but I began to learn about the complex mechanisms that drive cancer. One day, I approached my robotics coach and told him I was interested in biology research. One of the girls on my robotics team had done some physics research at a local university, so I thought maybe I could do the same.

Remarkably, my robotics coach helped me to start cancer biology research at my own high school. One of the biology teachers had a Ph.D. in genetics and she helped me to design my first experiment. Of course the high school biology lab did not have all the tools of a large research lab, but we tried our best. I wanted to study how different molecules in the body interacted to turn genes on and off in cancer cells. I slowly

read research papers, learned lab techniques and tried to make a dent in my research question. When I got to college, I had a leg up because I was already comfortable reading scientific papers and thinking critically about scientific questions.

During my junior year of high school, I was so excited about biology that I skipped physics to take an extra biology class. When I finally took physics, I realized I loved it — even more than biology. I started to think about biology in terms of physics. After all, we look at cells, tissues and organisms in a microscope using light, and the interaction between the biological parts and the light is physics! The application of physics to biological systems, also known as biophysics, was an exciting mix of everything I loved: biology, engineering and physics.

> **I figured out early on that it's important to surround yourself with people, and especially girls, who also love to learn. Joining an all-girls robotics team was one of the best decisions I ever made.**

I applied to college as a prospective biophysics major. Most colleges and universities do not have a biophysics program, so I planned to double major in biology and physics. I applied to a wide range of schools. Ultimately, I chose to attend Wellesley. Wellesley is a small college outside of Boston with fantastic professors, small classes and extensive cross-registration programs with other schools in the area. I was able to do research and take advanced courses at engineering schools like MIT, which was just down the road.

Right now, I am a first-year applied physics graduate student at the University of California, Berkeley. The distinction between applied physics and physics is pretty blurry, but I often tell people that I want to invent useful technologies using exciting, new physics. For example, before electronics were everywhere, in smartphones, laptops and even in your microwave, some impressive scientists figured out the physics of the tiny elements that together make our machines run. As we need faster, better and entirely new technologies in our lives, we will also need new physics to make these devices.

My area of expertise is light. In particular, I study how we can use light to investigate new materials for devices, and how we can use creatively designed materials to control light. This field is called photonics, and it is somewhere in between physics and electrical engineering, my favorite place. While big electronics and computer companies are already using photonics every day to design better laptop screens

Education

B.A.,
Wellesley College,
Class of 2016,
Major: Physics

Ph.D.,
**University of
California, Berkeley,**
Anticipated Class
of 2021,
Applied Physics

"My area of expertise is light. In particular, I study how we can use light to investigate new materials for devices, and how we can use creatively designed materials to control light."

and send information faster, a large part of the photonics community resides in universities around the world. At universities, physicists study the fundamental interactions between light and objects, and engineers figure out how to use these interesting phenomena in practical devices.

As a graduate student, I spend my days between my office and my labs. Our labs are scattered with different tools that help us to fabricate, visualize and test materials and devices. When we are in the lab, we wear blue flame-resistant lab coats and gloves for protection. Every day, I spend time solving problems, learning more physics and talking with my labmates about how to explain or understand my results. Graduate school is challenging because we consider difficult questions and have long hours, but it is wonderful to learn so much.

Most people in my lab studied electrical engineering, materials science or physics in college. As Ph.D. students, we are all training to be researchers, but with many different long-term goals. My dream is to work on a research team in a large company on a big, exciting, collaborative project. I want to be part of a big collaboration with lots of people working toward one goal. On a daily basis, researchers work in small teams on their own projects, but ultimately, everyone wants to make progress in one area. I work best in a collaborative environment, so this sounds perfect for me.

I figured out early on that it's important to surround yourself with people, and especially girls, who also love to learn. Joining an all-girls robotics team was one of the best decisions I ever made. For the first time, I had friends who shared my love of learning, and we had so much fun together. With them, I discovered that science and engineering can (and should!) be social. We often picture a scientist as a man in a white lab coat working alone, but doing science is definitely not like that! In the lab, I spend lots of time talking with my coworkers and figuring out what is going on with our experiments. We take breaks, we have lunch together and we help each other in the lab. Make sure your friends also love to learn. These girls will be your biggest support! •

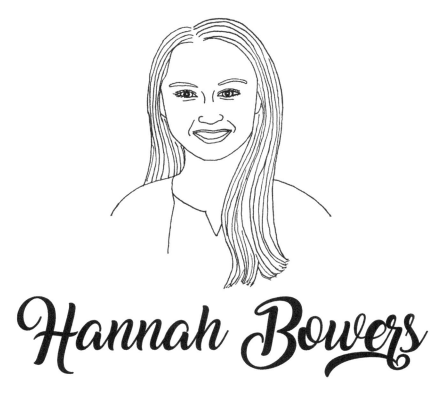

Hannah Bowers

System Safety Engineer

Most everyone knows someone in the military. Depending on where you live, you might even see signs that say, "Support our Troops," or yellow ribbons attached to trees or painted on buildings.

Often, these brave men and women who serve in the armed forces are put into situations that can be dangerous, and it's important to find ways to help keep them safe. My job as a system safety engineer (SSE) is to make sure that the people who are defending our country can do their jobs effectively and safely.

My job is to conduct system safety engineering on a weapon that is found on a naval ship which protects our nation by sea. What this means is that I evaluate, or assess, the risk of a project to assure that a system behaves as needed, even when mechanisms fail. All technology comes with a risk. The only way to build a completely safe system is to not build it at all. Since this isn't an option for the military, a SSE is brought onboard to help support informed decision-making processes. It is my job to make sure employees, the environment and equipment do not become injured or damaged.

About Me

I was born in Fredericksburg, Virginia and have one older brother.

Since horses are my favorite animal, it's understandable that horseback riding is my favorite pastime, and easy to understand why I loved reading the novel series created by Lauren Brooke, "Heartland."

Education

B.S.,
Sweet Briar College,
Class of 2015,
Major: Engineering Science

Working on a research and development naval base, I put my engineering-science degree to use by watching over those who risk their lives for our country.

One highlight of my job is that I assist with testing that is performed on the naval ship. This is super exciting for me because I get a chance to really see what I've created be put to use. Recently, I got to visit a ship in port and work in the command and control areas. Being able to be a part of the testing and having hands-on involvement with the weapon module was beneficial because I was working alongside military members. Knowing that the projects I work on help keep them safe was a very humbling experience. Most of all, what I like best about being a SSE is that I work on the entire project from start to finish. Plus, I help provide ideas to ensure that a system is designed and created to the best of its ability in order to function properly.

> **Working on a research and development naval base, I put my engineering-science degree to use by watching over those who risk their lives for our country.**

SSEs are involved in all parts of all testing, maintenance and events connected to the project. We must be present throughout the entire life cycle so that we can be sure the project stays safe. If a problem arises, we must find the source and a solution so that it does not happen again!

System safety engineering is a growing field that has only been around for a few decades. It's still very new, which means that there are so many career opportunities for those interested in technology. While I'm employed as a SSE within the U.S. government, SSEs are also employed in private industries. System safety is just one method of communication that is used by engineers working on a system. I help to decide if the risks involved in the system are acceptable for a project.

Growing up, I always liked Legos, building with my hands and problem-solving. I always really enjoyed planning out and then completing Lego projects. In school, I enjoyed math more than other subjects. Little did I know that my interests in problem-solving, conceptual design and math would eventually guide me toward a STEM career. Once I got to high school, I started to take more math, design and even a couple of programming classes. I started thinking about pursuing a STEM field in college.

"System safety engineering is a growing field that has only been around for a few decades."

My Favorite Things

The color green.

Ice cream.

Christmas.

Dr. Brinkman, a Sweet Briar College professor. She allowed me to grow as an engineer and challenged me to always work hard.

The beach as a vacation destination.

I attended Sweet Briar College and majored in engineering science. This engineering degree consisted of a mechatronics design, which means I studied all different types of engineering. My classes were split between mechanical engineering, electrical engineering and computer science. This broad approach to my major has served me well. I was exposed to so much information that I felt comfortable refining my interests. I was able to take many different classes involving different types of engineering. This degree has also allowed me to apply to a more diverse set of jobs than just a mechanical engineer, giving me more options when searching for a job upon graduation.

Growing up, I always liked Legos, building with my hands and problem-solving. I always really enjoyed planning out and then completing Lego projects.

When I graduated from college, I didn't even know what a SSE was. This was yet another benefit of my degree. There are so many jobs out there that I had never heard of, but they're jobs for which I'm qualified and can perform. This means that my job potential is limitless and I will always be able to challenge myself to find new things that interest me. That's the wonderful thing about studying a STEM subject. It's an opportunity to expand an interest into a really cool career. I found mine by studying engineering. And now I'm engaged in work I find interesting and rewarding. •

Janelle V. Reynolds Fleming

Oceanographer

Not everyone starts out with an interest in STEM.
At least, that's not how it happened for me.

I was almost not accepted into a private middle school because my math scores were so low. However, when I was in seventh grade, things just started to click. I'm not sure if the material was presented differently or there were different teaching styles, or if I had matured, but I took an early math exam and scored the highest in the class. From there, I was put in the accelerated program for math and science and really enjoyed it. It was also in seventh-grade Earth Science that I completed a project on tides. I grew up near the ocean and was both awed and frightened by the enormity of it and the animals that lived within. For this project, I monitored the tidal cycle near a local bridge for a month and reported my findings. This experience really opened my eyes to the cyclical nature within the environment.

While in high school, my favorite class was biology, and this was mostly because of the instructor. She was a hard instructor and made us learn all the Latin derivations of the scientific names we were learning in class. I didn't do well in class until we started modules in botany. Again, something just "clicked," and I loved it.

About Me

Hailing from Florida, I so enjoy scuba diving, and fortunately this is a skill that comes in handy as an oceanographer. Plus, I also teach scuba diving and science diving courses as part of my occupation.

I have two siblings and my favorite vacation spot is anywhere my family is located.

"I also teach scuba diving and science diving courses as well as provide community outreach and education."

My first major, for the first three weeks of Wesleyan College, was vocal performance. As much as I enjoyed this major, I really felt unchallenged. I was looking for something that was inspiring, not safe. That first year in college was an expansive one for me. I took several classes like psychology and sociology, which I had never even heard of before. It wasn't long; however, before I realized that math was where my heart was. I believe that Wesleyan provided the opportunities to allow me to explore what subjects were most important to me.

Much of my time involves manipulating large data sets, primarily relating to weather conditions, like storms and hurricanes. As a mathematician, this is most enjoyable!

While in college, I saw an internship advertised on the department bulletin board. This internship was for the fall semester at one of the Department of Energy research laboratories. I applied with the support of my main advisers and was accepted into a program at a national laboratory in Tennessee. This internship opened my eyes to the possibilities of conducting research. I worked on a mathematical model of neural networks for the fall semester. At the end, I presented my findings in a research paper and gave an oral presentation. This was my primary introduction to graduate-level work. I knew that research really intrigued me and that regardless of the occupation I selected, research would be involved.

Today, I'm an oceanographer. I decided upon this occupation because I was looking for a career that had meaning and also leveraged my passion for mathematics and the

environment and my interest in research. I became interested in oceanography when I was in graduate school, and quite by accident. I was attending Texas A&M University and studying computational mathematics. I took an oceanography class for fun and quickly became hooked. I decided to continue on for my Ph.D. in physical and biological oceanography, specializing in coastal biology and physics with an emphasis on data analysis, numerical modeling and oceanographic instrument development.

In its simplest terms, oceanographers study the ocean. Oceanography is encompassing, as there are many disciplines that go into the study of the ocean. Depending upon your area of interest, you'll have many career options.

··

Today, I'm an oceanographer. I decided upon this occupation because I was looking for a career that had meaning and also leveraged my passion for mathematics and the environment and my interest in research.

··

Biological oceanography, or the life within the ocean, is a broad term and covers many plant/fungi/animal/bacteria/protista interactions within the ocean. Physical oceanography analyzes the mechanical drivers of the water within the ocean, records how the water and atmosphere interact, including the travel patterns, determines how and why they flow in any particular direction and predicts flow patterns based on mathematical equations and known constituents.

Other disciplines include chemical oceanography, which investigates the chemical components of the water column, the organisms that live in the water column and the chemicals they produce. A water column is a vertical slice of the water body that extends from the surface to the bottom with a known area. There is also geological oceanography or the geology of the ocean, which seeks to understand questions about the composition of sand, rocks, the crust under the ocean and why these structures form.

After completing my Ph.D. program, I traveled to New Zealand to complete a two-year post-doctoral appointment at the University of Canterbury in Christchurch studying the larval transport of the green mussel, Perna canaliculus, a commercially important species. Upon our return to the United States in 2006, my husband and I started a consulting firm, Seahorse Coastal Consulting, to fill a gaping need in environmental consulting. We provide various consulting services including research,

My Favorite Things

Madeleine L'engle's book, "A Wrinkle in Time."

I love the following colors in combination: purple, green and blue.

I never get tired of eating chocolate mousse.

Thanksgiving.

My biology teacher in high school, Marcia Grady.

Leopards are my favorite animals, followed by octopuses.

Education

B.A.,
Wesleyan College,
Class of 1994,
Major: Mathematics

M.S.,
Texas A&M University,
Class of 1996,
Computational
Mathematics/
Oceanography

Ph.D.,
University of North
Carolina at Chapel Hill,
Class of 2003,
Physical and Biological
Oceanography

education and outreach. We also develop software and provide technical support for this software. One main product has been the ADCIRC Surge Guidance System (ASGS) that is used to predict storm surge associated with major storms and is used in the southeastern United States.

Much of my time involves manipulating large data sets, primarily relating to weather conditions, like storms and hurricanes. As a mathematician, this is most enjoyable! I love taking data and turning it into useful information. Another component of my work includes conducting marine research which entails designing scientific studies to answer specific questions, deploying and retrieving scientific instrumentation, downloading the data stored on the instrumentation, learning the different organisms in both temperate and tropical locations, training scientists on these organisms and how to collect data and disseminating this information to scientists and non-scientists alike. I also teach scuba diving and science diving courses as well as provide community outreach and education.

Many people find the ocean fascinating and understandably so. While humans have been studying the oceans since time began, we have so much more to learn and understand. Early on, ancient civilizations monitored the tides and the moon as a way to determine the best fishing strategies for their villages. Interest in a systematic approach to studying the oceans began in the early 20th century, fueled by conflicts such as World War I and World War II. During this time, the U.S. government helped establish many research organizations at several universities by investing funds in the study of the oceans.

If you're thinking about a career involving the ocean, know that jobs within the industry are unlimited and can include careers like marine fisheries observers, marine fisheries modelers, aquarists, researchers, educators, ocean advocacy leaders, oceanographers for the Navy, meteorologists, coral reef biologists, sea grass biologists, ocean chemists, etc.

Possible STEM majors that would apply to oceanography include mathematics, physics, chemistry, biology, geology and statistics. Helpful skill sets include communications (to help communicate your results to stakeholders), public speaking (again, to help communicate your results to stakeholders) and business (to help give you the financial capacity). If you would like to lead your own research projects, then a master's degree and more likely, a Ph.D., will be required. It's best to major in a major STEM field, like listed above, for your bachelor's and then to specialize for a master's or Ph.D.

The human spirit inspires me. So many people, whether young or old, are enthusiastic about the oceans and its environment and have excellent ideas on how we can make things better. If we can understand how the world is currently working, we may be able to help maintain it. •

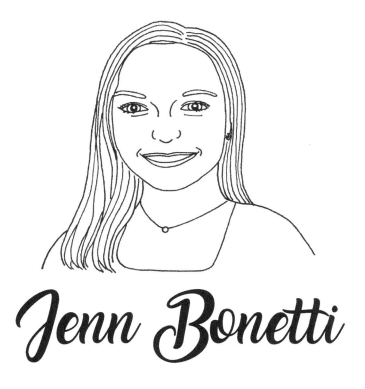

Jenn Bonetti

Forensic Scientist

When a crime is committed, or suspected to have been committed, there is generally physical evidence that can tell the story so that the events can be recreated using actual scientific analyses rather than relying on eyewitnesses.

This is where I come in. I'm a forensic scientist. Forensic scientists play an important role in our justice system by proving guilt or innocence. I feel that I am making a real contribution to society with the work that I do.

Studying forensic science was a natural choice for me. I've always loved puzzles and solving problems, and found chemistry intriguing. I knew that I could not make a living by doing jigsaw puzzles all day, but forensics offered a way for me to use that problem-solving process and apply it to other areas.

I specifically work in the controlled substances section of my lab, also known as the drug section. When a suspect is assumed to possess or sell a drug, the unknown substance is sent to my section so that we can figure out whether any drugs actually are present, and confirm exactly what they are.

About Me

I was born in Kingston, New York and I have one sibling.

I love red velvet cake and Christmas.

Reading, dancing, singing and puzzles rank high on my list of fun things to do.

"I am constantly inspired by the people that I work with. I am surrounded by some of the most intelligent people I have ever met, so it motivates me to do my best work every day. I'm also inspired by the knowledge that my work has a real impact on the lives of people in the community."

Attention to detail is very important in any section within a forensics lab. We often need to be able to get cases done quickly while still getting accurate results. Our results have a large impact on the lives of the people involved. It's also helpful to have a sense of natural curiosity. Every case is different and each case is like a puzzle that I get to solve.

It's also important to have integrity. We need to be able to testify to our results and give the community reason to trust that our results meet the expected level of quality that is necessary for a court of law. Along those lines, public speaking abilities come into play quite often since we need to be able to explain our scientific analyses in a manner that can be understood by those outside of the profession. I've always loved being involved in theater, which is incredibly helpful in this sort of profession.

Any natural-science major can be applicable to forensics. For my specialty, a degree in either chemistry or forensic science is the most common. For those more interested in

DNA, a biology degree may be more helpful. Many scientists can be very successful in this field with a Bachelor of Science degree, although it is growing increasingly common to have a Master of Science degree, either in forensic science or in a natural science such as chemistry or biology. For some disciplines, especially toxicology where drugs are detected in bodily fluids, a Ph.D. can be required.

....

I remember always loving math and science courses throughout elementary and middle school. My father was an engineer and would take me to "Take Your Kid to Work Day" every year.

....

Most of my day is spent in the laboratory analyzing casework. This is one of the things I love most about this profession. I love not being in an office all day! Each case is different, so every day is a little different. Generally, I start by sampling cases. This means that I open the sealed evidence, document what the evidence actually is, weigh the substance and then take a representative amount of the sample to analyze before resealing the evidence in its packaging. Once I have a sample to work with, I begin to analyze it. This involves screening tests which give me an idea of what types of drugs may or may not be present. From there, I can determine how to proceed. It's similar to a puzzle or a scavenger hunt where I take different steps along the way based on what my initial tests show me. Once I have completed the analysis, I then type up my results in a Certificate of Analysis. After review, the case is complete.

I remember always loving math and science courses throughout elementary and middle school. My father was an engineer and would take me to "Take Your Kid to Work Day" every year. This was a fantastic introduction to the world of STEM. It always seemed so captivating. I also have early memories of a family friend quizzing me with various math puzzles, like asking me to count backwards from 103 by sevens.

I loved learning about how things worked and why things were the way they were in the world around me. When I got to high school, I couldn't put my finger on the reason, but I was extremely excited to study chemistry. It might have been from watching Bill Nye as a kid or just random tidbits of information that I picked up along the way, but I just had a feeling that I would really enjoy the class. Sure enough, I found that chemistry just clicked. From balancing equations to reaction mechanisms, I loved feeling like I was solving puzzles that had practical applications. Since that was what I loved so much about it, it would seem only natural that I would eventually discover forensics as a way to use my chemistry knowledge in a practical manner.

My Favorite Things

"Name of the Wind" by Patrick Rothfuss and the Harry Potter series.

The color blue.

My Organic Chemistry professor in college. He was probably the most intelligent individual I have ever met, but also one of the funniest and kindest. He was a huge inspiration. It takes a special person to make a whole class love Organic Chemistry, and he was able to do it!

Vacationing in Bermuda is the best!

Horses.

Education

B.S.,
Cedar Crest College,
Class of 2011,
Major: Chemistry/
Forensic Science
Concentration

M.S.,
Cedar Crest College,
Class of 2012,
Forensic Science

I knew that I wanted to do something with chemistry, but I had no idea what I wanted beyond that. I knew a little about forensic science because my sister was going to college for it, but, as is common for many high school students, I had no clue what I wanted to do for the rest of my life. It's a scary decision. I figured a chemistry degree would give me a lot of options. I went with a forensic science concentration because the field sounded interesting and I wanted to learn more, but I knew that if it wasn't for me, the possibilities were nearly endless with a chemistry degree.

The most challenging step on my path to my current career was finding the courage to realize that my first job after college was not my ultimate goal. It was a great first job, and I was extremely grateful to be working at all, but I realized that I yearned to be in a lab rather than mainly at a desk in an office. It was a difficult decision because I loved the job and the people I worked with, but I knew that I had to try for my dream career. It was an exhausting job search, and there were many days where I felt like I would never find what I was looking for. It really can be easy to take it personally and feel like you aren't good enough, but that's not the case. It's just a matter of finding the right fit. Now looking back, it feels like I spent so much time stressing and worrying for no real reason!

I am constantly inspired by the people that I work with. I am surrounded by some of the most intelligent people I have ever met, so it motivates me to do my best work every day. I'm also inspired by the knowledge that my work has a real impact on the lives of people in the community. The fact that real lives are affected by my ability to obtain accurate results inspires me to be the best scientist I can be. •

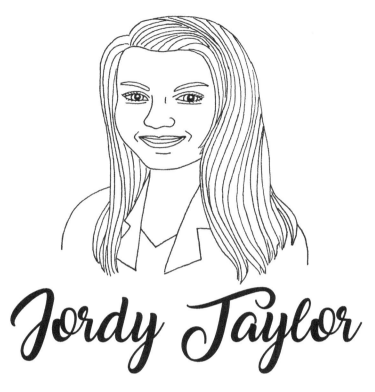

Jordy Taylor

Marine Biologist

*I've always been drawn to sharks, and I knew early on
that I wanted to be a marine biologist.*

My mom used to take me fishing on a pier near where I grew up to see my "fish friends." She also would take me to the local aquarium. Fortunately, it was located right down the road from my house, so it was super convenient to visit. I wanted to make sure they didn't acquire any new animals because if they did, I really wanted to name one "Spot." Living in the Panhandle of Florida had a significant influence on my future, since everywhere and everything was ocean oriented.

When I was 10, I encountered a shark and at first, I was nervous/scared. After watching this animal for several minutes, my nerves became curiosity. Since that day many years ago, I have been engaged in many activities to further appreciate marine biology and to learn more about sharks. In high school, (middle school was not really my stardom), I took as many biology classes as I could. I became close with my marine biology teacher; two years after I took her class, I volunteered my free period and my lunch to help her with labs, dissections and extra activities/field trips, so I could get more exposure. I even presented a few shark talks (shark finning) to my peers to spread the word about shark conservation and why it is important for students to know about sharks.

About Me

I was born in Fort Walton Beach, Florida and have three siblings, one full brother and two half brothers.

I love fossil hunting and the great hammerhead shark (Sphyrna mokarran) is my favorite animal.

"My career goal is to be employed as a researcher by a nonprofit lab that focuses on conservation, either for sharks and/or other cartilaginous fish, including rays, skates and sawfish."

Despite my passion and love for sharks, they were not the only things in my life at that time that I decided to pursue. When I was in high school preparing to graduate, I had to look at which college would suit me best, and it came down to who offered me the best scholarships, who gave me the best opportunity to excel at being "Jordy." At this point in my life, my No. 1 priority was where I could play lacrosse and showcase my passion for the sport. I had been playing for several years at this point, was offered several athletic scholarships, and was ranked as one of the top players in the state. It was important to me that I fulfill my thirst for the game while going to college, and pursue sharks simultaneously.

When I decided to go to Converse College, I was one of those "undecided" students who came in with the optimism of a small-town southern girl who could "achieve anything if she put her mind to it." Quickly, my peers, teammates and the president of the college had such a positive effect on my life. Those that surrounded me encouraged me to do my best. I always knew I wanted to be a marine biologist, but when I was 18, playing college lacrosse was everything to me. After being at Converse for a year, it came to that oh-so-difficult time to choose my major and it hit me. I had no idea how I was going to study marine biology, let alone sharks, at a landlocked school that didn't offer a marine biology major.

I had to swallow my pride and major in biology. I always had this reluctance to feel the need to settle, and at 19, that's exactly how I felt. I thought biology didn't encompass my true passion and potential. What I didn't realize is that majoring in biology was the best decision of my college career. By the end of my junior year, I

knew I was going to graduate school to further my education in marine biology. I sought out the best marine biology programs, and I dug into the literature to learn about various research avenues, so I could also seek out those programs.

I didn't know exactly what I wanted to study about sharks, but as a rising college senior, I didn't care. All I wanted to do was be surrounded by the biggest, best shark researchers available. I wanted to be completely surrounded by knowledge and sought to learn about my passion. During my research, I stumbled across some population genetics and phylogeny studies involving elasmobranchs, which intrigued me. I kept digging and found a prestigious researcher conveniently located in my hometown of 15 years, Charleston, South Carolina. I reached out to him, expressed my interest in the field in which I knew so little about, but explained I was enthusiastic and optimistic to learn. I drove to meet with him and toured the lab and facilities. After returning to Converse, I became obsessed with getting into the College of Charleston's Marine Biology Graduate Program and becoming one of this professor's students. Four months later, after relentlessly editing cover letters (which really stressed me out because it's pretty difficult relaying your passion about something without being cheesy) and chasing down professors to write letters of recommendation, I got my acceptance call from the Marine Biology Graduate Program. I was one of 17 selected out of 250 applicants for the program. The call came one hour before our first lacrosse game of the last season of my career. I cried with joy and spent the time before the game hugging it out with my teammates in the locker room.

I recently graduated with a master's degree from the College of Charleston, where I studied marine biology and also conducted research. My career goal is to be employed as a researcher by a nonprofit lab that focuses on conservation, either for sharks and/or other cartilaginous fish, including rays, skates and sawfish.

. . . .

A lot of people believe the job of a marine biologist is swimming with dolphins at a marine mammal park or going out and playing with fish on a boat, but it's so much more than that.

. . . .

As a graduate student, my research focused on investigating quantitative approaches for identifying isolated fossil shark teeth using tooth shape. I used geometric morphometrics, or shape analyses, to identify extant sharks using the shape of their teeth. With the trends laid out by the extant forms, I used this as an approach to identify unknown fossil teeth.

My Favorite Things

My favorite book is "Eragon."

The color gray blue.

Mint chocolate chip ice cream.

Christmas.

Mrs. Westbrook, my marine biology teacher in high school, as I'm most appreciative of her marine biology inspiration.

Vacationing in Iceland is the best.

Education

B.S.,
Converse College,
Class of 2014,
Major: Biology

M.S.,
College of Charleston,
Class of 2017,
Marine Biology

My research was thrilling because it was something I love doing and I found extremely interesting. This research was very specific and tailored to the lab that I worked in, the Chondrichthyan Tree of Life lab. Our central aim is to document the diversity of living and fossil sharks, rays and chimeras using anatomical, DNA and fossil data. Our lab collects shark and ray samples from all over the world. These samples are analyzed to look at which animals are breeding, migration patterns and to see how distinguished populations are from one another. All this information allows us to understand the conservation needs specific to various populations and species of sharks and rays.

We also look at evolutionary trends in these animals. Discovering which are the closest relatives to a specific animal and how their DNA material differ from one another is useful in determining what environmental pressures cause evolutionary change and how the DNA is influenced by the environment and/or genome. This, in turn, can be used by fisheries/governments to enforce laws for protecting those species in need which are susceptible to environmental pressures, particularly those brought on by human influence.

A typical day for me consists of going into the lab and reading over my notes and some publications for a few hours before prepping the lab for my work. I digitize teeth needed for my study and then sit down to do the tedious computer work, which is a necessary part of the job. Other activities include going into the field for collecting. Animals are caught either using rod and reel, bait traps or a long line, and once caught, a fin clip is taken and preserved on ice until we bring it into the lab. I will typically do some collecting or fieldwork for a breather and to get a break from the lab.

A lot of people believe the job of a marine biologist is swimming with dolphins at a marine mammal park or going out and playing with fish on a boat, but it's so much more than that. There are several distinct fields of marine biology including fisheries biology, fisheries science, population genetics, marine science or doing very specific research in a lab. Marine biologists can also encompass two or more fields, which is what I did with comparative anatomy and paleontology.

Throughout my life, I have never stopped asking questions. I constantly asked my parents, aquarists, friends, advisers and everyone else questions that have led me to endless possibilities. I think this life isn't just about me. It's about what I leave behind for future generations to learn from. So remember to keep asking questions. Questions wake us up and prompt new ideas. They perpetuate an understanding and further questioning, which opens you up to new people, exciting places and fantastic ideas. Anything that you go into, go humble. The most important rule to being successful is knowing nothing. If we knew everything, how would there be any room to grow? •

Karen M. Davis

Technology Executive

I never really thought I was an exceptional student. In my teen years, I decided that science classes were a problem for me (along with PE!).

However, I continued to take math classes along with many literature classes. My favorite topic was anything that involved reading, such as a class on Shakespeare. During high school, despite really good grades in algebra, I struggled with geometry and had a teacher who told me to avoid math in the future, whenever possible. Going into college, I decided on being an English major, though I did take calculus in my first year at Cedar Crest College. That quite possibly was the class that changed my life.

College calculus was taught by an excellent professor and all of a sudden, math concepts made a lot of sense. It was as if an entirely new world opened up. After my first year at college, that same professor advised me that though it was fine to be an English major, having a math degree would add options to future career plans. She told me that employers know people with math degrees can think logically. So, I ended up majoring in both English and math. Way back when I went to college, there were very few computer science programs and almost no programming classes taught except in engineering schools. I was one of the only math majors in my graduation year that was not also an education major.

About Me

I was born in Texas and
I grew up in Boston,
Massachusetts.

I have five siblings.

One of my favorite
hobbies is singing.
I also love creating
beaded jewelry, which
I have featured on
my website:
Wired Up Jewels
www.wiredupjewels.com

"My career has been an exciting adventure, a cross between engineering, computing and management and includes working at various prestigious organizations within different industries."

A local steel manufacturer interviewed on our campus even though we didn't have an engineering program. As a math and English major, my employment choices seemed to be limited to being a bank teller, heading into the exciting world of insurance sales or the position offered to me as an industrial engineer. I had no idea what an industrial engineer did, but I accepted the position and was excited for a great adventure.

I enjoyed working at my first company, but around the same time, the U.S. steel industry was encountering financial issues. As a result, my employer reduced operations and soon enough, I found myself working at a large car manufacturer in Dearborn, Michigan and then in Albany, New York, again as an industrial engineer. In these positions, I had the opportunity to work with automotive manufacturing plants as well as utilize computers in my work. This was really the first time I had an opportunity to work with computers at work. Next, I moved to a large company which specialized in consumer, textile and hospital products. Though I started as an industrial engineer, I soon found myself with opportunities in other areas; I held jobs with titles that included industrial engineering, quality engineer and cost accountant. I eventually ended up working in manufacturing systems. Ultimately, I became responsible for the data processing and computer systems in all the manufacturing plants.

Up until this point, I had worked in industries which were almost all male. I decided that a move into the computer industry would benefit me. At the time, computers

beyond the mainframes were pretty new, so it was a progressive industry, and even better, there were some women employees. I found a position in a large computer company, where I once again held a variety of roles. Over the course of 14 years, I had the opportunity to manage people as well as work on computer hardware, quality assurance, systems and software development, database application systems and client support.

Currently, I'm in technology management, employed by a nonprofit organization that provides our clients with research and technical services, much of which is for the U.S. federal government. Our mission is to deliver the promise of science for global good.

I've been with my company for 18 years. During this time, I've worked on business information systems with an internal company focus, and now I do work that is focused on systems for clients. Recently, I was named business group chief information officer (CIO) and VP, research computing. My new job is an expansion of my previous role of VP, research computing division (RCD). In the VP role, my division aims to be a preferred provider of information, data and technology solutions to a balanced portfolio of internal and external clients. RCD applies proven and emerging technologies to develop novel solutions that meet the research and implementation challenges of public and private sector clients worldwide. The division does software development, deployment, data integration, data management and bioinformatics for external client projects. As part of that, I also manage a large five-year project for a government agency — that project includes providing a grantee performance management and reporting system, along with training, technical assistance and analytics for agency staff and grantees. As business group CIO, I am responsible across the business group for working with our information technology services organization to ensure our business needs, business strategies and our external clients' project and technology needs are met. One specialty area is systems and data security, specifically security related to compliance with government regulations for systems for the U.S. government. We do work both in the United States and internationally, specifically in Africa.

. . . .

One aspect of my current role that I truly enjoy is being able to be a mentor to more junior staff as well as do outreach to other women in STEM fields.

. . . .

My team is comprised of individuals skilled in programming, informatics, math and computer science. Those who are in management positions also have skills/degrees in management, business and a wide range of scientific backgrounds, such as economics.

My Favorite Things

The color red.

Almost anything that includes chocolate.

Thanksgiving.

Mrs. Jane King — she is the one who encouraged me to do what I was good at, not just what other people told me I was good at.

Cats.

As an avid reader, I have a long list of favorites. Unfortunately, it's difficult for me to choose the one I like best.

Education

B.A.,
Cedar Crest College,
Class of 1977,
Double Major:
Mathematics
and English

M.S.M,
Worcester Poly Tech,
Class of 1988,
Information Systems

Important abilities, in addition to technology, include collaboration, negotiation, communication and project management, along with technical skills.

Most of my days are spent working with staff in my division and across the organization as well as with clients. A typical day might include a client meeting, reviewing a proposal that will go to a client for possible new work, and taking care of employee issues. The work environment in my organization is very collaborative and team focused, and this translates into working with smart and innovative staff to deliver on the organization's mission. Recently, I had the opportunity to participate in a Women in Technology mentoring event, and presenting and speaking at a CIO conference.

One aspect of my current role that I truly enjoy is being able to be a mentor to more junior staff as well as do outreach to other women in STEM fields. I've had the opportunity to speak in multiple venues where I'm able to reach women in STEM fields. I'm able to offer insight into my experience as a woman in STEM, and in this way, I hope that I'm giving back to the STEM community at large.

My career has been an exciting adventure, a cross between engineering, computing and management and includes working at various prestigious organizations within different industries.

As I've progressed in my career, I have found that I not only like variety, but also having challenging opportunities, and most importantly, being able to make a difference. Seeking out other people, skills, knowledge and the abilities to get the job done have helped push me forward. It's been my experience that there will always be people who doubt my abilities, and it's been my choice to either listen to them or not. Following my interests has helped me to learn and pursue new avenues of exploration.

Generally, I've found that when someone discourages me from doing something, that discouragement has more to do with the other person and less to do with me. In my life, not everyone has been my No.1 fan or my loudest cheerleader, and that's okay. I've simply surrounded myself with the people who help to encourage, support and cheer me on to success, and that's made all the difference. •

Kate Fehlhaber

Neuroscientist

*I don't remember exactly when I decided I wanted to be a doctor,
but I do remember the first time I saw a human brain.*

In grammar school, my parents enrolled me and my siblings in summer school. At the time, I was bitter about it, but now, I am very thankful for these opportunities. We got to choose whatever classes we wanted to take, and after third grade, I chose medieval history (I recall being addressed as "Lady Katie" and thinking that had a nice ring to it) and a human anatomy class. The only two things I remember from that class are dissecting a sheep heart and touching a human brain — an experience that left a lasting impression.

Did you know that your brain only weighs three pounds but contains as many neurons as there are stars in our galaxy? It needs that many neurons because your brain controls every aspect of who you are and how you interact with the world around you! As you can imagine, when studying the brain, things can get complicated really quickly. Especially when you're trying to answer big questions like, "How do we think? How do we store memories? What happens in neurological disorders, and how can we fix it?" If you are innately curious about how things work, then you will love neuroscience. There is so little known about the brain that you will be able to explore your curiosity for practically forever.

About Me

I was born in the beautiful state of California, and have two incredible brothers.

Since I really love colorful things, I'm going to have to say my favorite color is "rainbow."

"With a degree in neuroscience, there are many different career paths you can take."

I am a newly minted Ph.D., having graduated from the neuroscience program at the University of California, Los Angeles. Neuroscience is the study of the brain and nervous system. Neuroscientists study the brain at all different scales from large-scale changes in neuronal network activity to nanoscale modifications to DNA. Therefore, neuroscience involves the application of many different kinds of sciences, including biology, chemistry, physics, engineering and computational sciences. This highly interdisciplinary atmosphere creates a collaborative environment where specialists work together to solve complicated neuroscience questions. One of my favorite things as a neuroscientist is being able to apply ideas from other fields to my own projects.

With a degree in neuroscience, there are many different career paths you can take. The skills you will learn in graduate school will make you an excellent critical thinker. Quantitative analyses of scientific findings make you comfortable with handling data. Many neuroscientists stay in research, but others choose jobs in business, consulting or working for nonprofits.

For me, my passions in art and science have seemed difficult to meld into a single job title. When I began graduate school, I felt that we were not getting much training in being able to talk about science to the general public, so in 2012 I started a neuroscience education and outreach website called Knowing Neurons. What began as a blog has grown into an educational resource for which my fellow students and I were awarded the Society for Neuroscience Next Generation Award. It's been incredibly rewarding to see my passion project grow and blossom. Only recently have I realized that my ideal career would be one that melds art and science as a creative science communicator.

From a young age, when anyone asked me, "What do you want to be when you grow up?" I would respond, "A doctor," without hesitation. I don't remember exactly

what prompted this interest, but I knew I wanted to help people. I spent hours looking through pages of "Eyewitness Books," completely engrossed by the scientific illustrations of the insides of sharks, cats and humans. I was intensely curious about understanding how living things worked, and I'm grateful to Bill Nye and "The Magic School Bus" for helping to satiate my hunger for knowledge.

In high school, I took AP Biology and spent my free time shadowing a pediatric orthopedic surgeon. Thanks to this doctor's incredible generosity, I spent time in the clinic and observing surgeries in the operating room. Soon enough, I felt confident to accurately diagnose most of the children who came to the clinic after only a few minutes of interaction. I remember thinking that I had found my calling. When I applied to college, I knew I would be a premed major, but didn't know which major to choose. I'd been reading a lot about the brain, and I was fascinated by how little we knew about it, considering your brain is what makes you who you are and allows interaction with the world. So, I chose neuroscience.

> **During this time, I realized that I might be better suited for science, since I was always asking why things worked the way they did and creating experiments to test my hypotheses.**

I had no idea what kind of college I wanted to attend, so I applied to a hodgepodge of schools. The final decision was between UCLA and Scripps College, and after touring both campuses and talking to current students, I chose Scripps. Both schools had great science and premed programs, but I am happy I chose Scripps because of the unique opportunities it offered. The campus community was tightknit and classes were small, so I got to know my classmates and professors on a more personal level. The academic environment of Scripps College was generally supportive and not driven by direct competition, so I developed a strong sense of community which has definitely shaped who I am now. Moreover, the liberal arts education at Scripps kept my well-rounded interests in arts and literature strong when I could have simply become hyper-focused on science, and I am constantly grateful for this gift of an open mind.

One of the key turning points for me happened after my second year at Scripps College when I was awarded a summer fellowship to conduct research in a neurobiology lab at UCLA. This was my first attempt doing experimental science, and I absolutely fell in love. What was meant to be a "résumé builder" turned out to be

My Favorite Things

James Joyce's book, "Ulysses."

When it comes time for dessert, count me in for Trader Joe's coffee ice cream. Yum!

Photography — I always have a camera with me.

Celebrating New Year's.

Felix Schweizer, Ph.D., my professor at UCLA. He taught me to be a critical thinker, a balanced person and a fearless individual.

Joshua Tree National Park is the best vacation spot.

Cats — I would have so many if I weren't so allergic!

Education

B.A.,
Scripps College,
Class of 2009,
Major: Neuroscience

Ph.D.,
**University of
California,
Los Angeles,**
Class of 2017,
Neuroscience

really fun! My time in the lab was so rewarding that I opted to continue my research project the next summer, and I wrote up my findings in my senior thesis, for which I won an award.

After graduating college, I took a few gap years to take the MCAT and apply to medical schools. I was lucky enough to get a job as a laboratory technician in the same neurobiology lab at UCLA, so I was able to continue my research project and even learn new techniques along the way. During this time, I realized that I might be better suited for science, since I was always asking why things worked the way they did and creating experiments to test my hypotheses. After much deliberation, I decided to apply to graduate programs in neuroscience instead of medical school.

This was not an easy decision. For my whole life, I had said I wanted to become a doctor! Not much had changed though. What I wanted as a doctor and what I want as a scientist is to help people, only now it's at a more fundamental level. As a graduate student, I directly applied the scientific method to my ideas. Every day I got to learn about the latest and greatest scientific discoveries, and then I got to apply that knowledge to my work. As a scientist, I am literally on the cutting edge of understanding how things work!

I recently finished my Ph.D. in Neuroscience at UCLA, and I do not know exactly what my career path looks like, but I do know that I will be flexible to take opportunities as they arise if they feel right for me. Wherever I go, I will also strive to better myself and my ability to help others. •

Kathryne Stockinger

HVAC Engineer

Have you ever put your hand in front of an air vent and felt hot or cool air coming out of it? Part of my job as a mechanical heating, ventilation and air conditioning engineer (HVAC) is to make sure that the air coming out of the vent is the correct temperature it's supposed to be.

After all, cold air in winter or warm air in summer isn't going to help you feel comfortable. What would happen if the air was the wrong temperature? How could you fix it? My role as a mechanical engineer is all about solving problems like these.

I am a mechanical engineer for a large infrastructure firm in Washington D.C., specifically a mechanical HVAC engineer. The advancement of transportation and infrastructure is a substantial issue for our nation and I couldn't be prouder to be at the front lines of solving the issues.

One major project I am working on in my current position is the replacement of many chiller plants and the corresponding systems for a large metropolitan transit system. This project will revamp the transit stations' air conditioning and ventilation to make a more comfortable environment for the transit riders. I always find it fascinating to see the "guts" of the rail stations where all the machinery is held.

About Me

I was born in Portland, Oregon and have five siblings.

My favorite book is always changing! Most recently, my favorite is "Rise of the Rocket Girls." One of my favorite books when growing up was "Misty of Chincoteague."

Education

B.S.,
Sweet Briar College,
Class of 2015,
Major: Engineering Science

M.Eng.,
University of Maryland,
Anticipated Class of 2020,
Engineering Project Management with a Graduate Certificate in Mechanical Engineering

"While I did not originally plan to become an HVAC engineer, I am glad that I took a chance on the position."

It is captivating to me to trace the transfer of energy from a large cooling tower of water to the cool air you feel coming out of a vent. When an individual walks into a heated or cooled building, they very rarely realize the immense quantity of engineering hours it took to make that space's temperature the perfect level of comfort.

Generally, I am responsible for system design calculations, sizing and specifying equipment, creating engineering drawings and conveying design decisions to the customer. Since beginning my position as a mechanical HVAC engineer, I have had the opportunity to be on various design teams, perform complex calculations, learn about heating and cooling systems and frequently visit job sites. There is a great deal to learn about HVAC and mechanical engineering in general. I have only learned a small sliver of what there is to know, but each project teaches me something I am able to use on the next project.

One reason I enjoy my job is because I don't have a "typical day." My daily tasks are constantly changing. Every project I work on presents itself with new challenges. This means that I'm constantly reassessing my skills and working on the job to develop new ones.

If my job sounds like fun to you, the best thing you can do to prepare for a career in mechanical engineering is to challenge yourself in your math and science classes while in middle and high school. Many times when I was in school, I heard my peers say, "Why do I need to take this math class? It's not like I'm going to use it in the future!" Yes, you may not be solving quadratic equations in your everyday life, but you will constantly be problem-solving, and this is why math and science classes are so important.

Becoming a mechanical engineer requires a college degree and it's best to major in mechanical engineering. However, if that is not possible, there are many other options. My alma mater is a small liberal arts college that offers one well-rounded engineering degree. My degree is in engineering science, but I focused in mechanical engineering

by taking many mechanical classes. Some of my friends in the same program decided to focus in civil or environmental engineering by taking classes in those subjects. Other mechanical engineers major in mathematics or physics and then pursue a master's degree in mechanical engineering. In most cases, to be a mechanical engineer, you need at least a bachelor's degree. If you are more interested in research, then a master's or doctorate degree may be required.

From the early days of my education, I have always been interested in STEM, especially mathematics, but during middle and high school, I never could decide what I really wanted to do for my career. At one point I wanted to be a veterinarian, and then the next moment I wanted to be a marine biologist. This was challenging for me, because I felt like I should know what I wanted to do. Once I graduated high school, I settled on studying premedical in preparation to become a doctor. It wasn't my first love, but it was an acceptable career for a girl interested in STEM.

....

If my job sounds like fun to you, the best thing you can do to prepare for a career in mechanical engineering is to challenge yourself in your math and science classes while in middle and high school.

....

During my first semester of college, I took both biology and math. My adviser explained that I was most likely taking my last math class but the first of many biology classes. Since I did not enjoy the biology class nearly as much as the math class, I decided to re-evaluate my major, and that is when I went to speak to the head of the engineering department. Engineering seemed both exciting and challenging, so I figured I would give it a try. I can honestly say that was one of the best decisions I have ever made.

While in college, I interned for a petroleum company that specialized in deep-water drilling. After college, I worked for a nuclear energy company for 1½ years and I absolutely loved working in the nuclear industry. However, I was looking for a change of location and I found myself in an HVAC engineering position. While I did not originally plan to become an HVAC engineer, I am glad that I took a chance on the position. It is surprising what you will discover you enjoy by simply giving something new a try.

I am excited to continue learning every day and take on new engineering challenges. I plan to continue my education by earning my master's of engineering in project management starting fall of 2018. While I love the engineering work I do, I also really enjoy leadership roles, and I believe obtaining this degree will help me have the best of both worlds. •

My Favorite Things

The love of my life, my husband!

The color purple.

Trader Joe's Cookie Butter Ice Cream.

Horses and horseback riding!

Hiking with my dogs.

The outdoors.

Christmas.

My first engineering professor in college was my best teacher.

Vacationing on the Oregon coast.

Running races, including marathons and 10Ks.

Kelsey Barta

Test & Evaluation Engineer

When I was young, I loved playing with Legos and building things.

I really enjoyed working with my hands and loved to see my designs come to life. Unlike some of my peers, in elementary and middle school, my favorite subject was math. Math made sense to me.

When I entered high school, my parents encouraged me to participate in an engineering-pathway program offered at my school. This program focused on many different aspects of engineering, and it included taking a different engineering course each year. I really enjoyed these classes, because it gave me a chance to spread my science wings. One thing I noticed right away that really surprised me was the lack of girls in the program. The program was open to any student who was interested, but each year, out of about 25 other students, there was only one other girl in my class. The lack of female participation in the program was both startling and unexpected. I didn't understand why more girls weren't interested in engineering.

About Me

Seattle, Washington is my birthplace.

I have one brother.

My favorite teacher is Dr. Bethany Brinkman (Sweet Briar College) because of her passion for teaching and for the amount of time and energy that she puts in to ensure that each of her students succeeds.

"My job is the testing and evaluation of a naval defense system."

Looking back, I don't think it was that girls weren't interested in engineering; I think it was just that they tended to stay away from it because it's a stereotypical male profession, and therefore they couldn't see themselves as a future engineer. If it weren't for the influence of my parents, I probably would not have seen myself as an engineer either. They saw my interest in math and science at a young age and encouraged me to follow my passion.

I graduated from Sweet Briar College in 2015 with an undergraduate degree in engineering science and a minor in math. My Sweet Briar education was very well rounded. Sweet Briar is a liberal arts school with general education requirements for all students to complete courses across many different fields. This allowed me to not only gain the skills and knowledge required for a career in engineering, but it also provided me better insight into the overall influence of engineering on the rest of society.

> **Looking back, I don't think it was that girls weren't interested in engineering; I think it was just that they tended to stay away from it because it's a stereotypical male profession, and therefore they couldn't see themselves as a future engineer.**

Right now, I work in the defense industry. My job is the testing and evaluation of a naval defense system. Navy ships have a weapon system onboard that is used to defend the ship and the sailors from an incoming attack. My job involves testing this system to make sure that it's working properly.

Before each ship deploys as well as throughout a ship's lifecycle, testing is done to make sure that the defense systems are working correctly. This is really important to ensure that the lives of the sailors who are on the ship are as well protected as

possible. I work on both ends of a test event. This means that I work on analysis before and after the event. I run computer simulations before the event to predict what is going to happen. I want to show the test conductors that the test is going to be safe while also effectively testing the defense system. After a test, I work with a team to look at data from the software system to verify that the defense system is working correctly. If we find that something is broken, we will document the error and what needs to be done to fix it.

There are two components to this defense system: hardware and software. The hardware systems are the physical weapons that are used to defend the ship. These include things like guns and missiles. The software system is a collection of code that tells the hardware systems what to do, or in this case, tells the weapons when and where to fire. My job involves testing this software system through real, live tests.

My favorite thing about performing this work is the impact that it has. It's incredibly satisfying to know that the work I do on a daily basis is contributing to our overall national security and to keeping the Navy sailors who are deployed on these ships safe.

··

I like to relate my work to solving a puzzle. I first have to find all the pieces of information that I need to solve the puzzle and then I need to figure out how all that information fits together to find a solution.

··

The defense industry is responsible for the research and development, production and servicing of weapons and military technology. Defense contractors are the companies that produce the weapons, while the government is involved in buying and selling the weapons. The government is also in charge of testing the equipment that is produced by the defense contractors. My company works with both the government and the defense contractors to evaluate the performance of these tests. If anything is broken, then we work with the defense contractors and the system designers to fix the problem.

There are many opportunities to work in STEM within the defense industry. For my job, a bachelor's degree in a technical field like engineering, math, computer science or physics is needed. A variety of technical fields can be applied to this line of work. For example, any experience with computer programming skills would be useful, as data analysis often involves some amount of coding. A background in electrical engineering

My Favorite Things

The book "Freakonomics."

The color blue.

Ice cream.

Playing lacrosse.

The Christmas holiday.

An Iceland vacation.

Wolves.

Education

B.S.,
Sweet Briar College,
Class of 2015,
Major: Engineering
Science

M.S.,
Johns Hopkins University,
Anticipated
Class of 2018,
Mechanical
Engineering

and knowledge in electromagnetism, radio-frequency engineering or signal processing can be beneficial in understanding many of the ship radar systems that are being tested. A strong foundation in mechanical engineering can be used to help understand the mechanical components and systems on the ship.

Another favorite part of my job is that no day is the same. My work is incredibly fast paced, so it feels like I'm always working on something different each day. This keeps me on my toes and makes sure that I fully apply myself to each situation. I always have to be thinking about how to solve the next problem. I like to relate my work to solving a puzzle. I first have to find all the pieces of information that I need to solve the puzzle and then I need to figure out how all that information fits together to find a solution. It's very satisfying when I do put all the pieces together to "solve the puzzle." On occasion, I have had the opportunity to travel across the country to attend test events or to present my analysis results to other organizations. I love having the opportunity to travel to the live test events in order to be able to actually see the defense systems operating.

As an engineer, I think it's important to embrace a culture of lifelong learning. In order to perform my job effectively, it's important to have a good understanding of how the system being tested works. I have to try to learn as much as I can from the subject matter experts in order to gain a better understanding of the systems being tested. I also take every opportunity that I can to sign up for classes in order to continue my education. I'm currently enrolled in a master's program for mechanical engineering at Johns Hopkins and anticipate graduating in the spring of 2018. •

Kimberly C. Davis

Methods Development Chemist

Ever since my first Science Olympiad, which is a science quiz in which schools are able to compete against one another, I have loved science.

The Science Olympiad gave me the chance to test my science knowledge against other kids I didn't know, and it was an amazing experience. I carried my passion for science through high school, where my favorite classes were chemistry and science. I never imagined majoring in chemistry in college. That is, I never imagined it until I went to Meredith College, where I started school with a major in criminal justice. We were required to take a basic chemistry class and I fell in love with the idea of solving problems on my own. I knew that I was meant to be in a lab.

Meredith College professors were absolutely instrumental in shaping my future career. They helped me find research opportunities and I was able to perform graduate-level research as part of the Howard Hughes Medical Institute Summer Program. I was also a teaching assistant in undergrad for the lower-level chemistry classes, where I discovered my love of teaching people chemistry concepts. I carried that love of teaching into my job as a supervisor for a chemistry group in a QC (quality control) pharmaceutical lab.

About Me

I was born in Morganton, North Carolina and have three siblings.

For me, the best vacation spot is anywhere on the Outer Banks of North Carolina.

Coconut cream pie and Thanksgiving are some of my favorites.

When I started at Meredith, I was married with a small child and a full-time job. During the first two years of undergrad, I worked full time. During the last two years, I worked part time. It was challenging to manage everything I needed to do, but somehow I was able to make it work. Scores of baby sitters helped with that, and my professors always understood when my son needed to come to class on the rare occasion.

Now, I am an analytical chemist. I work in a research and development role for a large medical device company. I use my working laboratory knowledge, critical thinking, reasoning skills, math knowledge base and data interpretation skills to complete my projects.

As an analytical chemist, I design (often referred to as methods development) and execute experiments that test medical devices for volatile compounds and heavy metals. Specifically, I look for materials in my company's products that might harm the people who use them. For example, if someone is using a container to hold a blood sample, I make sure that the sample will not be altered by any materials that it could absorb from the container. I work with what chemists call "extractables and leachables" (E&L) testing.

As an analytical chemist, I design (often referred to as methods development) and execute experiments that test medical devices for volatile compounds and heavy metals.

For my job, chemistry knowledge is essential as well as a four-year degree. Biology majors have been successful in similar roles within a pharmaceutical lab. For my role, the data interpretation required for compound identification is a steep learning curve for those without a chemistry background.

Analytical chemists use instruments to perform tests on chemical substances. In addition to chemistry and instrumentation knowledge, an analytical chemist must also have strong computer and statistical skills. With this knowledge, they have many career opportunities. Analytical chemistry can be found in industry, academia or the government.

While I work in the medical device industry, other industries also employ analytical chemists, including medical or pharmaceutical companies, consumer products companies, fuel companies, agricultural organizations, food companies, companies that make plastics and polymers, the cosmetic industry and the textile industry.

"Even though I spend much of my time in a lab, my job lets me help people every day through my ability to solve problems."

A medical device company makes products used in the health care industry such as instruments, machines, implants, surgical or examination tools or any other products used to help people. These products can find what is wrong with someone and help them get better. Medical devices also can be anything from a medicine bottle or a Band-Aid, to a pacemaker or an artificial hip. Before any medical device can be used or even tested on a patient, it must be tested in a lab to ensure that it meets the FDA's safety standards for that kind of device.

The medical device industry is constantly finding ways to make current devices better as well as looking for breakthrough devices that will improve a patient's quality of life. My company makes many products used in the operating room, from antiseptic rubs to surgical instruments, to anesthesia face masks. We also make insulin syringes for diabetic people and we even make lab products so that hospitals or clinics can diagnose their patients quickly and accurately. We research and implement safe ways to dispose of used medical products to help both patients and medical professionals stay safe. Our goal is to provide health care professionals with the tools they need to save lives.

For me, the workday starts with the preparation of a device for testing. Typically, devices are placed in various solvents to extract, or leach, compounds from the materials. The extractions are analyzed with techniques called gas chromatography (GC) mass spectrometry, liquid chromatography (LC) mass spectrometry or inductively coupled plasma mass spectrometry. These processes have big names, but basically the techniques separate, identify and measure the chemicals or metals in the extractions.

Education

B.S.,
Meredith College,
Class of 2006,
Major: Chemistry

M.S.,
**University of NC
Wilmington,**
Class of 2012,
Chemistry

The majority of my work is interpreting the information from the chromatograms from the GC and LC work. I also provide the origin of the species, if possible. A formal report is then written for the client, who will then be able to use the device for clinical testing. It's great because finally, all those years of chemistry lab reports pay off!

The work I do impacts people's lives directly. The devices that are entering the market are life changing for diabetics, children, heart patients and so many others. I have an active role in helping these people because without my testing, we would not know which devices are safe to use. I get to see a device that could help thousands of people go from an engineer's mind to a patient, and I know that I am an essential part of the process that made it happen.

I love the autonomy in my work. I get to plan and execute my projects based on my training and scientific judgment, and I get to see the finished product make it to the market for patients. I also get to see many exciting advances in the medical device industry long before they hit the market. I am on track to be a supervisor for a group in the E&L group, which makes me excited for my career's future. I love helping junior scientists learn their jobs and the science behind what analytical chemists do.

Even though I spend much of my time in a lab, my job lets me help people every day through my ability to solve problems. My work is challenging and intriguing, as I know that what I do is making the world a healthier place for everyone. Although I did not always plan to become an analytical chemist, I am glad that my career has led me here because I love working in the health care field, helping people live longer, stronger and happier lives. •

Kristina Sorrells

Mathematics Instructor

Imagine being involved in an all-girls robotics team.

You would want to make sure you had lots of creative and smart girls on the team to help you design and build a great robot. You would also need to have a good teacher adviser. There's where I come in. I'm a faculty mentor and coach at an all-girls school in North Carolina. The program started in 2013 because my school was looking for more ways to get girls involved in STEM fields. I'm also a math educator and department chair at the school, which is a day/boarding school with students from around the globe, spanning 11 different countries.

When the program first launched, one of our first tasks was deciding on a team name. The school is big on sisterhood. We work hard to develop the spirit of working together, helping one another and being available for support. In brainstorming a name, an odd notion occurred to us. Did you know that one of the main pieces in a computing system is called a motherboard? The motherboard works to connect and control most of the main systems in a computer. The notion we found odd is that a female name (mother) was used to describe the "brain" or "foundation" of the computer.

About Me

I was born in Staten Island, New York and have one sibling.

Yellow is my favorite color and I love ice cream — my favorite is orange and vanilla.

I'm a big fan of Jane Austen's book, "Pride & Prejudice."

Christmas is my favorite holiday and I receive much joy from crocheting and knitting.

> "Everyone can master mathematics, and my job is to make sure that my students are not afraid of math."

To us, this was odd, only because technology is considered a primarily male field. The founding team members settled on the name Sisters of the Motherboard to emphasize collaboration in all STEM areas. Much of our first year was spent learning the names of all the parts, determining which programming language to use and just trying to get something built.

The Sisters of the Motherboard participated in one qualifying competition that initial year. The members of the team were nervous, excited and proud of what they had built. The Sisters' robot, named Phoenix after the mythical bird that rises from the ashes to become something new and strong, was only half the size of the other teams' robot. The Sisters came in dead last in competition. However, the Sisters did earn the Motivate Award at the qualifying competition for enthusiasm, passion and commitment. Our team learned so much from the competition and seeing what was possible through trial and error throughout the first year.

The second year the team brought fresh enthusiasm, new ideas, a whole new programming language to learn and the excitement of power tools. The team also went from six girls to 14. The girls knew the point of the program was to learn and tinker and explore. When planning this robot, named Sassmantha for her sassy foot action, the Sisters brainstormed ideas, researched engineering design concepts and created a plan of action before building. The Sisters went to two qualifying competitions and at one of these, earned the Inspire Award, which meant an automatic place in the state competition. The Inspire Award is earned by a team considered to be an inspiration to other teams. This team is able to communicate their experiences, enthusiasm and

knowledge to other teams, sponsors, their community and the judges. That year they came in 14th overall out of about 60 teams in North Carolina, quite an improvement from dead last! In the past two years, the Sisters have only gotten better and have grown and continued to impress the judges. The Sisters were even able to participate in the World Robotics competition in 2017.

I've always found math and computer programming interesting. In sixth grade, everyone at my middle school was required to take a keyboard class and a computer-programming class. The keyboarding portion was not very interesting, but when we got to programming, everything made sense. The process was logical to me. Take a big problem, break it into smaller pieces, then find a way to put the pieces together so they "talked" and solved the problem. I had a female teacher who made a point to say that learning programming is important for everyone.

> **I had an opportunity to see global positioning systems (GPS) put to use, learn how computer programs were written to analyze collected data and interact with various engineers. The internship opened my eyes to the power of STEM in our lives, essentially just how much STEM is around us.**

I attended a very large high school in San Antonio, Texas. There were computer-programming classes, but I was unable to take them due to scheduling conflicts. However, I had the opportunity to have fantastic experiences in my math courses and science courses. Eventually, I decided to attend college at Salem College in North Carolina.

Through the encouragement of several professors at Salem, I applied and was accepted for a summer internship program at Argonne National Laboratory just outside of Chicago. I had an opportunity to see global positioning systems (GPS) put to use, learn how computer programs were written to analyze collected data and interact with various engineers. The internship opened my eyes to the power of STEM in our lives, essentially just how much STEM is around us. Also, I saw firsthand how important it was to be able to talk, write and explain STEM. The writing and explanation portion is just as important as the data collection and programming.

Interesting to note, I did not originally plan to teach, so I earned my bachelor's degree and master's degree in mathematics without getting a certification. I began teaching

Education

B.S.,
Salem College,
Class of 1996,
Major: Mathematics

M.A.,
Wake Forest University,
Class of 1998,
Mathematics

without a certification which made my math knowledge strong because I was learning it for the sake of learning it, not to specifically teach it to other people. The math I studied was more varied, so I was able to learn more about the numerous connections between math topics and ways math is used in and can be seen in our world. I went back to school to get my teaching certification in order to be eligible for a Doctorate in Curriculum and Instruction.

In graduate school at Wake Forest University, I had an experience that cemented my desire to pursue teaching more seriously. As part of my teaching assistantship, I was assigned to work as a tutor for a man who had returned to WFU after leaving to play professional football. He returned in his late 30s to complete a math course. He was great to work with and really desired to have his degree completed. Since he had been away from math for a while, we spent time going over basic concepts and learning the new material for his course. Filling in the math holes took time and sometimes creativity. I had to adjust my explanations until he and I came to understand each other and find a rhythm in our work. As a teacher, I had to learn to find his language and translate my language to fit his. This process came to reflect my own teaching philosophy of working to fit the needs of the students.

To me, teaching is about sharing knowledge, passion and curiosity. Everyone can master mathematics, and my job is to make sure that my students are not afraid of math. This means I need to listen to my students. I need to know what interests them, what makes them nervous, and find a way to make the course content relevant to them. I'm here to ensure their math success.

Fortunately for me, the students are always willing to try a new learning environment, which encourages me to try new ways to teach and reach them. I am constantly impressed and inspired by these young ladies who come from across the globe to learn in a different country. The day students are also impressive because they leave "mainstream" education to come to an all-female high school.

Teaching mathematics allows me to share more than algebra and calculus information. We can discuss logic, find patterns and explore connections between other disciplines. No academic discipline is truly separate from each other. We need to understand how all things connect, and try to demonstrate and impart that to students, to empower our students to make those connections themselves! •

Lauren M. Lazaro

Weed Scientist

*If you've ever planted a garden (vegetable or flower),
you know how quickly weeds can take over.*

Weed management is an important part of gardening, especially if you are looking to have an abundant harvest. Many home gardeners spend countless hours pulling weeds to accomplish this task.

But what happens when a farmer has weeds? With so much acreage, pulling weeds would be impossible. Instead, farmers need a different solution and this is where I come in. I'm a weed scientist. My end goal is to reduce the amount or completely get rid of the weed species in a farmer's field through various approaches, and teach that farmer how to keep the weeds from coming back by using different approaches to manage their farms.

As a weed scientist, I study weed biology/ecology, harvest-weed-seed control and herbicide-resistant weed species in agronomic row crops like corn, cotton and soybean. I set up field and greenhouse experiments to test how a weed species will react to a proposed treatment, which could be the use of cultural, mechanical or chemical control, competition with other weed species or an environmental stressor like a

About Me

My birthplace is Shreveport, Louisiana and I have one sister, Kristin.

I'm most appreciative of Dr. Linda Fink — she took the time and made the effort to help me decide on my future. Dr. Fink even tailored a class toward botany; something that I was unsure was my interest at the time. Today, she keeps up with my work and progress, and is someone who I can still turn to for advice if needed. She helped launch my career in STEM.

fire or drought. I am unique in my field because I am traditionally a plant ecologist, so I look at the same problem in a different way than a traditional agronomist.

Agriculture helps feed the world and we need to make sure that farmers can accomplish this in the best way. To meet this lofty goal, agriculture keeps improving as the industry listens to consumers along the way. For example, today a larger number of consumers are interested in sustainable agriculture (using farming techniques that protect Mother Earth and its inhabitants) and for health reasons, prefer eating organic produce. This new consumer interest results in the demand for more organic farming. Interesting to note is that while weed scientists play an important role in conventional farming, they play an equally important role in organic farming.

To keep the industry moving forward, the agriculture industry needs people to look at and understand all the ins and outs associated with each problem and figure out a solution to fix it. Not for just one farmer or one field, but for a region, country or the world.

. . . .

When I was young, I never thought about becoming a weed scientist! I did not even realize such an occupation existed.

. . . .

My days vary between the growing season and the off season. The growing season is planting to harvesting (typically late spring to early fall). During those days, we are planting fields, setting up our field trials, collecting data, maintaining our research areas or harvesting. I tend to get up earlier than later so that we can beat the heat in the summer time. I work primarily in four different cropping systems and I am either conducting my own research or helping out another person in the lab with their research.

During the off season, I conduct experiments in the greenhouse, analyze data, write reports and attend professional conferences on the experiments that we conducted that season in the field. I also teach a class each semester and help mentor the graduate students in my lab.

I love working with a large group of people with mixed backgrounds in STEM and collaborating on a daily basis. Each person brings something to the table that allows us to develop and carry out unique and exciting research goals. Field research is definitely one of my favorite things to do. I love to be outside. I do not always like the

"Agriculture helps feed the world and we need to make sure that farmers can accomplish this in the best way."

more statistics-oriented parts of my job. When a project is finished, the data has to be analyzed and written up for publications, reports or conferences. My statistics skills are not as good as I would like them to be, but I am working on it.

The STEM majors for this field are endless. Majoring in biology, chemistry, agriculture, molecular biology, math, environmental sciences, ecology, wildlife ecology, botany, plant biology or engineering would be a good idea. Each one of these fields brings a vital and important aspect to the overall field because weed science as a whole is not one dimensional.

Regardless of the career field you go into, to me, the list for being successful is all the same. You have to have passion for what you do. Loving your job makes it fun, easy and not like a job at all. Adaptability is a big one for me. Field research rarely goes according to plan, so you have to be able to think on your feet and come up with a solution. Staying up to date on the newest research, techniques or procedures is very important. I do a lot of scientific reading to make sure that I am current with what is going on in my field. Being able to communicate well with others is important on several levels.

When I was young, I never thought about becoming a weed scientist! I did not even realize such an occupation existed. For me, my world revolved around horses and I spent as much time as I possibly could on my horse. I've been riding horses since I was 4 years old, and continued on through college. All that time, I was determined to become a large-animal vet so that I could take care of my horses. My parents noticed my interests and put me into STEM summer camps that focused on math and science. All the while, my dad would take me on nature walks around our property to show me all the different flowers and plants blooming.

Education

B.S.,
Sweet Briar College,
Class of 2009,
Major: Biology

M.S.,
Southern Illinois University,
Class of 2011,
Plant Biology

Ph.D.,
Southern Illinois University,
Class of 2015,
Plant Biology

When I went to Sweet Briar College, I knew that I wanted to get a degree in biology with a goal of going to vet school. What I didn't expect is not being able to handle the vet surgeries — specifically the sight of blood. I found this out the hard way during one of my summer internships. Fortunately, this happened before the start of my junior year, so I had time to re-group.

Unsure of my career path and looking for options, I decided to enroll in an Introduction to Botany class during my junior year. I instantly loved the material, but I wasn't sure if I really liked botany or the new professor. My adviser and I came up with a plan to find out. I took a Field Natural History course next, and it ended up being my favorite class at SBC. This class focused partly on botany, and primarily on wildlife ecology. This was the turning point in my career. After that semester, I knew that I wanted to go to graduate school for botany with a focus on ecology. All those walks with my dad suddenly took on new meaning as I realized I'd been aware of botany for a long time.

After I graduated from SBC, I went to Southern Illinois University, Carbondale, for my master's in plant biology, where I studied invasive species in grasslands. There, I discovered that I was not a huge fan of studying grasses. So, for my Ph.D., I was given a great opportunity to work on an agro-ecology project that was co-advised through my current department. I had never worked in agriculture before, so when I found out that my research assistantship was through the weed science lab group, I was a little worried. I soon found out that I loved working on a project that focused on my ecology background and on something new. From there, I moved to the University of Arkansas where I was a postdoctoral research associate in the weed science department.

My interest in botany unfolded into an agriculture career as a weed scientist. While at this time I am still a little unsure about my career goals, I know I have different options. I can go into academia, become a consultant or go into industry and work for a company. Either way, I would still like to conduct research.

Even though as I was growing up I never saw myself in an agriculture career, I'm glad I discovered this career path because I like knowing that the work I do helps to feed a hungry world. •

Lindsay Davis

Manufacturing Engineer

As long as I can remember, I've been really competitive at everything.

When I was in kindergarten, I wanted to learn everything faster than the other kids. Once the other kids learned to read, I wanted to learn math first. I would practice multiplication tables at night. I heard that harder math classes used letters as numbers, so I tried to figure out algebra in the first grade. Don't worry, I wasn't a super genius — I didn't come up with anything that resembled any kind of math. I just really liked being able to do stuff other kids couldn't.

Growing up, I had a single mom and no siblings living with me, so I watched a lot of television while my mom was working. I would say television highly influenced my life. While watching shows, I noticed that the really successful and interesting characters knew what college they wanted to go to, and they knew what they wanted to be when they grew up. In middle school, I didn't know what I wanted to do or where I wanted to go to college. The other students in my class were starting to figure that out.

So my competitive nature emerged, and I needed to know what I was going to be when I grew up. I recalled when I was younger and drawing a house, someone had told me that you can't just put the closet here or the bathroom there. It wouldn't work. I assumed there was a complex method

About Me

I was born in Corpus Christi, Texas and have one sibling.

I love giraffes, unicorns and Italian greyhounds.

My favorite vacation spot is London!

Glitter is my favorite color and my favorite holiday is Leap Day.

I think if I went to another college, I wouldn't be an engineer, largely due to the incredible professors that were at Sweet Briar when I was there.

"Engineering allows me to channel my fierce competitiveness solving problems that other people can't solve. Whenever people say something cannot be done, I see it as a dare to prove them wrong, rather than a roadblock."

that determined how and where each room would be laid out in a house. That was fascinating to me at the time and I wanted to be that person. Eventually someone told me that the closest thing to what I was describing was an architect. I told my mom with full confidence that I wanted to be an architect. My mom was very supportive, despite knowing nothing about my newly declared passion.

We went to the local bookstore to look at architecture books. When I flipped through the architecture book, I realized I was just looking at pictures of old buildings. How boring! I wanted something harder. I wanted to be the one who knows where the bathrooms go in the buildings, not what the buildings look like on the outside. Finally, my mom explained to me that a structural engineer is the person who decides those things. So that's what I decided to be.

Prior to my career decision, I decided that I wanted to graduate from Dartmouth. I wanted a serious school that would look good on a résumé when I got out of college and needed a job. Completely randomly, I chose Dartmouth. It looked like it was an amazing Ivy League college with all kinds of recognitions as such, but it wasn't so high profile like Harvard or Yale. So it was decided, I was going to Dartmouth and I acted as such.

Then it was time for college. Having fallen in love with Sweet Briar College (SBC) while attending an on-campus program for high school girls interested in engineering, Explore Engineering, I was no longer thinking about Dartmouth, and instead found myself with a genuine passion for engineering. I loved learning how to make cool stuff and professors were willing to help explore your creativity. It was because of this program that I decided I wanted to go to SBC and become an engineer.

With my college and career decided, I eagerly awaited the college's admissions decision. Needless to say, I was ecstatic when I received my acceptance letter. I was on my way to becoming an engineer!

In my first engineering class, we were challenged to create a boat out of 20 pounds of cardboard and 50 feet of duct tape. We had to sail the boat across the lake as part of the homecoming festivities. I worked tirelessly on my boat for a few weeks, and after the race, my team walked away with a clean sweep. Our boat won every category (by default). Since the other teams' boats sank, mine was awarded the best design and best overall. I was thrilled!

> **While being an engineering student required a lot of work, a lot of refusing to quit and a lot of problem-solving, it wasn't impossible. Plus, being at an all-women's college removed the fear and shame of asking a dumb question in class, and instead installed a sense of community.**

Most of the assignments in engineering were project based so you had a purpose behind the math, and at the end of the assignment, you had a great story to tell. I created a cardboard boat, electronic dice, a door alarm, a jukebox, a useless machine (a little wooden box with a switch and when you flip the switch, a little arm comes out of the box and turns off the switch), a Simon game with a twist, a unique ski lift, a life-size fully functional Game Boy costume and many more projects.

While being an engineering student required a lot of work, a lot of refusing to quit and a lot of problem-solving, it wasn't impossible. Plus, being at an all-women's college removed the fear and shame of asking a dumb question in class, and instead installed a sense of community.

My senior year, I had to prepare to enter the real world. I could either go to grad school or get a real job, and I couldn't afford grad school. Moving back home with my mom wasn't an option, so I absolutely had to find a job. I applied everywhere I could think of and got very few interviews. I was offered a job as an operations engineer with a large cellphone company, and it paid well, but I didn't like the job at all. The day before I absolutely had to accept the position, I received a rejection from a robotics company I really wanted to work for. That was my last lead, so I decided I had to accept the boring job and move to North Carolina.

I was sitting in the dining hall looking at the rejection email, pondering my decision, when a business professor I knew asked if I had accepted a job yet. I told him the situation and he said he knew of a company nearby that was looking for an engineer. I told him I'd love to interview, but I had to answer the other job really soon.

My Favorite Things

The book, "Alice in Wonderland."

Cookie dough anything is my favorite dessert.

Hobbies, such as sewing, crocheting and crafting.

All my professors at Sweet Briar, especially in engineering, were absolutely incredible. They were able to change the way they taught the subject so that each person would understand it better. They went out of their way to help you after class if only you asked. They checked in if you missed a class to make sure you were okay. They stayed late to help with a project. All-around wonderful teachers who truly would do anything to help their students learn.

Education

B.S.,
Sweet Briar College,
Class of 2013,
Major: Engineering
Science

I was called in for an interview that week. I wanted a design engineering position, but there were none available. Instead, the company recommended I start out in manufacturing to gain experience making products. The company manufactured circuit boards and gave me a number of reasons why working for a small manufacturer would be better than working for the large cellular company. I didn't need much convincing and accepted the job without hesitation.

Manufacturing engineers work to create a plan, make tools and set up resources to efficiently make a product quickly, cost-effectively and without causing any delays.

However, sometimes delays can happen anyway, either due to a mistake in the plan or to some unforeseen event. Then the manufacturing engineers have to quickly fix the problem in limited time. This process starts by asking a lot of questions. The test engineer can investigate the test and tell you if anything has changed. The project manager can tell you if the designers changed anything for these circuit boards. The purchasers can tell you if parts were substituted. The machine operators can tell you if anything different happened while making the board. Once the manufacturing engineer has tracked down the right people and asked the right questions, you compile it to create a complete picture, usually focusing on what's different between these broken units and the ones that have all passed.

Being organized and experienced is definitely helpful in creating an initial plan on how to keep things from going awry; however, just as important is the ability to quickly gather information, think about a problem and solve it when things do inevitably go wrong. Manufacturing engineers typically have a degree in industrial engineering or manufacturing engineering, although any engineering major will give you the skills necessary to succeed as a manufacturing engineer. You just need to be able to think, and be able to learn on the job. Most of my job is complex problem-solving like the problem above. Although I don't do calculus or differential equations ever, the problem-solving skills that you learn in upper-level math classes are necessary to be a successful engineer.

Engineering allows me to channel my fierce competitiveness solving problems that other people can't solve. Whenever people say something cannot be done, I see it as a dare to prove them wrong, rather than a roadblock. •

Liza Sanden

Environmental Scientist

I found myself in Alaska at age 22 on a lark, seeking some fun and adventure.

Seemingly unrelated happenstance and choices led me to exactly where I am now. I don't remember not wanting to go into some STEM career, though over the years, I've had different ideas of what that might be. By early high school, I'd settled on wanting to go into some field of biology or perhaps biochemistry.

Some of the most influential experiences I had were science-based summer camps through the Duke University Talent Identification Program in high school. These were also outdoors-based ecology courses and stoked a sense of adventure and love of the outdoors in me.

I entered college knowing I wanted to study biology and ecology. I chose a college based on two things — the availability of scholarships and the need for a hands-on science program. Wesleyan College gave me a large scholarship and multiple opportunities to not just study science, but to have practical, hands-on experiences. I am tremendously grateful to have had professors as mentors who encouraged, and even required, independent inquiry and research. I had opportunities to intern with an environmental

About Me

I was born on an East Coast U.S. Navy base and have one sibling.

I guess you can say that I really like birds; "Sibley's Field Guide to Birds" is my favorite book, my favorite vacation spot is anywhere with lots of birds, my favorite animals are ravens, and I'm an avid birder.

organization doing both fieldwork and data-based number-crunching and analysis as part of independent study courses, and conduct forest ecology research as part of an honors thesis. It was great to see science as both fun and somewhat boring — because it is both.

Most of my upper-level biology courses were four students or fewer. This was an amazing opportunity to have to prove one's understanding of the concepts. It also allows for a very thoughtful and thorough critique of one's work by the professor. This was invaluable in transitioning from academia to a career. I have often shared that I am incredibly thankful to have had reports and other documents mercilessly marked up in red ink by a professor, rather than gotten off with an easy grade only to have a professional document criticized by a boss or client. I will gratefully admit that I am fortunate to have in-house editors who offer expert reviews of my reports.

My STEM education is the basis for not only my job, but also my recreation and hobbies. A science-based life is one fascinated by observation and study. I want to know more and do better daily. Professionally, my favorite part of my work is when I am working on a project where I passionately believe that our product will protect or improve either the environment or people's lives.

> **My STEM education is the basis for not only my job, but also my recreation and hobbies.**

I describe my job as "Jill-of-all-trades" in environmental science, since at any given time I might be doing something different. Most often I am an all-hazards emergency planner for anything ranging from oil spills, hazardous-materials releases, earthquakes, pandemic influenza, wildfire or flooding. I am an environmental scientist and geographic information systems (GIS) analyst. I also do environmental assessment and remediation and response fieldwork, which means I get to travel all over Alaska and assess environmental problems, report on them and help to respond to them in some way. Because I do not have a straightforward title, I often joke I am the "Disaster Diva."

I work for an environmental consulting firm. Most environmental consulting firms are multidisciplinary and composed of staff with different skills and professions. A consulting firm is hired by a client to provide professional services on a specific project. I have worked mostly on projects for federal and state agencies and local governments. I love that my job changes significantly year-to-year, and even week-to-week. I love the

"Over the last 14 years,
I have had to learn how to be
a field chemist, hazardous-
materials technician, wetlands
biologist, incident command
systems specialist, mapmaker and
planner for disasters of all types,
natural and man-made."

mix of computer-based work, fieldwork, hands-on instrumentation (environmental sampling and monitoring equipment) and meetings.

Over the last 14 years, I have had to learn how to be a field chemist, hazardous-materials technician, wetlands biologist, incident-command-systems specialist, mapmaker and planner for disasters of all types, natural and man-made.

I do not have a typical day. Much of my job is coordinating with my client, colleagues, partner agencies and the public. I attend a lot of meetings and participate in frequent teleconferences. I typically travel a few days a month, often to places in Alaska I would not get to venture to otherwise, allowing me the chance to cross the Arctic Circle, and wade in the Bering Strait and the Gulf of Alaska. On these trips I have seen whales, muskox, bears and moose. Travel for work can be tiring, and it can be hard being away from my family, but I appreciate the opportunity to see new places and meet new people.

Education

B.A.,
Wesleyan College,
Class of 1999,
Major: Biology

As this is a very multidisciplinary line of work, almost any type of STEM major will be required as well as beneficial. Having a broad background in the physical sciences provides the baseline for continuous learning. I am very grateful for having a liberal arts STEM degree. The writing skills and communication skills that are required for a liberal arts program are utilized every day, more than any single STEM subject. One of the most poignant pieces of advice I received from a professor was that a bachelor's degree does not prove you are educated; rather it proves that you are educable. This, incidentally, came from a professor of philosophy and religion, but who served on my thesis committee and remains a mentor to me.

> **I describe my job as "Jill-of-all-trades" in environmental science, since at any given time I might be doing something different.**

Outside of my occupation, I am a volunteer naturalist at a local nature center and a bird guide. When I was just out of college, I took a full-time volunteer position here and have been a volunteer ever since. I was recently named Volunteer of the Decade for interpretive education — one of the highest honors I have ever received. As a volunteer naturalist, I lead hikes and classes. Especially as a mom of two, my favorite programs are family-friendly hikes, taking kids out to explore nature and teaching them to look and listen for hidden treasures of flora and fauna. I feel very passionately that learning to observe our natural world is critical to learning to make observations and insights into other lines of science and technology, and to the functions of culture and society. A unique opportunity of observations of the natural world is that it can be practiced every day and can form the basis for physical excursions, and mental relaxation and renewal. Once a person is in the habit of observing, it is a habit not likely to be broken, regardless of the circumstance.

I've occasionally felt somewhat jealous of people who have grand or at least specific long-term goals, but I am just not one of them. Every time that I think I know exactly what I want to do next, life throws a curveball, whether these are unexpected changes of circumstances or changes on my own whim. I'm excited to find out where I will be 10 years from now — because I have no idea. I have not planned a journey or destination. I just hope that I make thoughtful decisions at the intersections on slightly crooked paths. I look forward to that journey. It will be fun. •

Lorraine Amory Soisson

Molecular Biologist

Before I was born, my family emigrated from Syria,
a country no one had heard of in those days.

By today's standards, my parents were not educated. My father grew up in Syria and he had the equivalent of a sixth-grade education when he arrived here. My mother was born to Syrian immigrants and left school at the start of World War II to help with the war effort. She eventually attended night school to earn her high school diploma.

Many of my female cousins who emigrated when they were in middle school were married off to men they barely knew while they were in high school. My uncle, the patriarch of our family, saw nothing wrong with continuing the traditions from Syria even though we lived in the United States. When I entered high school, he started to try to arrange marriages for me. Thankfully, my parents left it up to me, and I wanted nothing to do with marriage.

I was always good in school, but I really had no one to talk to about available educational opportunities. I liked math and science and had a wonderful advanced biology teacher, who saw how much I loved the chapters on genetic engineering and molecular biology. She encouraged me to consider going to college

About Me

I was born in Allentown, Pennsylvania and have two brothers.

The teacher that had the greatest impact on me was my Advanced Biology teacher, Roseann Leonzi (Whitehall High School, Pennsylvania), who recognized my love for science and helped guide me into my career.

> "The goal of my work is to develop a vaccine to protect children and pregnant women living in Africa against malaria."

to study something like that. Both fields were new then, and there weren't many programs. Most were at large schools, and I didn't think my parents would agree to send their daughter so far away for college.

My older brother was two years ahead of me and majored in engineering at Penn State. He would be a junior the same year that I would be a college freshman. I thought I might be able to convince my parents that I could go to Penn State, since my brother could look out for me. I'm not sure that comforted my parents much, but I applied and was accepted into Penn State's molecular biology program.

Meanwhile, my biology teacher talked to me about Cedar Crest College, a small liberal arts college in Allentown, Pennsylvania. Even though I had grown up nearby, I'm not sure I ever heard the name. Cedar Crest had just started a genetic engineering program. I heard "private school" and thought "expensive." I knew we couldn't afford much and knew nothing about scholarships, so I never told my parents.

One day I came home and my mom told me a professor from Cedar Crest had called — she was the cousin of my biology teacher. But it was already April! The deposit check to Penn State was written and ready to be mailed. We went to visit Cedar Crest and I fell in love. The campus is beautiful, the faculty seemed approachable and interested and the students were excited. The trajectory of my life changed that day — but I'm not sure I realized how much.

As a freshman, I met other students who were interested in all sorts of science and health fields. The more I talked to everyone, the more scared I became and wondered if I was smart enough. My family was nearby and that's where I envisioned raising a family one day. If I majored in genetic engineering, there were

no jobs in the Lehigh Valley. I knew I wanted to help people, so I decided to be a medical laboratory technician to be able to work locally. My faculty adviser was not thrilled, but I persisted.

During sophomore year, I met with her to declare a major. She asked me what I would do if there was a sick patient to be treated who had astonishing blood-test results. I told her that I would want to figure out what was wrong with the patient. My adviser was tiny and so mild-mannered, but she stood up and said in the loudest voice, "That's not your job! You give the results to his physician and never find out what happens to him." Well, I didn't like that idea, so genetic engineering it was!

Once again, my life's course changed significantly. My mentors helped me realize that my ultimate goals would require an advanced degree, much to the chagrin of my uncle, who was still stopping by my parents' house with pictures of men who might still be interested in marrying me even though I would have a college degree. My parents weren't too supportive at first, but my dad said that if I wanted to further my education, I should. Pretty forward-thinking for a Middle Eastern man — I have to give him credit. So off to the Johns Hopkins University School of Medicine I went. Many of my family members were simply resigned to the idea that I wanted to further my education.

. . . .

Currently, I am a scientist working for the U.S. government. I advise on the direction of research on malaria-vaccine development.

. . . .

So, I pursued a Ph.D. in biochemistry, cellular and molecular biology. At Johns Hopkins, the majority of students in my classes were men. The majority of my professors were men. I had to work hard to accomplish my goals.

My Ph.D. work focused on developing a vaccine for schistosomiasis, the second most prevalent parasitic infection worldwide. The disease doesn't exist in the United States, but more than 200,000 people in Africa are afflicted. My research took me to Africa. It was there that I realized how little I knew about our world and how desperately I wanted to help change it for the better.

My education, both at Cedar Crest and Johns Hopkins, opened so many doors for me to a life that I could never have imagined. As I was finishing my Ph.D., I thought about how I could most directly help people, which is my passion. I heard about and applied

My Favorite Things

Vacationing in Punta Cana, Dominican Republic.

Elephants.

The color purple.

Chocolate cake.

Crossword puzzles.

Christmas.

The book, "From the Mixed Up Files of Mrs. Basil E. Frankweiler."

Education

B.S.,
Cedar Crest College,
Class of 1988,
Triple Major:
Genetic Engineering
Technology, Biology
and Chemistry

Ph.D.,
**The Johns Hopkins
University School
of Medicine,**
Class of 1993,
Biochemistry, Cellular
and Molecular Biology

for a fellowship program at the State Department where scientists worked alongside policymakers to ensure sound science-based decision making. My application essay detailed my experiences growing up and the lessons I learned in Africa. I explained that it was so important to consider the experiences of those who were affected by poverty, disease and lack of education, regardless of whether they were born in the United States or in a lesser-developed country. I had the opportunity to work with United Nations organizations on health and science policy and programming and to travel on U.S. delegations to various international meetings.

Currently, I am a scientist working for the U.S. government. I advise on the direction of research on malaria-vaccine development. The goal of my work is to develop a vaccine to protect children and pregnant women living in Africa against malaria. We do not have any laboratories at my agency. Instead, I use my program's funding to build partnerships with other agencies or with companies or academic research facilities and direct our joint research program toward the goal of developing a vaccine to protect children.

Malaria is the most prevalent parasitic disease in the world, and it has been around as long as humans. We have some drugs that work well, but they are expensive, and over time, the parasite develops resistance against the drugs.

My job involves everything from vaccine discovery, manufacturing, getting regulatory approval and testing of vaccines to see if they work in animals and in people. In malaria, we are lucky to have a challenge model, so we can test to see if the vaccine worked by infecting volunteers in our clinical trials with the parasite. Of course, we watch the volunteers very closely and treat them with drugs we know will be effective as soon as they show any symptoms or we see the parasite in their blood.

I never would have expected any of this when I was in high school. The experiences I've had remind me that all of this happened not because I planned or even wished for it. It happened because I was not afraid to take opportunities when they were presented to me. •

Lucia A. Perez

Astrophysicist

When I was maybe 8 years old, I remember going to the Museum of Natural History in New York and seeing a show about black holes in the planetarium.

I had a very visceral reaction. I was equally terrified and amazed at the sheer hugeness of galaxies, of the immeasurable strength of black holes and of the expansive darkness of the universe. I felt tiny, powerless and fascinated at the extent of what I didn't know and couldn't understand. That fixation has driven my entire intellectual journey.

I was born in Caracas, Venezuela. My family moved to New York when I was 6 years old because of the shifting politics, and we've lived here ever since. My grandmother is one of my role models. She was a lawyer, and through her tenacity and endless capability for love, she gave my father and his siblings new opportunities in the United States, and continues to be the lynchpin of our family.

My parents both have master's degrees and they prioritized education. They encouraged me to read and took me to lots of museums and supported me in whatever I chose to do. I remember when I got home from my first semester at Wellesley College, I told my parents I wanted to major in astrophysics, and they said, "That's great! What is that?"

About Me

I was born in Caracas, Venezuela and have three siblings.

My favorite color is purple and I enjoy painting.

I loved reading the Harry Potter series.

"Astrophysics is simply amazing; especially when one considers how much there is left to learn about the universe. It brings together physicists, statisticians, chemists, biologists, philosophers and more, to answer the deepest questions we have about the universe."

I think the greatest influence on my education as a whole was Prep for Prep. Prep for Prep is a New York program that connects smart kids of color in underserved neighborhoods to the private schools of the area. In Prep's academic boot camp, I succeeded the most in math. Through Prep, I attended the Nightingale-Bamford School, an all-girls school in New York. Math and science were some of my favorite subjects and most of my teachers were women. I was lucky that I didn't get any pushback from my interest in STEM as a budding student. All my classmates were girls and most of my teachers were women, so the idea that girls can't do science never really had a chance to take root in my psyche.

....

With a degree in astrophysics, you can really do anything!

....

I remember clearly the first time I took physics in high school. I spent the fall semester of my junior year at The Mountain School, which is a semester school in Vermont. It was an incredible experience that gave me a really unique connection to the environment, all while giving me awesome academics. The Mountain School is co-ed, so my physics class had three girls and 19 boys. There, I did feel some of the pressure that I'm sure other female scientists felt. I was never outright discouraged or insulted, but I felt like there was a spotlight on me, simply because of the gender imbalance. That was also the first time I'd really struggled in a class, but I was stubborn and eager to master the material, so I worked with my teacher every morning until I could do it.

Even though physics was the first class that was actually hard for me, I really liked the challenge. When I got to college, I planned to major in physics. I took an astronomy

class for kicks my first semester, and I loved it so much that I decided to turn my physics major into astrophysics.

Astrophysics is simply amazing; especially when one considers how much there is left to learn about the universe. It brings together physicists, statisticians, chemists, biologists, philosophers and more, to answer the deepest questions we have about the universe.

With a degree in astrophysics, you can really do anything! You gain excellent quantitative skills and problem-solving from physics, and diverse coding abilities from applying the physics to astronomy. You can go into banking (particle physicists use the same coding programs as Wall Street does!), or engineering or any other career that uses math. Getting a degree in astrophysics teaches you how to think about difficult abstract things using quantitative tools — those kinds of skills can take you anywhere.

When college application time came, I was hesitant to apply to women's colleges; but I applied to Wellesley at my counselor's insistence since the application was free and Wellesley is among the top five liberal arts colleges in the United States.

When I visited Wellesley during the Spring Open Campus weekend and met students and other prospies (prospective students), I got that feeling that I mattered and that Wellesley wanted me to succeed, and that it would support me in that. I could immediately see that a strong feeling of community and intellectual curiosity came from every crevice of that gorgeous campus, and I could see myself being happy and thriving there. I didn't feel that at any of the other schools I visited.

. . . .

A big part of science is overcoming setbacks and modifying your approach.

. . . .

And the all-women environment was exactly what made Wellesley so incredible! I went to an all-girl's school from seventh grade on, and I loved the care that the teachers gave to each student and the environment of community and encouragement. I felt like I mattered as an individual, and that people believed in my ability to succeed.

After graduating from Wellesley, I was awarded a Fulbright Student Research Fellowship in South Africa, with a focus on astronomy. The Fulbright is run by a specific office in the Department of State, and these fellowships focus on promoting diplomacy and positive international relations through professional person-to-person

My Favorite Things

Ice cream for dessert, please!

Christmas.

Dr. Irene Mata from Wellesley, super engaging and an incredible ally.

Vacationing in Italy is the best!

Giraffes top my list for favorite animals.

Education

B.A.,
Wellesley College,
Class of 2014,
Major: Astrophysics

Ph.D.,
Arizona State University, Anticipated
Class of 2022,
Astrophysics

connections. The Fulbright caught my attention because it offered me a unique way to get more experience in my field, explore a new region of the world and immerse myself in a different community within the field of astrophysics.

My project was quite unique; most people do work in health, or economics or sociology. Hard-science Fulbrights are relatively rare. I worked under the most-prominent black South African astrophysicist, Thebe Medupe, Ph.D. He and I began working on studying the pulsations of stars. We combed through databases to find evidence of large pulsating stars, but our search didn't turn up any candidates. A big part of science is overcoming setbacks and modifying your approach.

Another reason that I chose to do my Fulbright with this astrophysicist is because he does a lot of work promoting astrophysics in his community. Each July, he runs a program that encourages other black South Africans to continue in astronomy and teaches them the skills they need to do research. Promoting diversity in astronomy and STEM is something I'm passionate about, and it was great to see how this work is done in other communities.

> There's a myth that to be a physicist you need to be a genius — but that isn't true! You just need to be curious, decent with a computer and willing to try new things. I think a lot of young women will see a B or C grade and tell themselves they can't do it. This is so tragic considering how many boys will get a B or C grade and power through to become the next generation of scientists.

I'm now pursuing a Ph.D. in astrophysics at the School for Earth and Space Exploration at Arizona State University. The program averages six years. The first two are mostly coursework and preliminary research aimed at making you a well-rounded and knowledgeable scientist. The remaining years are dedicated to thesis research, where you seek to discover some knowledge that's never been done before. At ASU, the astronomers, planetary scientists and experimentalists that create the tools of those fields are all under one roof. This leads to a very interdisciplinary approach to the space and earth sciences, which appealed to me a lot. It means that in the same department, I can help build the telescope that I'll use to do my astrophysics research.

In my first year, I took several classes to delve into the details of astronomy. I also started work on the research that should feed into my thesis with my advisers. I've been working on the clustering statistics of high-redshift star-forming galaxies with the end goal of studying the early stages of our universe's evolution and helping guide some telescope missions. I'm also visiting Germany to work on my second project, studying magnetic fields around galaxies with a low-frequency telescope array. I'll take classes for another year, take my qualifying exams, and then dive into my dissertation work.

I'm not exactly sure about my career path. I like the idea of being able to do scientific research while doing outreach and science advocacy, especially out in popular culture. Or, I might end up working for NASA as a mission scientist or working on large astrophysics problems with one of the national laboratories. Part of graduate school will be working with and learning from people doing these things and more, and figuring out what will work for me.

If you're interested in astrophysics, my suggestion is to take as much math as you can. Learn physics as early as you can and go for it! If you want to do it, you can do it. It'll be hard, but you can do it. You might feel like you can't do it, but I'm here to tell you, you can.

There's a myth that to be a physicist you need to be a genius — but that isn't true! You just need to be curious, decent with a computer and willing to try new things. I think a lot of young women will see a B or C grade and tell themselves they can't do it. This is so tragic considering how many boys will get a B or C grade and power through to become the next generation of scientists.

The biggest challenge for me has been mental. I've had times in my career where I've started to self-sabotage a little bit because I thought I wasn't good enough and wouldn't succeed. Luckily, my penchant for planning ahead, my moderately above-average intelligence and the support of my community helped me get over those bumps and continue to reach new heights.

Now, I keep moving forward and continue to reach for the stars! •

Lydia Bussiere

Fuel Cell Engineer

On a whim, I signed up for my first engineering class.

It was called Engineering for Everyone and something about the course listing caught my eye. That one class opened my eyes up to things that had never occurred to me. On a whim, I'd taken the course not realizing that it was going to shape my future.

In high school, I was one of those people who genuinely liked learning. I was lucky, school wasn't too hard and not one single class was exceptionally challenging. Unlike many people I knew, I was able to simply enjoy the process of learning. That said, I didn't really have a favorite subject. I liked math, but I also enjoyed history. I loved reading and writing, so all my English classes were great, too. Toward the end of high school, many of my peers were already sure of what they wanted to study in college. That wasn't exactly the case for me.

About Me

I'm the only child in my family and was born in Northampton, Massachusetts.

My high school math teacher, Ms. Young, was my favorite teacher. She made it easy to learn a lot of hard math!

When I started applying to colleges, I mostly looked at smaller liberal arts schools, figuring that I could take a wide variety of classes and decide on a major later. I chose Smith College for a lot of reasons, but honestly, the engineering program wasn't one of them. I didn't even know about it! But when it came to choosing classes for the first semester, an introduction class to engineering caught my eye. It seemed interesting, so I decided to go for it.

And I'm so glad that I did. In the span of one semester, I built a miniature house capable of heating itself through solar energy that could maintain a comfortable indoor temperature on a brisk December day in Massachusetts. I learned about the technicalities of heating and cooling, why the largest windows should be on south-facing walls, how to program a microcontroller, which are like mini computers, and how to use a laser printer. But more than that, I learned about troubleshooting, working through an issue in a systematic way until you've figured out how to fix it. It was like the puzzles that I had loved as a kid, but on a larger scale. I realized that I could spend my days coming up with creative solutions to tricky problems, and I loved it.

· ·

In the span of one semester, I built a miniature house capable of heating itself through solar energy that could maintain a comfortable indoor temperature on a brisk December day in Massachusetts.

· ·

Energy consumption is at an all-time high, and will only increase over time. The solution is not to restrict or limit consumption, but to create solutions that are sustainable and environmentally friendly. With increased demands, the good news is that STEM can be looked to for solutions, and for those interested in the energy field, studying a STEM-related subject will be advantageous.

Energy comes in many forms. It is associated with electricity, and while electricity is an energy form, it's not the only one. The remarkable thing about electricity is that there are many ways to create electricity in our world today. A lot of those use non-renewable energy sources like coal and oil. These sources can be harmful for the earth, creating unwanted pollution in our air. The future is going to require cleaner and more renewable energy sources. That's where I come in.

I work for a company that manufactures green energy sources, namely hydrogen fuel-cells and stationary hydrogen fuel-cell power plants. The fuel cells we make are

> "Green energy and sustainable technologies have always been important to me, and I know that wherever else I go in my career, I plan to continue to work toward a better, healthier world."

My Favorite Things

Whales.

Cheesecake.

The color blue.

"The Hitchhiker's Guide to the Galaxy" by Douglas Adams.

Playing the guitar.

Christmas.

Spending my vacations in Blue Hill, Maine.

each about 10 feet tall and three feet square. There are four fuel cells per power plant; each power plant is the size of a tractor trailer and can produce 440 kilowatts of continuous power. To put that into perspective, one kilowatt represents the amount of energy needed by a 1000-watt device, such as a clothes iron or microwave, to operate continuously for one hour. The fuel cells made by my company use hydrogen for an electrochemical reaction that creates electricity, clean water and heat.

When I started with the company, my role was two-fold. We are a 24/7 manufacturing operation, so there's always someone working. This is great for energy production, but it also means that there are always issues that come up. In order to keep the manufacturing floor running, I support fuel cell testing. If a fuel cell is performing poorly during testing, I work with the manufacturing team to figure out what went wrong. I also help diagnose problems that come up once the power plant is installed in its permanent site. Along with supporting manufacturing, I am also involved in new product development and design.

Education

B.S.,
Smith College,
Class of 2012,
Major: Engineering
Science

Recently, I was moved from our engineering department to our service engineering department and received a new title, service engineering project manager. As a test engineer, I was focused on day-to-day operations in our manufacturing facility. As the project manager for our service engineering team, I'm focused on long-term reliability and efficiency improvements for our fleet of power plants in the field. I also assist with some of the issues that come up in the field. It's a project management role instead of a hands-on role, so I do miss getting dirty in the factory at times. However, it's good experience and it's been interesting learning about how the product that I tested in the factory actually functions once it is delivered to the customer. My experience in the factory has also helped when trying to look at cross-functional ways we can improve our processes and our products.

> **I work for a company that manufactures green energy sources, namely hydrogen fuel-cells and stationary hydrogen fuel-cell power plants.**

I'm happy to say that I have, so far, found jobs that allow me to feel creative and challenged on a daily basis. Not only that, but my current job also allows me to feel as though I'm making a difference, however small, in the health of our planet. Green energy and sustainable technologies have always been important to me, and I know that wherever else I go in my career, I plan to continue to work toward a better, healthier world. •

Maria Hristova

Software Engineering Management

You would think that coming from a family of engineers (both of my parents are engineers, as was my maternal grandfather), I would have actively recognized my aptitude for STEM subjects as a young girl. This couldn't be further from the truth.

In fact, I tried to actively steer away from it as I wanted to do something else besides what everyone else in my family was doing.

However, I do remember being very interested in biology and medicine. I spent a year in middle school at a math-focused school. I even started taking programming classes when I was 9 years old.

The majority of my high school career was spent slinking in the back row of all the science and math classes, which were requirements for me to graduate, but weren't the primary focus of my interests. I spent a lot of time writing for the newspaper and participating in the theater productions, drifting further and further away from any science interests.

About Me

Hailing from Bulgaria, I have one sibling.

My favorite book is "Microserfs" by Douglas Coupland.

I enjoy vacationing in Maui, Hawaii and my favorite animal is an octopus.

"The technology field is changing, and I have seen it happen even during my career. There are more opportunities than ever for women to advance in this field and our achievements are being recognized and celebrated more every day. Come join me!"

At college, I took all sorts of classes at Bryn Mawr and absolutely loved my art history classes. I had to take some mandatory science and math classes to fulfill my requirements, and begrudgingly excelled at them. As much as I had wanted to do something else besides math or computer science, I also realized that it might be useful to pursue a subject which I did well in, especially at Bryn Mawr, which was extremely competitive.

I had a fantastic computer science professor who encouraged me the entire four years I was there and who is personally responsible for me eventually graduating with a degree in the field. I had opportunities to do research during the summer and to be in a cocoon of support, which eventually translated into the confidence that allowed me to have a successful interview at a major software company and land a job there upon graduation. I had thought a lot about pursuing an advanced degree in the field, but decided to try out the industry instead. I have been in it ever since, and I am not going anywhere.

I work in software engineering management. This means that I manage a team of developers who work on delivering a software as a service product. In turn, this allows our customers to securely share documents in a virtual space online. I work in software, so it is just like that show "Silicon Valley." Except when it isn't, which is every day.

I love working in teams, trying to solve really difficult technical questions. It always amazes me how much more can be achieved when a team works together rather than everyone plugging away on their own. The notion of the "lone coder" is extremely outdated and no longer represents our industry.

There are days when I am in meetings all day and I am constantly talking and switching between different projects that we are working on. As an introvert, having to communicate all day can be exhausting. That said, it is also extremely rewarding when you watch the projects that your team has been working on go live and see customers "in the wild" use them.

I work in an open-space office where the entire team sits together in team "pods." The teams consist of developers, quality assurance and product owners. We practice a method of software development called Agile, in which we meet daily in the morning to talk about the progress that we made over the previous day and if there is anything blocking us from progressing further. It is a highly collaborative and team-focused approach which allows us to ship product to our customers as soon as we have a working viable version of it.

> **I am really inspired by examples of excellent teamwork and when people are able to get together and collectively produce something which is better than the sum of all of their individual efforts.**

Hiring is a big part of my job, so I think a lot about the skills that make people successful in this job. The ability to learn and a natural curiosity are probably at the top of my list, along with problem-solving aptitude and the ability to persevere when no obvious answer emerges. Being able to work in a team of people and to constantly integrate other people's feedback on your work is critical for long-term success.

I am really inspired by examples of excellent teamwork and when people are able to get together and collectively produce something which is better than the sum of all

My Favorite Things

The color black.

Chocolate chocolate with more chocolate.

I own and run a craft distillery in my free time!

Deepak Kumar, as he made it possible for me to graduate with a degree in computer science.

Education

B.A.,
Bryn Mawr College,
Class of 2002,
Double Major:
Computer Science
and Mathematics

of their individual efforts. As much as I like and have come to accept that I am an introvert, I also get very inspired from simply interacting with people during problem-solving. There is a real technical high when I walk out of a brainstorming session when we have come up with a path forward for a problem that previously seemed unsolvable. It doesn't have to even be the "right" direction — so often the problems that I come across don't have clear technical answers. I am simply inspired by the technical process, and I feel incredibly fortunate to be a part of it every day.

....

**As an introvert, having to communicate
all day can be exhausting.**

....

More than anything else, I use my critical thinking skills, the majority of which are very closely related to my STEM education. Second to that, I rely heavily on my ability to learn new things and integrate them in my work — being a STEM major at a liberal arts school gave me the skills to keep my mind open to new ideas and to pursue learning as a mode of day-to-day operation rather than a distinct process with a beginning and an end. And lastly, I use data to guide me in my decision-making process as one would use the results of an experiment when proving a hypothesis.

I plan on following my career path as far as I can take it. My goal is to be a vice president of engineering or a CTO (chief technology officer) at a startup one day. I feel incredibly fortunate that my mother is an engineering manager and that I had that example to rely on throughout my entire career. I had a mentor, an outstanding engineering mind and a mother all wrapped up in one, and that made it possible for me to envision myself in these roles, even though throughout my career there have been few women in leadership positions at the companies I worked for. I talk to a lot of women thinking about going into the tech industry and to some who are in it, and I always try to convey that it is, in fact, possible to excel and hold some of these positions.

The technology field is changing, and I have seen it happen even during my career. There are more opportunities than ever for women to advance in this field and our achievements are being recognized and celebrated more every day. Come join me! •

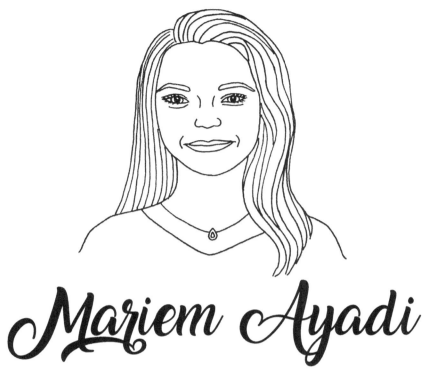

Mariem Ayadi

Software Engineer

I like the feeling of being limitless.
I like having a career with unlimited options.

Once I realized that by being a software engineer, I could work anywhere and in any industry, and solve a breadth of different and ever-changing kinds of problems, I was hooked.

In my occupation, I use computers to find creative ways to solve all sorts of problems, even problems from the real world. The computer becomes a tool; my tool to "write" or rather "code" my ideas. An example can be given using social media. Have you ever wondered how the computer somehow magically recognizes your friends' faces without you having to do all the hard work? That cool feature is developed by software engineers in the field of artificial intelligence (AI) or machine learning, which are fancy words for the art of teaching computers to learn from repetition.

Programming simply means using computer language, like typing "4/2" to ask the computer to divide four by two. A software developer/engineer is good at communicating with computers to make them accomplish the tasks they have in mind. But a software engineer's job is not only limited to using a

About Me

I was born in Tunisia and have one sibling.

I most enjoyed a trip to the southern part of Tunisia. I fell in love with Matmata (not far from the neighboring towns where the Star Wars early episodes were filmed). But my favorite vacation spot is the Yucatan Region in Mexico.

Even though I wear a lot of black, I would have to say that dark blue is my favorite color.

"Computer science also taught me to never give up. Even when you think that an application is completely broken, miracles do happen."

computer to solve mathematics problems; they can also use a computer to program a video game, a website and all sorts of cool smartphone applications.

I like that I am able to use my creativity. Think about your favorite website or app. Is there a feature that you wish existed? As a software engineer, you could make that feature! Software engineering allows for a lot of creativity; it is a career that encourages you to combine your technical knowledge and imagination in order to innovate.

The most straightforward approach to becoming a software engineer is by majoring in computer science. As of today, a bachelor's degree qualifies you in many industries that employ software developers. A master's degree or a higher graduate degree is optional for an entry-level position since you learn and grow so much on the job.

In computer science, you will often hear about peers who have started coding at an early age. Is it intimidating? Of course it is. But I did not let that stop me. Growing up, we all have different interests and that should not prevent us from continuously exploring new ideas and passions. I decided that I was equally capable of learning this skill set; I was equally capable of being great.

Computer science also taught me to never give up. Even when you think that an application is completely broken, miracles do happen. You just have to befriend the internet and continue looking for the clues! It's very much like being a detective.

I believe that I have always been drawn to mathematics. Literature, history and geography are interesting and very important, but as a child, I felt that these subjects involved far too much memorization. I would forget everything I learned the second the test was over. I felt I was more drawn to mathematics.

From middle school to high school and to this day, I have and I am still known for asking millions of questions, and with mathematics, I felt satisfied by the answers.

I would dig further and further until I had no more "why" questions. Practice felt rewarding. When I would learn about a topic for the very first time, it would feel so ambiguous and impossible to comprehend, very far from being enjoyable. But while the challenge would feel frustrating at first, somehow every time it would eventually start feeling gratifying.

In Tunisia, my home country in North Africa, mathematics was a popular branch of studies that girls and boys pursued equally. Mathematics and science were also the most highly regarded academic paths. It seemed that every parent's dream was for their child to become an engineer or a doctor. I tend to disagree with that mindset as I truly believe that all academic paths should be equally respected. In fact, I wish I had taken more nontechnical courses. Nevertheless, I am happy that I had decided on my own to dive further into mathematics out of personal conviction and interest, as opposed to family pressure.

. . . .

In computer science, you will often hear about peers who have started coding at an early age. Is it intimidating? Of course it is. But I did not let that stop me.

. . . .

My first internship was at a technology company that runs a website where users can search and book flights and hotels online. At that time, I had not considered computer science as a career, but loved the company culture and the people. It was a cool place! Over the years, I came to realize that I was indirectly impacted by my interactions with the software developers at the tech company. I was intrigued by what they did.

Wanting to investigate other career avenues for computer science majors, I also tried out research and went to Germany. I joined a university research group that was working on helping people gather very large amounts of data, which the industry calls Big Data. Big Data is used to make interesting conclusions by analyzing all sorts of mass data, from text, to photos and to videos. For example, have you ever noticed that a lot of the ads that you see while browsing the internet are generally about things you really like or have recently looked up? If so, then you've already encountered Big Data! Software engineers — sometimes called data scientists in this case — gather, and then analyze data about users, trends, etc., to help companies better understand their consumers. Other engineers might use Big Data to try to predict the next best-selling game or the cheapest time to fly to Hawaii!

My Favorite Things

The book "The Industries of the Future" by Alec Ross.

Anything with matcha.

Photography/oil painting (at least I try) and phoning an old friend out of the blue to catch up.

Professor Judith Keyler-Mayer. She is honestly the reason why I even ventured into learning German and somehow can speak it (to a limited extent, of course). She is my role model when it comes to breaking complex information into its simplest form.

Pet hamsters.

Education

B.A.,
Smith College,
Class of 2016,
Major: Computer
Science

During my sophomore and junior years in college, I had the chance to meet several senior women in the technology side of banking. They each had a unique and impressive career path. I was inspired. Since programming skills can be used in any field, after college, I decided to explore yet another completely different industry: finance. Today, I'm a software engineer at an investment bank.

Years ago, traders working at investment banks relied heavily on the telephone when communicating with their clients. When a client was looking to buy or sell a stock, they would call their trader (or sales contact at the bank) to convey their request verbally. After the phone conversation, the trader completed the necessary paperwork for the transaction to take place.

Fast forward to today where investment banks use the phone a lot less; many of the voice transactions are now conducted using computer applications instead. And that's where the software engineer comes into play! We use computers to help businesses run faster and more efficiently. I get to interact with the business or more generally, the user of an application, hear about what they wish the application could do better, and then my job is to turn those ideas into reality.

As you may have guessed by now, software engineers spend a lot of time in front of computers. But nowadays, so do many of us. Working at the office is encouraged, but many software engineers across industries also have the option to work from home. The advantage of working with computers is that you can carry them around with you. Visiting your grandmother for an extended weekend? Traveling overseas for a month? You will generally have the option to log in and do your job remotely from any of those locations. I prefer to work from the office because I get to share my ideas with other engineers. What may at first seem like a hard puzzle becomes easier when you share your thought process with other team members.

Coming from an international background, I speak a few foreign languages and I am truly passionate about communication. This has helped me connect better with the international members of my team. At my current job, I feel so lucky to be surrounded by people from all over the world, and that is by no means an exaggeration. Turkey, India, the United Kingdom, Bangladesh, Kazakhstan, Cameroon, Russia, the United States, Ireland, China — these are all countries that my colleagues sitting next to or across from me are originally from. My closest mentor at work once said, "I hope that the world will one day get along, just like we all do here." •

Marin Kress

Research Physical Scientist

Looking back, I see why I enjoyed that worm dissection
in my seventh-grade life sciences class.

I remember the day vividly because the preservatives smelled really bad, but despite the smell, it was neat to see what the inside of the worm looked like. Learning the names and functions of the different organs was cool because it was like this secret language that gave me the power to look at the worm and see how the pieces worked together. It was even more interesting when we learned how a worm could regenerate its tail if it was cut off, but only if it had enough of the head-end intact. It sounded like some sort of superpower to me, and it made me wonder what other sort of superpowers are out there in the natural world.

It may seem contradictory, but while I liked seeing the inside of things, I did not want to get my hands dirty or touch whatever smelly thing we had to dissect. I was careful about using different tools and going slow. At the time, I never thought, "I want to do this for a living" or "I'm going to study science later." I just thought it was interesting, and that made me want to do the reading and the homework, and so I did well in the class, but I didn't think anything of it.

About Me

I have an older brother and prefer to spend my vacation time in places with lots to see, like a healthy coral reef or New York City.

I love to scuba dive, and this comes in handy when exploring coral reefs.

I'm especially fond of peacock mantis shrimp.

By the time I reached high school, I was especially drawn to biology because it was so relatable to the world around me. I volunteered at a hospital in middle school and high school. It was basic stuff like helping people find their way around the hospital, but being in that environment made me think about the human body and disease. I didn't have a plan, or a specific job in mind, but that volunteer experience showed me that there are many ways to help people and be involved in medicine that don't require being a doctor, nurse or physical therapist.

I decided to go to Smith College in Northampton, Massachusetts, which is extremely supportive of the sciences. About one quarter of women there major in the sciences, so there was a large community of women doing all kinds of scientific research. At Smith, I met women who were doing research with professors during their first year of college because they already had expertise in some field. That set a high standard. I made friends with women who had amazing interests outside of their laboratory, too. Scientists can make art, play sports, learn foreign languages, tell funny stories or be amazing dancers. I had already decided to be a biology major, but I think Smith College and the great friends around me made me a more enthusiastic biology major.

· ·

I'm employed by the U.S. government within a federal agency that works on water-related projects.

· ·

My occupation as a research physical scientist is all about being creative, specifically, combining large data sets, looking through them in ways that no one else has done before and then telling people what I've found. It isn't what I expected to be doing when I was in middle school, high school or even in college, but I really enjoy it.

I'm employed by the U.S. government within a federal agency that works on water-related projects. Most of the data I work with is collected in order to keep shipping lanes open. This is a never-ending task because shipping lanes are underwater channels which often fill up with sediment washed off from land. Part of that data has to do with things like where the government places the sand that it has to move out of the shipping channels; sometimes they use it for beaches, or to build wetlands, sometimes it goes way offshore in the ocean. There is a lot of interest in understanding what is happening with sand and sediment movement all over the country, and how we can improve the process, but it doesn't always get analyzed and communicated in a holistic way.

"My occupation as a research physical scientist is all about being creative, specifically, combining large data sets, looking through them in ways that no one else has done before and then telling people what I've found."

What I like most about my job is that it allows me to do new things, and I get to use the skills I learned in school in different ways. I also get to meet people from all over the country and learn all about how transportation networks function to deliver everything from ice cream to computers. Understanding these networks is kind of like dissection, and I've always liked to figure out how things work.

An important part of my scientific training was learning how to carry out long and detailed procedures. That ability to design and follow a long series of instructions is something I use every day. I used to work in a medical research laboratory, and there you had to run experiments very carefully in order to be able to trust your results. I also had to be physically precise because I was working with biohazardous materials, and that training in precise thinking has carried over into other jobs and been very useful. I still carry out long precise protocols to get results, but my work now is computer based, so I don't worry about knocking over containers of blood or radioactive materials.

Education

B.A.,
Smith College,
Class of 2003,
Major: Biological
Sciences

M.S.,
**University of
Massachusetts
Boston,**
Class of 2013,
Environmental Science

Ph.D.,
**University of
Massachusetts
Boston,**
Class of 2016,
Marine Science
and Technology,
Concentration
in Ocean &
Human Health

I consider myself to be slightly introverted. I don't seek to be the center of attention in large groups. I'd prefer to be to the side just observing, which makes me patient. In school, I was often hesitant to raise my hand in class unless I was absolutely positively sure of the answer, and I didn't like having to raise my voice to be heard. Some people have naturally loud voices and seem to speak very smoothly; I am not one of those people, but I've gotten better with practice. Smith College definitely gave me space to grow in that regard; students were expected to speak up and contribute in class.

At work, my daily inspiration comes from trying to make a small part of the world better by providing a solid scientific reason something should change. Environmental issues are important to me since we only have one earth to live on, and thinking of ways to reduce pollution by being more efficient with resources, or how to support environmental restoration efforts, is something that I enjoy working on. The pace of change can be slow, because change in government happens slowly; but overall, I'm contributing to something I think is important.

There is a great quote I read once from MIT professor Nancy Hopkins that I like to share with people when I think about the future: "The field of science you fall in love with may be so new it doesn't even have a name yet." I think about that because when I was in college I liked genetics, microbiology and immunology, but I had no idea that there was such a thing as a personal microbiome. Now genomics research is so accessible because the price of equipment has gone down, and this whole new area of research on the microbiome has emerged. It's amazing!

I never liked the idea of limiting oneself to thinking that "doing science" or "being a scientist" only involves the type of work you see on TV or read about in the news. Being a scientist can involve working at the South Pole, searching for big sharks or tiny molecules, writing books or writing computer code or even making movies. I know scientists that do all those things. My own experience has taught me that if you like some topic but there isn't a name for it, just keep going and you'll get to create the job later because people need pioneers to explore and discover all the things we haven't yet imagined. •

Marina Biggio

Medical Device Engineer

Science rubbed off on me by chance.

In middle school, I was assigned to my science teacher's homeroom. I think the classroom had an affect on me because suddenly everywhere I looked, I saw something relating to science. Science allows me to be an independent learner. I have always been curious about the nature of everything around me. I love to think about what things are made of, how they work and what that means for the world at large.

I was most interested in how biology worked. Biological machines are the most fascinating machines of all because they exist, work and live all on their own. I also enjoyed science because I could take something I was curious about and I could research it, test it and learn about it all on my own! This gave me a satisfying and empowering feeling even at a young age.

An example of this was my first science fair project. When I got to high school, I was curious about whether medicine was safe for your digestive system or not because I'd heard a lot of different things. I decided to do an experiment where I grew healthy stomach bacteria in Petri dishes and put different types of medicine in the dishes to see if anything happened. When the experiment was done, I discovered that the medicine was killing healthy bacteria!

About Me

I was born in North Conway, New Hampshire and have three siblings.

My mom is my best teacher because her lessons made me who I am today.

"I like to think that improving the health of others can have a ripple effect."

For a long time, I thought I wanted a career in neuroscience because I am really interested in how people think and the biology of the brain. This is because there is a lot we don't know about the brain and the mystery of it is very intriguing. I also really liked using the computer, especially when it came to graphic design, creating things and thinking about 3-D shapes. I now realize this was the beginning of my interest in computer-aided design (CAD).

....

As a recent engineering graduate, I am aspiring to work as a medical device R&D engineer. The job of a medical device engineer is to brainstorm design ideas, create prototypes and test devices to be used during surgeries and medical procedures.

....

It wasn't until my senior capstone at Smith College that I knew what sort of job I wanted. I worked with two other students designing a mechanism for a surgical device called the Veress needle. This was a huge milestone for me because we were working on a real project with a well-known medical device company, and it was very similar to working as a medical device research and development (R&D) engineer. Getting a glimpse of what R&D engineering was really like helped me finally solidify my decision to pursue it as a career.

As a recent engineering graduate, I am aspiring to work as a medical device R&D engineer. The job of a medical device engineer is to brainstorm design ideas, create prototypes and test devices to be used during surgeries and medical procedures. A medical device engineer can work on devices for all types of procedures. Sometimes the job is to improve an already existing device, and at other times it is to create an entirely new device that no one has ever seen before.

In order to be successful, a medical device R&D engineer needs a variety of different skills. These include mathematics, computers and computer programs, designing and carrying out experiments, time management and project management, brainstorming and coming up with new ideas, problem-solving, taking things apart and re-assembling

them, basic biology and, most importantly, the ability learn on-the-go and to work with other people.

Most of these skills will come from an engineering education, but it's important to realize that some of the necessary know-how will only come from experience. An engineering education will get you far, but once you are working, you may need to teach yourself new things to succeed at your job.

To be hired as an R&D engineer for medical devices you usually need to go to college for a bachelor's degree in engineering. There are many different types of engineering, but the most common major needed for medical device engineering is mechanical engineering. Electrical engineering and biomedical engineering are also very common, and computer science majors also work on medical devices if the devices need computer programming.

Even more so, though, I am motivated by the thought of improving the quality of life of others, and I think the best way to do this is by lessening the pain that many people endure.

One of my favorite aspects of medical device R&D is brainstorming ideas for devices. It is one of the more creative sides of engineering. During this phase of the process, it's okay to come up with lots of crazy ideas, and none of them are considered wrong. After the best ideas are chosen, my next favorite thing to do is create the model of the design on the computer using the CAD program. CAD programs allow you to draw a very detailed 3-D version of the device on the computer.

I also really love working with people. Whether it is collaborating with other engineers, the surgeons who give feedback on designs or the people marketing and selling products, I'm always collaborating with other people to make the project happen. It's a good reminder that everything can't be done all on your own!

Medical device R&D engineering definitely has its challenges. For every success in a project, there will probably be more failures and things that go wrong. A huge part of designing a device is trial and error and re-doing designs to improve them. This can be difficult at times because it can get frustrating, but the important thing is to keep trying and pushing on. If you fail enough, you will have worked out all the bugs in your design by the end and will have a better, safer and more efficient device.

My Favorite Things

Reading
"The Dovekeepers"
by Alice Hoffman.

The color red.

Dark chocolate.

Weightlifting.

Thanksgiving.

Vacationing in Lake
Winnipesaukee.

Deer.

Education

B.S.,
Smith College,
Class of 2017,
Major: Engineering
Science

Also, the more difficult the design process, the more satisfying the feeling will be when you succeed and finish your device.

I am now finally at the point where I can start applying to jobs. I'm perfecting my résumé, having friends, family members and teachers look over my cover letters, and I'm applying for real medical device R&D engineering jobs. This is the moment I've been waiting for, and I am so very excited. I'm definitely nervous about putting myself out there, but in an excited sort of way. I feel like I've done everything possible to prepare myself for this point in my life and now all I can do is take the leap into the world of employment and hope for the best.

Moving forward, I hope to land a position and to continue my career as an engineer. I know medical device R&D engineering is the right place for me, and I also know that as I experience the workforce, I will gain an even better idea of my interests and my future goals for my career. Right now, I am just taking it one step at a time. As I move forward every day, I am motivated by my goal of creating financial stability for myself and giving myself the ability to live life to the fullest and be my very best person.

Even more so, though, I am motivated by the thought of improving the quality of life of others, and I think the best way to do this is by lessening the pain that many people endure. The world is constantly changing; the world of technology especially, is growing quickly. This is good news for the realm of medical devices. I want to put that technology to good use by keeping devices up to date and ensuring the best medical care for people all over the world. I like to think that improving the health of others can have a ripple effect. It is much easier to be happy, to live your life fully and to give to others if you are pain-free. I hope that lessening someone's physical pain can improve their ability to be happy and to make others happy in turn. This is, after all, the ultimate goal. •

Morgan Halley

Veterinary Medical Officer

When my parents bought my first toy doctor kit, I was overjoyed.

But, to their surprise, I never used it to play with dolls. I played "doctor" with my stuffed animals instead. I grew up imagining a future as a veterinarian before I could remember. The path that I inevitably pursued, however, was anything but typical.

As a veterinary student now, many of my classmates are planning to pursue the career we imagine when we think of veterinarians. They want to become "small animal" doctors for dogs and cats. For a long time, I was undecided about what I wanted to do in veterinary medicine; I knew I wanted to help animals, and I liked medicine, but putting people's pets to sleep was emotionally very hard on me. So I did a little research on the different career opportunities in the field of veterinary medicine.

It turns out there are a multitude of careers for veterinarians that most people don't think or even know about: wildlife conservation, zoological medicine, research and perhaps the most underappreciated — public health. And within the field of veterinary public health, there is an even more diverse range of opportunities. There are public health veterinarians who work as epidemiologists (studying disease outbreaks), field researchers, animal welfare advocates and food quality inspectors. My love of working

"While I knew I was interested in veterinary medicine from a very young age, it took me a long time to really settle on what exactly I wanted to do within the field of veterinary medicine."

with beef cattle, pigs, sheep and goats directed me toward the last category. I thought, "What better way to make an impact on protecting animal welfare and human health than to work on the front lines as a food animal inspector?"

Veterinary medical officers (VMOs) who work in food animal inspection have busy lives! In a given day, they might be expected to inspect holding and animal processing facilities to make sure the animals are treated well, while also looking for any sick animals that might have zoonotic diseases (diseases that can be passed from animals to humans). VMOs are also responsible for checking imported animals and meat products from other countries for diseases. In some instances, VMOs are called upon to travel and investigate disease outbreaks, collect data and analyze that data in a lab. A VMO is typically someone with great attention to detail, who likes problem-solving and has an interest in traveling. The hours are very reasonable, which is almost unheard of in most veterinary careers. Some of my classmates expect to go into careers where they might work 100+ hour weeks. VMOs have much more free time, which is something that appealed to me. Best of all, you are learning every day as a VMO and constantly seeing new things!

The path to a veterinary degree has been anything but easy — and I'm not done yet! I had to graduate from high school with good grades, and obtain a bachelor's in biological science. By the time I applied to veterinary school, I also had a few thousand hours of veterinary-related work experience in multiple fields (small animal, wildlife, large animal and laboratory animal), as is typically expected of most veterinary school applicants nowadays. It's worth mentioning that I wasn't a typical science-minded student from the very beginning. I enjoyed writing and history early on, and only later became interested in science — so if math and science don't immediately come naturally, don't worry! I also had several classmates who chose nonscience majors and went on to veterinary and medical school. By managing your classes closely and making sure you meet the entry requirements for veterinary school, it is certainly possible to change your major.

While I knew I was interested in veterinary medicine from a very young age, it took me a long time to really settle on what exactly I wanted to do within the field of veterinary medicine. I went to a tiny middle school (my graduating class was only

three students), and was the only girl I knew who was interested in science.

In eighth grade, I designed a project for the school science fair that involved testing to see if cats can be right or left "pawed," just as we are right or left-handed. My project found that they do, indeed, individually favor one paw! My project won the science fair, and I began thinking maybe veterinary research would be my "thing."

The transition from middle school to high school was hard for me. I went from a tiny school where I knew everyone to a class size of 400 where I knew no one. I took a few advanced English classes early on, but avoided taking advanced science classes until my junior year, when I decided to take Chemistry Honors.

I hated chemistry, but somehow I got through Chemistry Honors, and I did really enjoy biology and physics (both of which helped me succeed in college-level animal physiology and anatomy).

. . . .

It turns out there are a multitude of careers for veterinarians that most people don't think or even know about: wildlife conservation, zoological medicine, research and perhaps the most underappreciated — public health.

. . . .

During my senior year, I started working in my first veterinary clinic as an assistant, where I became immersed in the world of small animal medicine and quickly decided I didn't like it. I also began looking into colleges the summer before senior year, those that had strong science programs. I had a short-list, but then my guidance counselor asked, "Have you heard of Scripps College?"

I sure hadn't, and I sure am glad she asked, because that question changed my life. I turned my nose up initially to the idea of going to an "all-girls school," (I later learned that this term is demeaning and "women's college" is preferred) but something changed my mind the moment I stepped on campus to tour. Everyone seemed happy, people were out studying in the Southern California sunshine, there was a robust science program shared with three other colleges and the class sizes were small. I missed the small class sizes I had in middle school, and the faculty attention that comes from them. There was also something so empowering about being part of a class of very bright, supportive women who were motivated, diverse and interested in so many different things. My acceptance phone call is still one of the happiest memories of my life.

My Favorite Things

J.R.R. Tolkien's book, "Roverandom."

Playing the piano.

When it comes to teachers, my best teacher ever was my biology professor, Dr. Marion Preest. While I was at Scripps College, she introduced me to chameleons and shared her love of all reptiles.

Vacationing in Nicaragua.

Guinea pigs.

Education

B.A.,
Scripps College,
Class of 2013,
Major: Biology

D.V.M.,
UC Davis School of
Veterinary Medicine,
Anticipated Class
of 2019

As I hoped, Scripps' science program was instrumental in supporting my goal of a veterinary career. The small classes afforded me to get help when I needed it. They also enabled me to speak out and be more involved in class, which allowed me to develop close relationships with a number of my professors — three of which I still communicate with on at least a monthly basis. I began collaborating with two of them on research projects, which appealed to me. I worked on one project that looked at exercise metabolism in flying geckoes, and another that studied relative bone sizes in different bird species. I believe the relationships I built with these faculty members were hugely instrumental in supporting my desire to pursue science as a career — especially as I continued to struggle in chemistry, particularly Organic Chemistry.

So how did I find my way to public health? Actually, not until after college. I knew I wanted to take at least a year off between graduating from Scripps and going to veterinary school, and I hadn't yet gotten any large animal experience with cows, sheep, goats or horses. After some research on internships, I found myself on a farm in Hickman County, Tennessee, within a month of graduation. This internship was eye-opening and truly life-changing.

I worked primarily with beef cattle, and got a better understanding of how the food-animal industry works. The farm owners were also brilliant in that they encouraged us to read about pasture-raised animals and learn about proper processing facilities. It was there that I learned about Temple Grandin for the first time — she's a fantastic animal-rights and autism-awareness advocate who has worked to improve humane handling of food animals.

I became interested in veterinary careers that helped advocate for food animal welfare, and also learned quite a lot about food animals and veterinary public health from one of the farm owners who used to be a public health inspector.

Fast forward to the present: I am a second-year veterinary student at UC Davis School of Veterinary Medicine. Veterinary school is not like my undergraduate career at all. Every day is like a firehose of information blasting at my brain, and I'm scrambling for buckets to catch all of it! But it's wonderful to be learning skills that I will actually use, and inspiring to be surrounded by people who are interested in the same things as me. I'm also fortunate in that last year I was selected to be one of the first recipients of the Adel Malak Scholarship from the USDA Food Safety Inspection Service (FSIS). This scholarship provides me with financial support while I'm in school, which is much appreciated! The scholarship also means I have a job lined up working for the USDA when I graduate. I will be pursuing my dream — finally! While I don't know yet where FSIS will want to send me after graduation, I know that I will be working to improve the welfare of food animals and to also protect the health of the humans who inevitably eat them. •

Myra Lee Weiner

Toxicologist

Looking back over a nearly 40-year career in toxicology, I have surprised myself. I have succeeded beyond my wildest dreams by becoming a well-known professional in my field, having published over 40 peer-reviewed scientific papers, book chapters and review articles.

I have made more than 50 trips abroad to Europe and Asia working in my field and gaining an international reputation. After retiring from the industry, I have started my own consulting company that provides a source of scientific fun as well as an ample income.

Here's how I discovered STEM. When I was a young girl in middle school, I loved to explore the outdoors. The natural world became my means of understanding my environment and living things: frogs, bugs, caterpillars, snakes, mice, rabbits, were all fascinating to me. Collecting specimens and displaying them on a small shelf in our spare bedroom was one of my favorite pastimes. I thought of it as my own personal nature museum.

As a present on my 10th birthday, my parents gave me a small microscope. Soon, I was looking at organisms swimming in pond water, leaves, skin and other biological specimens. A new world opened

About Me

I was born in Brooklyn,
New York and
have one sister.

I'm appreciative of
my high school
algebra teacher,
Mr. Shapiro, because
he taught me to ask a
lot of questions!

"For me, the fun and challenge of being a toxicologist is solving a new mystery."

up to me through the microscope. I was hooked. Biology became my passion. My parents always encouraged my interests. Dad would take me to the physics laboratory in a local college where he taught. It was exciting to see all the instruments and be allowed to touch them and even to play with them.

In high school, I was excited about taking biology class. The term STEM was not used back in the 1950s, 60s and 70s when I was going to school, instead it was "science and mathematics." Each girl was on her own to find her place in an area of interest. Parents and caring teachers were the main advisers to encourage us. Otherwise, girls were not particularly encouraged to choose science or math as avenues for a career.

Girl Scouts helped develop my leadership skills and gave me the chance to study new areas. I was involved in Girl Scouts and camping from middle school through high school. It provided me with positive role models and encouragement.

. . . .

I'm a toxicologist. Toxicology is the study of the potential adverse effects on the body from chemicals, drugs, pesticides, food ingredients, air pollutants and consumer products.

. . . .

When it was time to decide on college, I knew that biology would be my major. My four years at Stern College for Women flew by, and I enjoyed taking every biology course in the curriculum and many of the chemistry courses, too. My female biology professors were also role models. I worked part time as an assistant in the chemistry laboratory. In a small women's college, I shined with good grades and a strong work ethic. The classes were small with a lot of opportunities to talk with teachers after class and dig deeper into the course material. There was no feeling of being "too smart" in front of boys, and my fellow female students sought me out to help them with biology before exams. I loved it.

By the end of four years of college, I finished my degree cum laude, but I had no idea what I wanted to do. In 1966, most women got married, or if they wanted a career, they chose teaching or nursing, neither of which appealed to me. Instead, I decided

"Girl Scouts helped develop my leadership skills and gave me the chance to study new areas."

to attend graduate school to learn more. Although I was not clear what I would do with a graduate degree, I realized that I needed to learn more before doing anything worthwhile. My college professors were not helpful in steering me on a future course, so I had to find out on my own where to apply to graduate school. No one prepared me or helped me to understand what job opportunities might lay ahead. I applied to only two schools in the New York City area.

My first interview at Downstate Medical Center (State University of New York) was an experience that I will never forget. I went naively to an interview in the pharmacology department without any preparation. A professor began by asking me technical questions about physiology. He kept asking harder and harder questions in rapid fire. To my surprise and relief, all my college physiology came back. I was able to answer all his tough questions correctly. His last question surprised me: "Why should we accept you? As a woman, you will probably get married and drop out?" Without showing my inner shock, I looked the professor squarely in the eye and said emphatically, "I plan to finish." Shortly after, I was accepted into its Ph.D. program with a full fellowship. So began the start of my graduate career.

After graduate school, I followed my husband of two years wherever he got a job. Then, I would look for a job. This worked well. I spent 29 years working for a large global chemical company in New Jersey. When I joined, I worked part time so that I could spend time with my three young children. As the children got older, I increased my hours to full time and took on more responsibility at work.

I'm a toxicologist. Toxicology is the study of the potential adverse effects on the body from chemicals, drugs, pesticides, food ingredients, air pollutants and consumer products. Originally, toxicology was developed to study poisons and how they act on the body. Today, toxicology is an important field of science used to guide decisions on safety for citizens. Government agencies, like the U.S. Food and Drug Administration (FDA) and Environmental Protection Agency (EPA) are charged with insuring the safety of food, water, air, drugs, cosmetics and other chemicals in which people may be exposed.

For me, the fun and challenge of being a toxicologist is solving a new mystery. For example, my company would like to sell a new chemical to kill weeds. What safety

My Favorite Things

"The Power of One" by Bryce Courtenay.

The color blue.

Peach cobbler.

Quilting and writing. I am currently working on my memoir about my toxicology career and life.

Thanksgiving.

Swimming at the beach.

Dogs.

Education

B.A.,
**Stern College
for Women,**
Class of 1966,
Double Major:
Biology and Chemistry

Ph.D.,
**State University of
New York, Downstate
Medical Center,**
Class of 1971,
Pharmacology

information do we need to be able to sell this new chemical to farmers and other people who might be exposed to the herbicide used on farms or their own gardens? We begin by checking EPA-required animal and cell-based studies. Next, we may design animal or cell-based studies to meet requirements and to answer questions about the chemical's safety and actions. After the studies are completed, we evaluate the results to insure that consumers, farmers and all others use the chemical safely for its intended applications.

Thus, the toxicologist has many tasks that require training and experience. She will need to have a strong background in basic sciences: biology, chemistry and often, statistics. She will need to think critically in designing new studies and in evaluating the results of the new studies. She will need to enjoy solving mysteries!

My career in toxicology spanned 38 years. After I went full time, I was eventually promoted to a senior toxicologist, and then to manager of toxicology programs where I supervised a staff of nine professionals. During the entire time that I worked, I always took continuing education courses to improve and update my knowledge.

Eventually, I passed a difficult exam to become a board-certified toxicologist, a diplomate of the American Board of Toxicology. The new certification credential added prestige to my résumé and allowed me to continue growing in my field. During my career, I also attended annual meetings in my field, usually the Society of Toxicology meeting, to continue to learn new techniques, skills and the latest information and to publish studies done for my company.

Nine years ago, the company where I had worked for 29 years offered me an incentive to retire at age 63. I accepted its generous offer. Since I did not feel ready to retire from science, I started my own consulting company, TOXpertise, LLC. Immediately, many of my customers from my former corporation asked if I could consult for them. Soon, my consulting business was in full swing. I had consulting contracts with about four different clients. Basically, I did the same type of "desk" toxicology that I had done when I was employed. I charged clients by the hour and kept records of my time for invoicing. The independent consultant job paid well and I could work from home at my own office. Emails and phone calls were the main ways of staying in touch with clients. It was a win-win situation.

Seven years ago, I applied for and was accepted in the elite Academy of Toxicological Science as a Fellow, an additional credential in toxicology based on active participation and accomplishments in this field.

I am still consulting as a retired person and enjoy the fun of solving toxicology mysteries. •

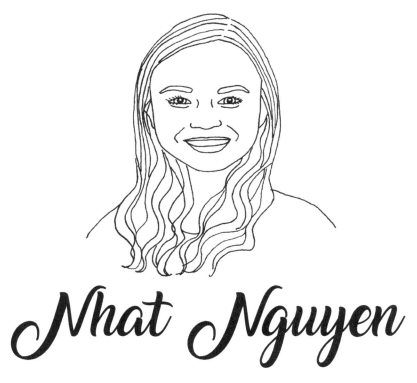

Nhat Nguyen

Financial Analyst

I enjoy working with numbers and interpreting their meanings.

It has always been fascinating for me to work through numbers to find mysterious answers to math problems. My math grades were always higher than my other subjects. The more I studied, the better I was at it; the more I enjoyed it, the more it made me want to study. In Vietnam, the kids who are good at math are considered smart. So, the better I was in math, the smarter I was perceived.

I have been interested in STEM since elementary school. I consider myself lucky that my parents are really supportive of my education. I still clearly remember early mornings when my dad helped me with algebra while cooking breakfast for the family. In my elementary school, I was unnoticed, but when I went to middle school, that started to change.

My high scores in math got me noticed. My classmates started asking for help with math problems. My logical way of thinking in math helped me significantly when I started taking physics and chemistry, so I performed well in these subjects as well.

About Me

I was born in Vietnam and have four siblings.

My favorite holiday is Tet (Lunar New Year in Vietnam).

Ms. Ban, my math teacher in second grade, was my favorite teacher. She was really supportive and caring, and that was even more so important for me when my parents moved to Ho Chi Minh City and I was still in my hometown.

"I hope one day to become one of the most well-known portfolio managers in the world."

In high school, I had no idea what I wanted to do with my life. High school students in Vietnam are required to take a national exam in order to get into universities. My parents encouraged me to pursue medical school to become a doctor. However, I was afraid of blood.

The closest thing to medical school without facing blood is pharmacy school. I have always wanted to find the unknown variables, so I thought I could work on finding an unknown drug to fight different kinds of diseases. To get into pharmacy school, the three exams I needed to take were math, biology and chemistry. Besides pharmacy, I also applied to an economic university since I was also interested in doing business.

My parents have their own business. I spent my childhood helping them in their business, so it seemed like a good career choice. I admire my mom for her strength, courage, boldness and wise judgments in business. I wanted to be like her. As strong and bold as she is, she is still influenced by society around her with the concept that women should take an easier path — the harder path, which I would consider more exciting, is for men.

I'm a financial analyst. In this role, I have the opportunity to work with data a fair amount of the time.

The required passing score for pharmacy school was 23.5 and I only scored a 23. I was shocked and shattered. However, my score for economic school was a 26 and the required score was only 17. Pharmacy was my first choice, but it was not an option in that year for me, so I went ahead with economics as a major.

I was happy with majoring in economics because I was interested in statistics, optimization, economic theory, advanced math and much more. My curious mind was fascinated with all the new knowledge. My parents, however, were not. My dad constantly told me to take the exams again, so eventually I gave in and retook them. I got a 26, but the pharmacy school requirements changed that year. I needed a 26.5 to get in. Being a pharmacist was not my fate and my parents didn't ask me to take the test again.

Today, I'm a financial analyst. In this role, I have the opportunity to work with data a fair amount of the time. The analysis helps me to understand what is going on in the market — what industries are doing well or not and why, or what companies are doing well and would likely do well in the future. If we put money into the right companies, our clients would benefit from the extra money and companies would have the money to make products and provide their services to the market. It is a win-win-win situation. Our clients are happy, we are happy, and companies who get to borrow or use the money are happy.

· ·

As a financial analyst, I always keep myself updated with current important economic and market events and especially what is going on with the companies that we invest in. I enjoy collecting data, analyzing and finding the meanings behind it.

· ·

The financial industry is a crucial part of the world's economy. It is a system of lending and borrowing. To be successful in this occupation, a financial analyst needs to have both quantitative and qualitative skills. Quantitative skills are important in analyzing and understanding data. Qualitative skills are important in filtering and understanding the information from the market, preparing research, communicating clearly with co-workers and clients and understanding clients' needs and wants. The financial industry is probably one of the most flexible industries in terms of hiring background. I find economics and math really helpful in my job; yet there are successful financial analysts who studied engineering, physics, chemistry, computer science or even art history.

While I was at the University of Economics in Ho Chi Minh City, I got to know a number of alums who went to study abroad. Many of them became successful in their business endeavors. The concept of studying in another country and learning about different cultures started forming as a dream. During my junior year, I decided to quit school at the university to start studying at Bunker Hill Community College.

My Favorite Things

The book, "The Snowball: Warren Buffett and the Business of Life."

The color blue.

Tae kwon do and watercolor painting.

My favorite dessert is flan.

Vacationing in Montreal.

Cats.

Education

B.A.,
Mount Holyoke College,
Class of 2014,
Double Major:
Economics and
Mathematics

I flourished at Bunker Hill. My major was business concentration with the idea that I would build a business in the future. I enjoyed studying different subjects, but math was always my favorite. Studying math is like building a house. The foundation needs to be strong before the house is built. When I graduated from community college, I spent a year working and applying to four-year schools. During that time, I got to know Mount Holyoke College. A friend of mine went there first, so I went to visit her. I fell in love with the school the moment I stepped on the campus. The atmosphere was quiet, peaceful and warm.

It was the best day of my life when I got the acceptance letter from Mount Holyoke College with a significant financial-aid package. Without the financial aid, my family wouldn't be able to pay for my last two years there, even if my parents sold their house.

While considering majors at Mount Holyoke, I got back to what I really enjoy studying — math — and the closest thing to business — economics. The liberal arts education gave me the flexibility to combine them together to become a "math and economic special major." I learned so much more about how the economy works and mathematic applications in economics. My professors were dedicated and supportive. I saw the joy in their eyes when they taught. The career center introduced us to the possible careers we could take with our majors. The love of learning brought my friends and me together to compete in a national economics competition. Even several years after graduation, we are still close friends.

During my junior year, I was actually not sure what my career was going to look like. I had many career tracks to pursue with my economics and math major. After analysis, with my interest in business, economics and math, I realized that the finance industry was the perfect match for me. My understanding about the economy and my quantitative approach to investment has been a tremendous asset to the firm and to my career.

I am lucky and privileged to say that I currently love what I do. As a financial analyst, I always keep myself updated with current important economic and market events and especially what is going on with the companies that we invest in. I enjoy collecting data, analyzing and finding the meanings behind it. I am lucky to have the chance to do that often at work. I may not directly apply my advanced mathematics knowledge in my work, but the quantitative approaches that I have developed through my math classes have been helpful for me to understand data intuitively. I learn new things and develop myself every day. I hope one day to become one of the most well-known portfolio managers in the world. •

Rhea Williams

Scientific Journal Editor

I was 7 years old the first time I remember seeing my grandfather, a radiologist, at work.

I was impressed by the big words he was saying into the microphone while studying the blurry gray X-rays hanging in the light box. In rapid succession, medical residents, technicians, nurses and administrative staff would pop into his small, somewhat cluttered, hospital office to ask for his guidance or just to chat. When I found out he studied science in college, I started to try extra hard on my science assignments with the thought that I might one day be just like him.

I joined the Science Olympiad team in junior high and took the science fair assignments seriously. In high school biology I became discouraged; I struggled with the tests because they seemed to require a lot of memorizing. Instead, I found more success in chemistry class and I was happy to learn that chemistry majors can get into medical school, too.

Besides chemistry, another favorite class during high school was yearbook. Designing the layout of the pages, cropping the pictures just right and catching mistakes in the captions became a passion. My diligence helped me earn the role of editor and I know this experience was part of what most interested me about publishing scientific journals.

About Me

I was born in Fresno, California and have four siblings.

My favorite vacation spot is Park City, Utah and my favorite book is "The Rosie Project."

"Don't tell anyone, but I still ask my mom to be another pair of eyes on my work sometimes."

When it came time to apply to college, I had my dream schools like Stanford (grandpa's alma mater) and Wellesley high on the list, but the right offer came from Salem College in North Carolina. At Salem, I became involved in several groups, including Lehman Scholars, Student Affiliates of the American Chemical Society and Women in Science and Mathematics. It does not sound like anything special, but it was probably the Salem "Jan-Term" offering that had the most unexpected and profound impact on my professional development.

Besides chemistry, another favorite class during high school was yearbook.

Salem students are required to complete an educational or career-focused internship during the month of January. There were some ready-made, local options, but none seemed like a good fit for me. Instead, I took the initiative to arrange new, never-before-hosted Jan-Term internships in my sophomore (Hurricane Katrina cleanup), junior (U.S. Environmental Protection Agency Green Chemistry Program) and senior years (Sundance Film Festival). The lesson I learned is to step up and pursue what you need and want. Take stock of your genuine interests, and then make a polite, but direct, request for what you need. Nobody can help until you know what you're looking for.

A scholarly scientific journal is essentially the In Style magazine for a specific field of science. Using much bigger words than you'll see in newsstand magazines, journals feature the latest cool research instead of the latest fashions, music or celebrities. I am a managing editor for three scholarly scientific journals. Responsibilities that go along with this title may vary depending on which company you work for, but it is generally a role that helps bring the efforts of many people together to meet deadlines through timely and effective communication.

Each of the 15 managing editors at my company has earned a doctorate degree in various STEM fields. For our editorial careers, we have now "left the bench," which means we are no longer researchers in a laboratory. Because scientific editors are authors themselves, we keep the researcher's perspective in mind every day. We share similar backgrounds to the authors featured in our journals, so we are qualified and feel comfortable talking with them about their ongoing research projects and experiences when publishing their findings.

There are different types of editors needed to create a journal issue. Some are "copy editors" while others are "content editors." Copy editing is what your teacher or parent does when you write a report for school, they change words or catch spelling and grammar errors. (Don't tell anyone, but I still ask my mom to be another pair of eyes on my work sometimes.) Editing for content involves deciding what research topic goes where in the issue, who writes what, which articles or stories to publish and which articles to decline.

> **As a managing editor, I keep things running smoothly, maintain open lines of communication and track the progress of different projects which must move forward simultaneously.**

Each day I am motivated by crossing things off a prioritized to-do list and accomplishing tasks that further the goals of my journals and our company. I like the wide variety of tasks I do and the people I engage with every day. I also like the global reach of my work. Just like group projects at school, sometimes I struggle with the group projects at work because I have to trust other people to come through on their piece of the puzzle. The good days definitely outnumber the tough ones, though.

My typical day includes looking at the status of all my "irons in the fire." This means emailing or coordinating phone calls with people all over the world, booking travel to conferences, reaching out to meet with university professors and researchers, preparing agendas for conference calls, leading project meetings, taking a gazillion notes, following up on the ideas mentioned and determining what can be accomplished or strategies to put in place given a timeframe and budget constraints.

I believe my success in this occupation is a result of my organizational skills, an ability to manage time efficiently and listen carefully, completing assignments on time, following up to confirm details and creatively solving problems that affect

My Favorite Things

The color purple.

Strawberry shortcake.

Writing cards on nice stationery and sending snail mail.

Thanksgiving.

Ms. Carbaugh, my math teacher, fifth-eighth grades, who has provided me mentorship and a listening ear since 1998.

Education

B.S.,
Salem College,
Class of 2009,
Double Major:
Chemistry and
Mathematics

Ph.D.,
**University of
Colorado Boulder,**
Class of 2014,
Chemical Engineering

others. As a managing editor, I keep things running smoothly, maintain open lines of communication and track the progress of different projects that must move forward simultaneously. While we are students, we measure success by making grades like As and Bs. As a professional, I know I am successful when I complete tasks on time (or early) and am satisfied with the quality of the final product. Maintaining the good reputation of my journals is a responsibility I take seriously.

My path to a career in science publishing was paved when I decided to continue into graduate school. I chose chemical engineering for my Ph.D. because it seemed like a broad and useful degree that would provide tangible, applications-driven energy research opportunities. At the same time, I found out that the broad "ChemE" field made it more difficult to decide on the right specialty. When I was just one year from my Ph.D. graduation date, I got serious about narrowing the options between industrial companies, national research labs and what are called "alternative careers." To learn more about each type, I started carrying out "informational interviews" with professional people in various positions. In all, I accomplished 40 interviews that year! It was very helpful to peek behind the curtain and hear what's really expected in different careers.

Ultimately, I decided to take my advanced degree and leave the bench in favor of scientific publishing. Every time I've moved on to the next phase (from junior high to high school, then from college to graduate school and now my first "real job"), I have had feelings like, "I thought it would get easier after I accomplished X or passed Y. So, why does it feel harder? You mean I have to start all over?" With each passing day however, I have realized that it is probably better this way. I now realize that challenges have helped me grow, personally as well as professionally. Plus, they keep things interesting.

While I did not ultimately pursue medical school, I am proud to join my grandfather in having Dr. before my name. Now, I have my own office where colleagues pop in to chat and seek my guidance. My career is still young and unfolding. I continue to make connections and talk to people about their unique career paths. I am also keeping notes on the parts of my work I enjoy most (or dislike) and what I need to improve on personally.

I now realize that it's okay not to have figured everything out at age 12, 14 or 18 even, and marvel at how wonderfully things have worked out for me. Back then, my main focus was trying to win my school science fair. The sense of success in a high school chemistry class replaced the disappointment with biology, led to broad experiences and an interest in green chemistry, energy and catalysis, chemical engineering and its practical applications.

I am grateful for each person who encouraged my interest in science and led me to study STEM subjects in college. •

Sanita Dhaubanjar

Hydrologist

With super curly hair that was almost always left in disarray, I was likened to Einstein from the very first day my cousin read a story about the great scientist.

The child-friendly sketch of the famous scientist flaunting his silver locks accompanying that story haunted me most of my childhood, yet normalized the word "scientist." More importantly, it planted the seed in my mind that being a girl can mean being a scientist. When I discovered a love for physics and trigonometry in middle school, it seemed natural for me to start saying "Einstein" with all honesty when asked the perpetual question, "What do you want to be when you grow up?"

Growing up, no one in my family studied past high school. However, my family owned a transportation business, allowing me ample opportunities to see trucks, tractors and other vehicles at work. The gender norms in Nepal allowed only the boys in my family to use the family garage as their playground. I grew up watching my dad and uncles take apart cars, fix punctured tires and weld damaged vehicle parts. I never got to learn any of the tricks the men in the family passed on to my brothers for driving around tight corners, fixing issues in the radiator or tinkering in engines. Though I did not actively learn much, passively it made me value the efficiency of a well-engineered solution. By the end of middle school, I had learned to differentiate between theoretical and applied physics

About Me

I was born in Bhaktapur, Nepal and have one older brother and one older sister.

My favorite dessert is freshly made yoghurt from my hometown.

My last name means yoghurt-seller in my native language.

and set my heart on the latter. At some point along the way I had also realized that Einstein being a man was quite important for his success in life, and me being a girl might be an issue. But with the passion I had developed for science and the unconditional support from my parents to follow my dreams, it really didn't matter. I didn't need a female role model.

I cannot recall exactly why I narrowed my dream down to aerospace engineering. As a teenager, I wanted to do something different, so I decided I would go to the United States to pursue that dream. Instead of following the traditional high school program in Nepal, I went to a highly competitive high school that followed the UK-based Cambridge University. Budhanilkantha was the best school for the program at that time and I must acknowledge it for bringing out the extrovert in me. At Budhanilkantha, I solved differential equations in my mathematics class while acing intramural swimming competitions, acting in plays, helping put together cultural programs and raising funds for an orphanage my club supported. All of this was new to me. The combination of applied sciences with extracurricular activities helped broaden my mind. I became more passionate and more outgoing — two skills that helped me make the best of my undergraduate years at Smith College. Besides helping build my personality, Budhanilkantha gave me the teacher that helped me discover the beauty in math and learn to love its complexities.

....

After spending nearly seven years abroad, today I am back in Nepal working as a water resources engineer or hydrologist.

....

After going to a top high school, going to Smith was not my first choice. It was one of my safety schools. Without realizing that Smith was an all-women school, I sent in my acceptance because it gave me the best funding. I was so busy looking into how to make the most out of the Five College Consortium, which allows Smith students to enroll in classes and activities across five colleges (Smith, Hampshire, Mount Holyoke, Amherst and UMass Amherst) in the area, that it was only a week before my flight that I realized Smith was all women.

If I tried to describe all that Smith gave me, I could write a novel. Smith and all the passionate (sometimes crazy) women I met there helped make me an activist. Smith taught me that everything we do is a result of and a precursor to privileges that are unevenly distributed in society. A traditional engineering degree could not have given me such perspective. My liberal arts degree in engineering made me realize that any

"As a Smithie, I learned to ask, 'Does my solution leave the world a better place?'"

My Favorite Things

The book "God of Small Things" as well as "Farewell to Arms" and "The Fountainhead."

The color deep ocean blue.

Swimming and trekking.

My high school advanced math teacher Mr. Lal Bahadur Rana because he made math seem like a piece of cake. He was fully aware that most of us were intimidated by the new concepts he was presenting, but he was very patient with us and helped me convert my fear of math into fascination.

Vacationing up in some mountains where I can sit and enjoy a cup of hot chocolate.

Dogs (I grew up with always having two or more dogs in the house. Currently we have four).

technical or nontechnical question can have more than one correct answer; but not all answers are socially or environmentally just and equitable. As a Smithie, I learned to ask, "Does my solution leave the world a better place?"

Aerospace engineering, though fascinating, did not give me the satisfaction of pursuing something socially engaging. Besides that, I was starting to utterly miss my home in Nepal, and going for aerospace engineering meant I could never really go back. There are nearly no jobs in aerospace engineering back home. When more than half the nation is struggling to put food on their plates and make sure their kids can go to school, investment in such areas like the aerospace industry is not big. My newly found activism and nostalgia pushed me away from my teenage dream to build flying machines and travel to space.

One of the first things we learn in Nepal in kindergarten is that we are the second-richest country in the world in terms of natural water resources. Nepal has more than 6,000 rivers and is considered the Third Pole due to the snow and glaciers that accumulate in our mountains. I grew up appreciating nature and all these water resources around me. It wasn't long before my desire for a more fulfilling aim in life directed my interests toward water-resources engineering. I loved my Fluid Mechanics class and was thrilled to discover that water engineering would allow me to combine my interests in fieldwork with working with differential equations and models. I could also learn a skill and help people along the way. I found my purpose and with that, my way forward. I have volunteered in Ghana, studied in Israel and implemented peace projects in Nepal — all because of the education I received at Smith.

In line with my plans to eventually return to Nepal, I hurried a bit in my selection of a graduate school. I chose to go to the Technical University of Denmark (DTU) near Copenhagen because I wanted to diversify my portfolio of experience. Northern Europe is considered a pioneer in water solutions. Two years at DTU challenged me plenty; I felt I lacked some of the engineering skills that my peers from technical

Education

B.S.,
Smith College,
Class of 2013,
Major: Engineering
Science

M.S.,
**Technical University
of Denmark,**
Class of 2016,
Water Resources
Engineering

schools seemed to flaunt. DTU's project-based coursework with student evaluations based on reports, presentations and oral exams allowed me to use my Smith skills to better show off the technical instincts I developed at DTU. I think softer skills are easier learned and better assimilated into our personalities at an earlier age, while technical skills can be learned and unlearned.

After spending nearly seven years abroad, today I am back in Nepal working as a water resources engineer or hydrologist. I'm employed by a nonprofit scientific research organization, focused on water and land-related challenges in developing countries. My work falls under the field of development, research and water management. Simply put, my employer performs research activities to support better water management for sustainable development in the global south. I feel lucky that my job perfectly combines my passion for engineering with the skills I have acquired. In my role, I am supporting two development projects on water resources management in western Nepal, which is the poorest region in the country and consists of the communities most vulnerable to climate change. My projects assess the state of existing water resources and conduct research to inform policies on how water resources development can be done in a sustainable, just and productive manner.

In a typical month, you will find me hiking the rugged hills of Western Nepal to gather field data and interact with local communities, or participating in workshops with key decision makers from the government to discuss visions for water resource management. With fellow hydrologists, I discuss ways in which to make our watershed model realistic given the data scarcity. The gender and social inclusion expert on the team reminds us of real-life factors that cannot be quantitatively included in our hydro-economic model, while our political experts analyze the political context under which our model outputs have to be considered. It is intellectually and personally fulfilling to be joining heads with national and international social and political scientists, and joining hands with local decision makers and political players to pave a better way forward for water management in Nepal. Today, more than ever before, I am following the passions ignited at Smith to promote scientific solutions that are socially and environmentally just. •

Sarah Schutz

Data Scientist

*While I loved math in middle school, I never thought that
I was good enough at it for it to become my career.*

The idea of thinking of ways to solve problems was always exciting for me. Unfortunately, my teachers in middle school never seemed to be very encouraging about my pursuit of math. Looking back, they seemed to focus on encouraging and supporting the boys in our class to love math and science more than the girls. Fortunately, this changed for me when I entered high school. There, I found supportive teachers who helped to cultivate my love of STEM subjects and today, I'm a data scientist. But actually, it wasn't just STEM subjects I grew to love.

My interest in economics started when I was in high school. I took an AP Macroeconomics class my senior year. Over the summer, my teacher asked us to read "Naked Economics: Undressing the Dismal Science," a book that puts economic concepts into terms anyone can understand. As I pored over the words, I found the author's message incredibly moving. In my earlier years, I thought economics was all about money and financial decisions. After reading this book, I realized economics is a way to solve problems and a way to interpret the world around us. On its most basic levels, it tries to describe people's motivations in response to scarcity, which is basically all the material desires people have and the economic limitations on those

My birthplace is Little Rock, Arkansas and I have two siblings.

My favorite color is yellow and I love vanilla and orange soft serve ice cream.

I receive great enjoyment cooking and I also have a cooking blog I run on the side: The Cutting Veg *thecuttingvegblog.com* and my Instagram account is *@thecuttingveg*

"I work to protect consumers from the negative effects of company mergers and deceptive practices in the health care industry."

desires. Economic study, therefore, can be transformational in understanding how people can take actions which might, at first, not make sense.

I decided to attend Barnard College in New York. I knew that once I graduated, I wanted to help people to understand the world around them. At first, I thought I wanted to be a physician, mostly because my dad, someone to whom I look for support and guidance, was a physician. However, after taking Organic Chemistry my first year, I realized that path was not for me. For a brief moment, I felt lost about where to go from there. However, after taking Introduction to Economics that same semester, I decided to continue to study the subject I had fallen in love with as a high schooler.

I'm employed as a research analyst at a government agency. Day to day, I write and clean code to analyze government data about the health care industry.

At the recommendation of my academic adviser, an economics professor, I became a research assistant. For two years, I helped an economist conduct research he was using to write a book. In particular, I looked at the impact of global trade policy in Argentina during the Great Depression of the 1930s. The experience allowed me to recognize I could channel my skills at problem-solving to evaluate government policy.

But I realized that in order to study policy in the way I wanted, I needed to strengthen my background in statistics and math. While Barnard did not have a statistics and economics major, the liberal arts education allowed me the flexibility to create my

own major. Interestingly, my desire to break the mold piqued the interest of the head of the economics department. In turn, she told students to ask me for advice on how to pursue an economics and statistics major. I found that creating my own major allowed me to pursue my interests more freely. I took many graduate-level statistics courses to help strengthen my quantitative skills. I wrote a senior thesis analyzing the effectiveness of health care policy. These experiences allowed me to realize that economics research was what I wanted to do as my career.

....

When I accepted my current job, I asked my supervisor why he chose to work for the federal government. He said, "It is because I am performing a service for my country, and I am proud of my contributions as a citizen."

....

I'm employed as a research analyst at a government agency. Primarily, my job consists of reviewing, analyzing and interpreting data to help protect consumers from anti-competitive business practices. More specifically, I work to protect consumers from the negative effects of company mergers and deceptive practices in the health care industry. Day to day, I write and clean code to analyze government data about the health care industry. Based on my analysis, I generate reports to recommend changes in policy to protect American consumers. Sometimes the days are long. It can be frustrating to be working on code that does not work the way I want it to. However, the satisfaction I experience once I've successfully answered the question I intended makes the job all the more worthwhile.

When I accepted my current job, I asked my supervisor why he chose to work for the federal government. He said, "It is because I am performing a service for my country, and I am proud of my contributions as a citizen." The work that I do and its effects on the general public inspire me to continue with my work going forward. Our agency exists to protect the American consumer from the effects of big business. It makes me proud to think my job helps to serve and represent the little guy, who might otherwise struggle against big business without our support.

While I spend a lot of my time in an office, I am never shut into a cubicle. I collaborate with other research analysts and economists to think of different ways to look at a problem. I am constantly learning from them, which is an aspect of this job I find incredibly rewarding and stimulating. I also have opportunities to inform my research with representatives and their staff in Congress.

My Favorite Things

"East of Eden" by John Steinbeck.

Thanksgiving.

My thesis adviser, Randall Reback, for igniting the passion in me to start thinking about doing economic research as a career.

Vacationing in Amsterdam is the best.

Elephants.

Education

B.A./B.S.
Barnard College,
Class of 2015,
Major: Economics/
Statistics

Many of the people I work with have master's degrees in statistics, mathematics or economics. Others, myself included, have bachelor's degrees in those STEM fields. Ultimately, my goal is to conduct my own research to answer questions about the economics of health care. To do so, I need to attend a graduate economics program and earn a Ph.D in economics. Studying for a Ph.D. takes an average of five years and is very academically challenging. While I know it is a long and academically-challenging commitment, I am confident that the skills I will learn will allow me to pursue my goals.

As a tutor in the economics and statistics departments at my university, many of the female students I tutored would tell me they "sucked at math." As women, often we are conditioned to feel that unless we are perfect or we can do it all, we are inadequate. I found myself encouraging these individuals to not sell themselves short based on others' expectations, especially if they have a passion for a subject. I explained that I found my understanding of math and economics has come after trying and failing numerous times. Sure, it sucks to feel like you don't understand the material. But it's important to remember that even if you don't get it right on the first try, that doesn't mean you're not good at math or any subject for that matter. Instead, practice, ask for help and practice some more. Eventually, it will click, like it did for me! •

Sarai Elizabeth Neloms

Fashion Engineer

I absolutely love shoes. I can't even count how many pairs of shoes that I have.

I love seeing how a great shoe can change someone's confidence. Developing the next big (and fashionable) running or basketball shoe is what I want to do. Not only would I enjoy this, but I can empower every girl who loves sports with an amazing product, so that she can feel like a champion.

It's an area I'm passionate about and a career option I don't think many young women know about. My desire is to bring light to a place where creativity and mathematical and technical experience can shine.

Sometimes it can be frustrating because fashion trends are extremely fast-paced, and can change at the drop of a dime. But that's what's the most exciting! I can figure out how to help someone feel confident while they are pursuing their dream. It's amazing to see a shoe you worked on worn by the biggest names in professional sports. Basketball, football, baseball and tennis players would be wearing something that I helped to create. Being able to create a product that helps someone to pursue their passion is my dream.

About Me

I was born in Augusta, Georgia and have three brothers.

When asked what my favorite book is, I reply, "It's a super tie between 'Tuesdays with Morrie' and (all of) 'A Series of Unfortunate Events'."

"My mathematics and mechanical engineering degrees are giving me the tools to achieve the career of my dreams!"

I had the opportunity to intern with a major sportswear-tech company where I focused on footwear development. It was amazing! The most exciting part of my internship was being able to launch a paint automation research project with the company and one of its robotics partners. In addition to seeing the engineering design process in action, I also learned practical business concepts. I got to work with a new innovation lab, and help shape some great ideas for the company's future. The skills I learned at my internship gave me knowledge to help with designing a robot for a robotics competition at Georgia Tech.

Having graduated from Spelman College with a bachelor's in mathematics, I'm now an engineering student at Georgia Tech. Every day, I am inspired by the power of my mind. I am learning so much at Georgia Tech and I know that when I finish, I'll be able to use my technical experience to build a life for myself, as well as service the community around me. My current career aspirations allow me to follow sports and fashion trends, and further fuel my eagerness to graduate.

School is tough sometimes, but I always remember why I am pursuing a degree in STEM. Once I begin my career in tech and sportswear, I eventually want to return to business school for a Master in Business Administration (MBA) degree. I then want to start a nonprofit organization that encourages young girls to love STEM, fashion and sports.

In order to work in sportswear and tech, you would need a STEM degree. Going to college to study a discipline like math, mechanical and/or industrial engineering, industrial design or information technology, etc., would be a step in the right direction. A career like this one would require a young woman who has a passion for sports, and the latest sports technology and trends. Specifically, for footwear,

she should have the desire to design/develop a revolutionary shoe that changes how people play sports.

I have two years until graduation from Tech, and I can say that every day I learn something new. Georgia Tech is an amazing place where tons of brilliant people study. Because I have already graduated from Spelman, I use the skills I learned there to get through Georgia Tech. There aren't many women in my discipline, specifically black women, so that's where my inner "Spelmanite" comes in handy. I don't just use my math skills, but the confidence I learned from Spelman has helped me to get the job done.

> **My middle school years were filled with ballet, piano, choral and drama classes. Along with these rigorous fine arts came rigorous academic courses as well. It was then that I realized I was an excellent math student and writer.**

In elementary school, I did not really fit in to any specific "friend group." I stayed pretty much to myself. I had always been labeled the "super-duper smart girl" because I was two years younger than everyone else in my class. I did not have confidence in myself which caused me to try to hide how smart I was from my classmates. But in the sixth grade, my mom encouraged me to audition for a fine arts school. I was one of about 100 sixth graders chosen to attend Davidson Fine Arts Magnet school; which is one of the top public schools in Georgia.

My middle school years were filled with ballet, piano, choral and drama classes. Along with these rigorous fine arts came rigorous academic courses as well. It was then that I realized I was an excellent math student and writer. My interest in STEM began with Earth Science in the sixth grade. We had to create a homemade planetarium, and observe moon waxing and waning (which provided me a great excuse to stay up late, too). Sixth grade was also the first year I presented in the Georgia Middle School Science Fair. I didn't win, but I did get an honorable mention. Confidence in my academic abilities strengthened and science became my favorite subject for the rest of middle school.

In the 11th grade, I was selected to take AP Calculus as a senior. Math had always been a strength of mine, but I had heard that AP Calculus was the hardest class in our whole school. So, at first I was going to settle and just take mathematical computations, a much easier class. When my math teacher noticed the change in my

My Favorite Things

Christmas!

The color navy blue.

Brownie batter ice cream.

Going to the movies.

Mrs. Rebecca Harris (my fifth grade teacher); she's my favorite teacher of all time because she always encouraged me to do my best. Mrs. Harris helped me to realize I loved school, and it was there that I gained a new affinity to learn new things.

Charleston, South Carolina is my favorite vacation spot.

Polar Bears.

Education

Dual Degree
Engineering Program

B.S.,
Spelman College,
Class of 2017,
Major: Mathematics

B.S.,
Georgia Tech,
Anticipated
Class of 2019,
Major: Mechanical
Engineering

schedule for the next semester, he asked to meet with me. He was concerned that I would be taking the easy way out, and wanted me to challenge myself because I was more than capable of doing the work. The rest was history. I graduated with honors from my high school, and got a lot of scholarships to go to college.

After receiving the award for the most outstanding student in my freshman engineering and computer science courses at Spelman, I knew STEM was the place for me. Having the opportunity to study STEM at Spelman where so many great black women had studied was truly an honor that I did not recognize at the time. The foundation and support I received from the professors and my Spelman sisters really pushed me to keep going even when the classes got hard. I also had a lot of fun! The Atlanta University Center (AUC) is a great place to meet people, make friends and figure out exactly who you are. Being a product of the AUC, when I transitioned to Georgia Tech, I was much more confident in myself as an engineer who could do anything anyone else could. Many times, when you don't see other people who look like you in certain academic spaces, it makes you feel as if you don't belong. I had to keep telling myself that I belonged here, despite all the challenges I faced (and that I am still facing). Yes, it will be tough, but that doesn't mean it isn't worthwhile.

This past summer (2017), I took one of the hardest classes in the engineering curriculum. I was placed on a team and we had to build a robot (from scratch) to compete in a huge competition at the end of the summer. I had never built a robot before, so honestly, I was terrified that I would not be of value to my team. But it turned out that I ended up being one of the team leaders that helped to get a lot of the hard work done. It was really satisfying to get to the competition and make it to the fourth round! We made it to the quarterfinals! And I got an A in the class. That just goes to show that hard work definitely pays off!

I would love to help other girls do the same thing! If I can build a robot from scratch, you can too! That's how I want to pay it forward. I want to show that STEM looks like me, and STEM looks like you. We are just as capable and equipped as anyone.

Learning to build a robot definitely reaffirmed my interest in STEM. It made me more excited to pursue a career in footwear development! If I can build a robot, I can build the next amazing sports shoe to cater to athletes around the world! My mathematics and mechanical engineering degrees are giving me the tools to achieve the career of my dreams! •

Seanne P. Buckwalter

Clinical Microbiologist

Not one single day goes by that I don't use my STEM education.

In fact, because of it, I've been successful at changing careers. Let me explain. When I graduated from Saint Mary's College, I was sure I wanted to be a forest ranger in a national park, preferably somewhere out in the western states. I had traveled extensively with my parents and fell in love with the mountains. I had a set of skills and an education that I thought would eventually get me there. I knew it would be quite a journey. Attaining a job in the National Park Service would be tough since jobs there are always in high demand.

But this was not to be. Today, I'm a clinical microbiologist, employed as a research and development technologist in a mycobacteriology and mycology laboratory. I work in one of the largest and most sophisticated clinical laboratory and pathology departments, housed within a prestigious not-for-profit health care organization.

About Me

I was born in Blue Island, Illinois and have five siblings.

My favorite dessert is crème brûlée and my favorite hobby is gardening.

This department is responsible for performing more than 20 million laboratory tests annually. We have the knowledge and expertise of almost 200 consultants and 3,000 employees, all who come from a wide range of professional roles. In turn, we support patient care ranging from the patient's bedside to laboratory and pathology services.

My job is to develop, evaluate and implement new tests, methodologies or products for the mycobacteriology laboratory. I assume responsibility for improvement of existing methods or implementation of new technology. I maintain complete and accurate documentation of data generated and work performed, and I prepare data for publication and peer review as well as participate in formal presentations.

Over the last 15 years, I have developed a number of molecular assays to help identify bacteria, also known as pathogens, which cause infectious diseases. The work I do is important because we are able to diagnose diseases more quickly than conventional methods. Faster turnaround times are ideal for the patient because not only do they get a faster diagnosis, but they are prescribed the right antibiotics for whatever disease they have.

Since I work with live mycobacteria cultures, I could land in the hospital or on months of antibiotics if I don't handle them properly. That is why we have labs that have air-controlled rooms, door locks and alarms; technologists are also required to wear respirators and other personal protective equipment and have yearly testing to make sure they are competent to enter such labs.

> **Over the last 15 years, I have developed a number of molecular assays to help identify bacteria, also known as pathogens, which cause infectious diseases.**

I love my job because it is challenging, and depending on the projects I am working on, can be different day to day. A person in my job needs self-motivation, attention to detail and excellent written and verbal communication skills. They should be capable of creating a method using reference material and adapting existing knowledge and procedures to develop new methods or products.

Growing up in a house that was built on an acre of wooded land with a creek and forest preserve meant that I was never far from nature. I was fascinated by the large deciduous trees on our property, especially the oak trees. I collected leaves, acorns, nuts and seeds; I climbed the trees and loved playing in the prairie. This interest would

"The work I do is important because we are able to diagnose diseases more quickly than conventional methods."

come of great use later on in life. My first recollection of becoming interested in STEM was in my own backyard.

Being as though I was always so close to nature, I went all in on a leaf project in my freshman year of high school. I collected leaves and then wrote about the characteristics of trees. I took so much pride in the fact that the leaves I collected were all from my family's property and this really started my interest in botany. And by my sophomore year, I knew I loved chemistry and experiences of identifying unknown elements through chemical reactions.

Saint Mary's was an easy choice for college, and that's not just because it's a family tradition. It's also a liberal arts college, and as a woman not really knowing what I wanted to do, it was a good fit. Needing to declare a major, I entered Saint Mary's as a business major. While in high school, I was thinking that I might take over my dad's business after college, so a business degree made sense to me. It did not occur to me that other options existed. However, this all changed once classes started.

During my first semester, I found myself in Biology 101 with Dr. Platt and Dr. Jensen. And while all my friends struggled with the course material, I became absolutely enthralled with studying cells, botany and human evolution. I changed my major in the second semester of my freshman year to biology and didn't look back.

During the remainder of my college years, I liked most of my classes. I had a great adviser who encouraged me to enroll in a variety of different courses. I especially loved the botany, taxonomy and ecology classes. I often had semesters where I spent nine hours a week with required lab work, and it was great. With my love of oak trees and a professor whose research focus was on tree taxonomy and white oaks, I

Education

B.S.,
Saint Mary's College,
Class of 1995,
Double Major:
Biology and History

M.S.,
Idaho State University,
Class of 2002,
Biology and Ecology

soon found myself with a senior project collecting leaves and using instrumentation and statistics to compare leaves within and between tree specimens. So, there I was, collecting leaves again for class.

I took unusual jobs for work during college. They were definitely not the typical college-kid jobs. For two summers, I worked at our local water and sewer department, where I helped maintain many parts of the plant.

Upon graduation, I was hired as a biological science technician at a national park. I worked with a botanist whose focus was on tallgrass prairie restoration projects. I collected vegetation data, organized and supervised programs for the local Junior Ranger Program, participated in capture-recapture studies for Karner blue butterflies, coordinated and participated in exotic plant removal projects, conducted E.coli tests on water samples and was a member of the fire team. This job was one of my favorite jobs to date.

However, I quickly realized that if I wanted to move forward in my career, I would need additional education. I pursued a master's degree in biology at Idaho State University (ISU) the following year. At ISU, I worked on my thesis and worked part time in a laboratory. I coordinated several post-fire vegetation development studies as well as evaluated vegetational data and attained extensive experience in identifying many plant species found in the sagebrush steppe. The end product? My master's thesis about vegetation after wildfires was completed in 2002, which allowed me to continue on my career path.

In 1998, I found myself following my husband to Fort Collins, Colorado. While I felt that there were many opportunities to use my skill set and education, jobs were hard to come by. I ended up getting an internship at a water microbiology lab, which turned into a job six months later. Although I had very little experience working in a water microbiology lab, my skills as a quick learner and a biologist kicked in. I coordinated and conducted all kinds of experiments I would have not otherwise been exposed to.

Sometimes I get asked, "If you have a botany and ecology background, why are you working as a clinical microbiologist?" I find that I love to tell my story. Each time I explain how I came to where I am, I realize that I'm right where I want to be. I usually end my story by saying, "I kept learning, adapting, changing and evolving, resulting in being able to embrace different STEM careers."

Looking back, I got the, "It will be a long journey" part right, but what I didn't know was that my journey was going to lead me to a completely different career path. •

Tiffany Q. Liu

Robotics Research Scientist

*Have you ever attended a robotics competition
or been part of a robotics team in school?*

If you have, you have experienced the fun and excitement of robotics. Watching as each team's robot competes in simple floor games and seeing which robot will get more balls into a basket is exhilarating. But did you know that robots can do other things?

If one were to get technical and define any form of automata as a robot, the earliest descriptions of one appeared way back in about the third century B.C. In 1202, an inventor by the name of Ismail al-Jazari created various automata that included a drink-serving waitress and a musical robot band. Leonardo da Vinci created the mechanical knight in 1495.

Today, robots are used primarily to do tasks people find repetitive and tedious or dangerous. In 1961, the first industrial robot was installed in a factory. From there on out, aside from the Japanese endeavors in humanoid — as in human-lookalike — robots, most robots could only be found behind giant cages as they worked on assembly lines.

About Me

I was born in Beijing, China and have no brothers or sisters.

I love desserts — it's difficult to choose just one because most of the time they're really good. Currently, the desserts I can't stop thinking about are red currant cakes and lemon ice cream....Not necessarily to be had together though!

"The field of robotics is a growing field with many career opportunities."

As robotics begins to employ techniques from artificial intelligence, machine learning and cognitive science, we are starting to see robots more and more outside of those cages. Right now, we see a lot of interest in household robots and autonomous vehicles.

In the field of robotics, I am specifically interested in creating autonomous robots that can intelligently reason about the world around them with respect to the tasks they must complete. This will be especially beneficial in applications where cost-effective robots address many tasks in unstructured environments, like health care robots, household robots and search-and-rescue robots.

I was first introduced to this field when I took a college-level class during a summer while I was in high school. It was a harsh introduction because I was so frustrated and lost as I tried to make my way through that class. Despite the rough start, I was not deterred from pursuing it further. Robotics was appealing to me.

I'm glad I did not give up, because today I am a Ph.D. candidate working in the Laboratory for Perceptual Robotics (LPR) at the University of Massachusetts Amherst College of Information and Computer Sciences. As a graduate student, I am currently involved in a team project under a National Aeronautics and Space Administration (NASA) grant, designing an architecture that allows a robot to model objects, reason over these objects and create assemblies using these objects. We use something called belief space planning to allow the robot to overcome uncertainties that could come from the environment or sensor noises. With this architecture, I am interested in having the robot determine when it is necessary to perform uncertainty updates with respect to a task that needs to be completed.

Science and technology have always fascinated me. My father came to the United States to pursue his doctorate in electrical engineering when I was a 1 year old, and

he proceeded to become a software engineer, so I always had him as a role model. My father's first job after graduate school was a position at Bell Labs, and I remember loving the days when parents get to take their children to work. The machines, blinking lights and lines of code were so intriguing to me. Of course, at the time I had no clue what any of those things did or what they meant, but I was excited to be a part of that world.

I was naturally drawn to math and science classes in middle school, and I was good in those classes. In high school, I was certain I wanted to study engineering and computer science later in college. I came from a very large public high school; my graduating class was just shy of 500 students. And even though I was taking the highest level classes, I never really felt like I was learning to better my knowledge or preparing myself for life in the real world; I felt like I was learning for the sake of passing exams, and with such large class sizes, teachers could not really do much else than follow the curricula and send as many of us through to the next stage as possible.

> **In the field of robotics, I am specifically interested in creating autonomous robots that can intelligently reason about the world around them with respect to the tasks they must complete.**

My high school offered two classes in computer science. I took both. I remember how imbalanced those classes were in terms of gender. In the first class, I was one of two girls; in the second class I was the only one. It never bothered me, nor was it shocking. From a young age, I have known that these were areas of study that were scarce in female representation. I wanted to be a change in that.

So by the end of high school, I was really looking forward to having access to more personal attention from the faculty and being able to take classes that I was actually interested in taking and learning from.

When I was considering places to apply for college, at first Smith was not on my radar at all. My mother pushed me to apply since she thought I could benefit from an education at an all-women's institution. Plus, the relatively close distance to home was appealing, so I started looking into the college and what it had to offer. I liked that it was a liberal arts college but still offered engineering as a major. The class sizes were small and the curriculum was open.

My Favorite Things

"The Phantom Tollbooth" by Norton Juster.

The color Tiffany blue.

Baking and crafting.

Chinese New Year.

My sixth grade teacher, Mr. Curren — he was strict and challenged us to learn in ways that went beyond what was called for by the public school curriculum. We would play fun competitive counting games, and we even learned how to do taxes by hand. He would design weekly puzzle competitions and gave us various reading assignments that ranged from novels to reading up on current events. I have always excelled in math and science, but I came out of sixth grade being a much more confident reader and writer.

A warm getaway during the New England winter.

Clydesdale horses.

Education

B.S.,
Smith College,
Class of 2012,
Double Major:
Computer Science and
Engineering Science

M.S.,
University of
Massachusetts
Amherst, College
of Information and
Computer Sciences,
Class of 2015,
Computer Science -
Robotics

Ph.D.,
University of
Massachusetts
Amherst, College
of Information and
Computer Sciences,
Anticipated
Class of 2018,
Computer Science —
Robotics

What really sealed the deal though was everything that happened after I submitted my application. The whole process still feels surreal and magical. One day my mom came running up the stairs shouting my name and handed me a haphazardly opened envelope. By this point I had already received so many acceptance/waitlist/rejection — mostly rejection — letters that I actually preferred that she just break the news to me instead of having to read it all myself.

I took the letter from her and before I could read past the first word of "Congratulations," my mom asked, "So does this mean you got in?!" I looked at her, puzzled, before I continued to read the rest of the letter, which told me that I was receiving the Jean Picker Engineering Fellowship. That was exciting but nowhere in the letter did it say I had been accepted.

I could stay in academia and start up a lab at a research university; I could join a research lab and become a research scientist in robotics; I could also join a robotics start-up company.

So, I looked back at my mom and shrugged my shoulders. I still was not sure. But the next day, I received a letter inviting me to Discovery Weekend, which gives prospective students a chance to visit the campus and experience what life at Smith would be like. I think it took about another week before I received my official acceptance letter.

Discovery Weekend was an eye-opening experience. The weather perfectly highlighted the beautiful campus, and I met some lovely and friendly students who genuinely seemed to enjoy being there. I got to experience the housing system, which I felt fostered a stronger community bond among fellow Smithies. So when it came time to matriculate, Smith really just had all the positive checkmarks of the things I was looking for (some I did not even realize I was looking for).

The next four years certainly did not disappoint. I took challenging engineering and computer science classes, as one would expect considering my majors. But the liberal arts education also opened my learning horizons to American studies and women's history courses. Smith is also where I met some of my life-long friends. Most of who were actually people outside of my major, which I attribute to Smith's unique housing system. Growing up as an only child, this was the closest I got to having sisters.

By the end of college, I was already seriously considering a Ph.D. in robotics. One summer, I stayed at Smith to work on a research project with a computer science professor who taught my robotics seminar. The project developed into my undergraduate honors thesis. After that summer, I was fairly certain I wanted to conduct research in robotics and applied to UMass Amherst in addition to several other research universities with robotics programs.

Robotics is a growing field with many career opportunities. I could stay in academia and start up a lab at a research university; I could join a research lab and become a research scientist in robotics (and these labs can be from a private company or funded by the government); I could also join a robotics start-up company.

My career plans are rather fuzzy right now, which scares me a bit considering that until now; I have always known what my next step will be. I'm leaning toward not staying in academia, but I am not ruling it out as an option just yet. On the one hand, the thought of being able to lead my own lab and continue to have nearly free reign over my research topic is appealing. But on the other hand, after being in graduate school for so many years, having a 9 to 5 job is pretty attractive as well. •

Vanessa Eliana Rivera

Cosmetic Chemist

If you're like lots of girls, you might have an interest in makeup.

Blush, lipstick, mascara and even eyeliner can be really fun to play with. At least it was for me. From the age of 14 until today, I've always loved cosmetics. Not only did I like experimenting with different looks, I really loved reading the ingredient labels on the back of these products. I always found myself wondering what the ingredients did in the product and the science behind why it was there in the first place.

In addition, I've always been interested in the function of skin. I mean, it covers the entire body, so it's pretty important. Protecting the skin from damaging UV rays from the sun is also really vital to making sure it stays healthy. However, the only career I knew of at that time that would accommodate my love for beauty products was a beauty editor for a beauty magazine. I figured I could write about all the beauty products and skin health that I love and get to try out new ones, too. Win-win. Another reason why a beauty editor career appealed to me was that my teachers in middle school and high school said that I was a very good writer. English class was actually my favorite class growing up. I did, and still do, love to write.

About Me

I was born in Edison, New Jersey and I have one younger sister.

Turquoise is my favorite color, and I love dark chocolate.

My favorite vacation spot is anywhere tropical.

"What I like best about my work is being an inventor of beauty products."

But once I saw the connection between science and cosmetics, I decided to change my career direction and study science.

Today, I am a cosmetic chemist working at a cosmetic ingredient manufacturer and supplier. Even though my employer does not manufacture or sell cosmetics, it's my job to make cosmetics using the ingredients that my employer is supplied, all the while showcasing what the actual ingredient does in a formula. While I'm not formulating cosmetics to sell, the cosmetics I create are used as a selling tool to show cosmetic companies how well the ingredients work in a formula so that they will buy the ingredients.

A cosmetic chemist is an exciting career because it is a mix of science and art. Not only do I get to apply my knowledge of science in order to make a good formula, but I also get to express my creativity by choosing different colors and textures for my formulas.

But once I saw the connection between science and cosmetics, I decided to change my career direction and study science.

In order to be a cosmetic chemist, a strong science background is needed. Most jobs require a four-year degree in a science field. The most popular science majors are chemistry, biology, chemical engineering and microbiology. There are some schools that even offer an advanced degree in cosmetic science. However, what is most important is on-the-job training. Once you get a job in the cosmetic-science field, it is essential to learn everything you can. Challenge yourself and learn what all the ingredients do and learn how to make all different types of formulas.

A typical day involves making batches of formulas and reformulating these batches until I get a perfect formula. For example, let's say I have a project to make a volumizing mascara. I think about what ingredients I will need to make a volumizing mascara and I write out a formula. I then make the mascara in the lab. Writing the formula and then creating the project is a lot of fun, but I also really enjoy the fact that I can test these products out on myself. So, if I'm working on the volumizing mascara, I'll apply it to my eyelashes to see if I like how it goes on, and if it really does what I want it to do. I also ask my colleagues to test the mascara and provide feedback. I use these comments and reformulate the mascara, if necessary. Usually the formula is not perfect on the first try, and that is fine because it is a learning experience to figure out what works and what doesn't.

....

I'm someone who had very little interest in STEM early on. It was not until I was in college that I took an interest in science.

....

What I like best about my work is being an inventor of beauty products. I now know what the ingredients do in beauty products and how to make skincare, suncare, haircare and color cosmetics! It is very rewarding (and cool) to go into the beauty section of a store and know that I have the knowledge and skill to make almost all the beauty products on the shelves.

I'm someone who had very little interest in STEM early on. It was not until I was in college that I took an interest in science.

My first year of college, I wasn't sure what to major in, but I was leaning more toward being an English major because I had been fixated on becoming an editor for a beauty magazine. It wasn't until the beginning of my sophomore year in college when I read an online blog about a cosmetic chemist career that I realized what my calling was! A cosmetic chemist job was exactly what I wanted to do, but I never even knew that kind of job existed until I read about it in a blog that day. I quickly changed my focus to science courses.

I chose to major in biological sciences because of my interest in learning about skin biology. I also took many chemistry classes. Wellesley College has a strong science program, and my professors were very supportive in preparing me for a successful career in the science field.

My Favorite Things

Cats.

Celebrating New Year's.

Fitness and nutrition.

My high school psychology teacher because he went the extra mile to support and guide me, especially during the college application process.

"The Success Principles: How to Get from Where You Are to Where You Want to Be" by Jack Canfield.

Education

B.A.,
Wellesley College,
Class of 2009,
Major: Biological
Sciences

If you're interested in becoming a cosmetic chemist, then it's important to do well in high school and graduate from college with a four-year degree in a science field. It would be very helpful to try to get internships in the cosmetics industry while in school because experience and on-the-job training is critical and will definitely give you an edge over other job applicants.

Networking and connecting with professionals in the cosmetics industry is also a great thing to do. One great way to do this is to get involved with your local chapter of the Society of Cosmetic Chemists, where you can learn more about cosmetic science and network with those who can help you get a job in the cosmetics industry. Your first job in the cosmetics industry may not be a cosmetic chemist job.

You may have to start in a different position and work your way up the ladder as you gain more experience and on-the-job training. I actually started as a lab technician and worked in various departments until I was offered a cosmetic chemist position. Be patient, and you will eventually get there. One day you may see the beauty products you created on the store shelves! •

Veronica Falconieri

Medical Illustrator

Take a moment and breathe in deeply. Imagine what your lungs look like as you do this. Got an image in mind? If you do, it's because at some point you saw the work of a medical illustrator, perhaps on the web, in a textbook or on a poster in your doctor's office or classroom.

Organs, muscles, nerves, blood vessels — these are all subjects of medical illustration. But these topics just scratch the surface of the modern medical illustrator's work. Today, we visualize complex surgeries, intricate cell and tissue structures, critical molecules in disease and more. We use illustration, animation, graphic design and interactive technologies to tell stories through images, and make complex concepts clear.

In fact, it's pretty hard for me to just write about it. An image would be so much easier!

About Me

I hail from Massachusetts and have one sibling.

My favorite vacation spot is Cape Cod and I love dark chocolate.

My favorite part of being a medical illustrator is constantly learning new things, both scientifically and artistically. When I get a new project, there's new science to learn (what the heck is a salivary canaliculus?), and often a new challenge in visualization (how do I show the 3-D relationship of a canaliculus to a salivary gland?). By far the most important "skill" you must have as a medical illustrator is a determination to keep learning and growing, even after school. The science and the visualization technology are always progressing, and it is important to keep up.

I really like pictures, which is one of the reasons I've always been interested in science. Textbooks and science classrooms are filled with them, and that makes it a lot easier to visualize complex information. Very often, if you open a textbook and pick any page, there will be a picture on it, and you can just look at the picture and get a good understanding of the information that's written in the text.

In particular, I've always had an interest in biology, mainly because so much of the subject matter is directly applicable to us! When I learned about cell biology, I could imagine my own brain cells currently working to learn about cells. Biology is something we are always experiencing, since we are biological organisms.

. . . .

My favorite part of being a medical illustrator is constantly learning new things, both scientifically and artistically.

. . . .

Art has always been an interest of mine, though I'm not sure I'm naturally talented at it. During high school, I started to worry that I'd have to pick science or art to study in college. I wasn't sure I could find a career that could include both of my interests. Fortunately in high school, I happened to hear about the medical illustration field and once I did, I knew what I wanted to do.

I went to Smith College because its open curriculum allowed me to study science, art and anything else I was interested in (Japanese, for example), as long as I filled the requirements for one major. Though I went to college thinking that it would just be a way to reach graduate school in medical illustration, Smith ended up being much more than that. I was able to get hands-on biology research experience, which has given me a unique competitive edge as a medical illustrator. It also let me know that I did not want to be in lab science for the rest of my life, which helped me rule out a graduate-research degree and affirmed my plan for a professional master's degree.

"By far the most important 'skill' you must have as a medical illustrator is a determination to keep learning and growing, even after school."

My Favorite Things

"The Fifth Season" by N.K. Jemisin.

The color purple.

Weightlifting.

Thanksgiving.

Mrs. Dunbar, my high school art teacher, who inspired me to be bold.

Any friendly dog.

Some medical illustrators come from a strong art background. For example, they attend art school, or major in art, and then fill in science classes along the way to prepare for a master's program in medical illustration. Others, like myself, come from a science-focused background, majoring in science in college and either minoring in art or developing their portfolio independently to prepare for graduate school. I decided to minor in Studio Art, which included developing a portfolio.

Many medical illustrators earn a master's degree at one of four certified graduate programs in North America. You can learn more about these at the Association of Medical Illustrator's website, www.AMI.org. There are also bachelor's programs in scientific illustration, and these can prepare someone for a master's program or the vast world of science visuals outside the medical niche. Though it is a less structured and in many ways more difficult route, some illustrators pave their own way, training themselves independently for medical illustration after already having started a career in science or art.

For graduate school, I decided to attend Johns Hopkins University School of Medicine's Medical and Biological Illustration program. The Hopkins program strongly emphasizes a solid foundation in traditional art techniques. As a stronger scientist than artist, I knew my skills would be an easier fit at some of the other programs. However, I wanted to work toward becoming a better artist, knowing it would help me in my future career.

$\mathcal{E}ducation$

B.A.,
Smith College,
Class of 2012,
Major: Biological
Sciences,
Minor: Studio Art

M.A.,
**Johns Hopkins
University School of
Medicine,**
Class of 2014,
Medical and Biological
Illustration

Certified Medical
Illustrator (CMI), Board
of Certification of
Medical Illustrators
(BCMI), 2017

I was expecting a challenge, but I didn't know just how difficult graduate school would be. I remember spending most of my first year self-consciously comparing my artwork to my peers'. The faculty in the program had me re-draw my planning sketches multiple times whereas my more artistically-inclined classmates would have only minor corrections. This could have become really overwhelming if I'd let it, but I refused to quit. I felt overwhelmed at times, but I kept working at it, because I knew I was growing as an artist. My second year was a bit less nerve-wracking, since I had caught up on my art skills, and I could apply those skills to more scientifically-complex projects.

At my current job, I work with researchers to visually analyze 3-D structural data as well as communicate their research through images and animations in presentations and papers published in journals. My co-workers are almost all Ph.D.-level scientists, with deep knowledge of biology, protein structures, microscopy and computational image processing. My STEM education, particularly my undergraduate experience, helps me speak their language and translate their work for visual storytelling.

The best moments for me are when I collaborate with one of my co-workers on a visual, and the way I have presented it causes them to realize something about their own data that they had missed before. In the future, I hope to continue collaborating closely with scientists as well as also grow my independent medical illustration and animation company, Falconieri Visuals. My company gives me an opportunity to work with a range of clients, design visuals for different audiences and learn about a greater variety of subject matter. •

Xiaotong "Phoebe" Jiang

Biostatistician

*Like many 12 year olds, I did not know what I wanted to do
when I entered middle school.*

I was born and raised in China where the curriculum involved nine subjects, and the coursework was heavy every day. At that time, I was struggling with fitting in the new environment and keeping my grades up. I did not have time to think about my future, or rather, I had no idea what to think about my future.

However, there was one thing I was sure about: mathematics and logic thinking. I had been fascinated by puzzles and logic problems since elementary school. Every time a puzzle was solved, I felt unbelievably satisfied and accomplished. I was never a child fond of reading, partially because I cannot sit quietly for that long and partially because I would rather go out and watch ants move candy. Puzzles, somehow, have this special power to help me concentrate for a long time before I figure them out.

I had probably the best math teacher in middle school. He was clear when explaining problems and always encouraged new solutions and thoughts. One day, he told me he was about to teach a special class designed for students interested in participating in the International Math

About Me

I was born in Qingdao, China and have no siblings.

My favorite colors are lilac and cyan and my favorite holiday is Chinese New Year!

Curling, swimming and scuba diving top my list of pastimes.

And although it is mentioned in the main text, I want to add my current Ph.D. adviser; Dr. Michael Kosorok to the list of outstanding teachers. He is one of the smartest people I know, but he is humble and gives very good advice, both professional and personal. Plus, he likes blackberries and thinks eating the seeds is a challenge.

"The information hidden in the data sets provides answers to many important health-related problems that could not be solved otherwise, and helps me to learn more about medicine and diseases from a mathematical and analytical point of view."

Olympiad (IMO), an annual exam for precollegiate students, covering difficult math problems beyond the level taught at school. Students had to take a test before taking the class. In order to get in, I bought a 500-page book of exercises. There were many times when I could not find a solution, and it was frustrating. Thankfully, failure did not discourage me. Instead, I focused on how to approach the problem.

After finishing the book in one month, I was fortunate enough to be one of the four girls who passed the test that year. The IMO class was mind-blowing. They asked harder questions in the area I was familiar with, and covered new materials such as combinatorics and probability, which was very advanced for middle schoolers. I often had to change my way of thinking, and it made me realize how little I knew in this deep ocean of mathematics. I became very eager to learn during my math class as well as learn about the application of math in other science classes. In the end, my score placed me in the top 1,000 in my province. It is

nothing worth mentioning now, but it meant a lot to the 15-year-old me at that time. Contrary to many young girls who claim that math is not their thing, I told myself, "Hey, you are good at this!"

Then it was time for me to go to high school. After the first year, students in China need to pick between the science path (physics, chemistry, biology) and the liberal arts path (history, geography, politics). Still a young girl who was not a big fan of reading pages and pages of books, I went with the science path because I found myself to be more of a learning-by-doing person. By doing practice problems, I learned concepts and theorems by heart. Looking back, I now realize that I started to head toward a STEM career at that time.

Another pivotal point in my life happened in high school: I decided to study abroad. I wanted to combine my favorite subjects, math and English language, and become better at both, which led me to the idea of studying mathematics in the United States. The application process was not easy for me because I was in another country with a different education system. My parents helped me with mailing and printing documents, but they could not help me choose schools and majors; it was a conversation between me and myself.

> **I was never a child fond of reading, partially because I cannot sit quietly for that long and partially because I would rather go out and watch ants move candy. Puzzles, somehow, have this special power to help me concentrate for a long time before I figure them out.**

Coming from a co-ed public high school of 3,000 students, I was tired of waiting in line to ask a teacher a question, a teacher who might not even know my name. I had always been longing for the closeness in small schools. After a long time of going back and forth, I accepted admission from Sweet Briar College (SBC).

Sweet Briar is a small liberal arts college located in a rural town at the foothills of the Blue Ridge Mountains in Virginia. During my time at SBC, I joined a community service club, co-founded a Chinese club, worked for the library and served as a tour guide at the Admissions Office for four years. I got to learn riding, fencing and yoga as well as celebrate traditional American festivals at friends' houses. As for my major, it was an easy decision, mathematics. Fortunately, all of the five math professors at Sweet

My Favorite Things

"The Sherlock Holmes" series by Sir Arthur Conan Doyle.

Matcha mille crepe cake.

Vacationing in Hawaii.

Definitely dogs.

$\mathcal{E}$ducation

B.A.,
Sweet Briar College,
Class of 2014,
Major: Mathematics

Ph.D.,
University of North
Carolina at Chapel
Hill,
Anticipated
Class of 2019,
Biostatistics

Briar were extremely caring, helpful and excellent in mentoring. There were always one-to-one meetings with faculty. Even now, four years after graduation, I still miss that homey environment where professors treat students as their kids and their doors are always open. This kind of closeness is exactly what I wanted.

Starting from the first summer after my freshman year, I worked on math projects with my professors. At first, I did not expect I would like the projects because I had no experience in researching, and nobody in my family has research experience. I discussed my work with students and faculty from partnering universities every week. Through these opportunities, I experienced the differences between regular classes and research, and I began to see the broader mathematical context for many of the topics I was pursuing.

During my busy college life, I read a few books on Big Data and got to talk with professional biostatisticians to learn more about their work. These resources piqued my curiosity and helped me eventually pursue biostatistics, a field that requires strong mathematical skills and passion for human health, both of which I have.

Biostatistics is the application of statistics (the science of data) in public health, medicine, biology and other health-related fields. Using simulation, modeling and statistical learning methods, biostatisticians are able to find structure in data and answer health questions in either the general population or personalized medicine. You may wonder if it is all about numbers and math. Not really. Biostatistics is more about the medical application: understanding what the numbers imply, finding relationships among risk factors and diseases and being involved in health-related decision making. The math part comes in theories, the building blocks of all analyses that biostatisticians (Ph.Ds in particular) need to know.

There was a lot that I wanted to learn about biostatistics, so by the end of my junior year, I applied to graduate programs.

The application for graduate school was somewhat easier than the application for undergraduate. I knew clearly what program to apply to and I was able to visit several departments in person. When it was time to decide which offer to take, the choice was apparent after several campus visits.

I joined the biostatistics department at UNC-Chapel Hill in 2014, enrolling in its Ph.D. program, and anticipate graduating in 2019 with a dissertation topic in machine learning. This program has afforded me the opportunity to work with many groups of brilliant professors and doctors on topics ranging from diabetes to

cystic fibrosis. It suits me well and offers me what I look for in a graduate program: demanding but comprehensive coursework, interdisciplinary research and many collaboration opportunities. Graduate school is an interesting place: it gives students unbelievably complicated work, yet nobody complains (at least explicitly), and almost all succeed eventually.

When I graduate, I know I will have many career opportunities. Biostatisticians are hired at various companies and work alongside a wide range of professionals, such as researchers, physicians and even software developers. Our work could be consulting in study design, data management, data mining, etc. Companies that hire biostatisticians include, but are not limited to, pharmaceutical companies, CROs (contract research organizations), hospitals, schools and research institutions, government, technology and software companies as well as banks and financial institutions.

My career goal in the long run is to go into industry and apply my graduate studies in biology and medicine as a successful biostatistician. Contributing to the improvement of human health care has always been meaningful to me; I like to help other people and play an indispensable part in the development of science and society. The information hidden in the data sets provides answers to many important health-related problems that could not be solved otherwise, and helps me to learn more about medicine and diseases from a mathematical and analytical point of view. •

Chapter Three

Sneak Peek Into Book Two

Introduction

With so many STEM women wanting to share their career stories, it was necessary to plan for a Book Two!

In Diane's journey to publish "Her STEM Career: Adventures of 51 Remarkable STEM Women," she's thrilled to report that she has met many remarkable STEM women interested in sharing their stories. These women are part of a global community that actively supports other STEM women while inspiring the next generation of female scientists, technologists, engineers and mathematicians.

Unfortunately, due to word count, Diane was not able to include all of them in this book. Nor was she able to include other information she initially envisioned — testimonials about the academic institutions where these women earned their undergraduate degrees as well as vintage college photographs of STEM women.

Having graduated from a women's college, Diane has firsthand experience on the effectiveness of single-sex learning environments. Women's colleges have always played an important role in the education of STEM women. This is why Diane encourages college-bound high school girls to investigate this effective educational option.

She also wanted to include vintage photographs of college STEM women. Vintage photographs remind us of the long-standing interest women have had in studying STEM subjects. In Book Two, expect to see many more vintage photographs — from the late 1800s to the 1970s.

Book Two, like Book One, will contain stories of STEM women. In addition to these stories, there will be new content, including alumnae shout-outs to undergraduate alma maters, vintage photographs of college STEM women and maybe even a surprise or two!

This chapter is all about getting a sneak peek into Book Two. Enjoy!

To be notified when Book Two is available, feel free to email Diane Propsner directly: HerSTEMCareer@gmail.com

The Remarkable STEM Women You'll Meet

Alisa Stratulat, Ph.D.

Materials Science Researcher

Smith College, Class of 2009
Engineering Science Major

Amber Todd, Ph.D.

Science/Medical Education Researcher

Cottey College, Class of 2003,
AS Degree

Mount Holyoke College, Class of 2005
Biochemistry Major

Candice M. Hughes, Ph.D., MBA

Science Entrepreneur

Mount Holyoke College, Class of 1986
Biology Major

Carley Przystac

Civil Engineer

Mount Holyoke College, Class of 2015
Environmental Studies Major

Darcy Dwyer, M.Sc.

Data Scientist

Smith College, Class of 2011
Engineering Science Major

Dee Mudzingwa, M.Sc.

Hazardous Materials Manager

Hollins University, Class of 2007
Chemistry and Spanish Major

Elizabeth Schlieper

Java Developer

Meredith College, Class of 2014
Computer Science Major

Felicia Harrsch

Clinical Pharmacist

Mount Holyoke College, Class of 2014
Neuroscience & Behavior Major

Flynn Vickowski

Zoo Curator

Mount Holyoke College, Class of 2014
Neuroscience & Behavior and Spanish Major

Jasmine Everett

Secondary Mathematics Teacher

Bennett College, Class of 2016
Mathematics Major

Jodie Pope Morrison

Science Executive

Mount Holyoke College, Class of 1997
Neuroscience & Behavior Major

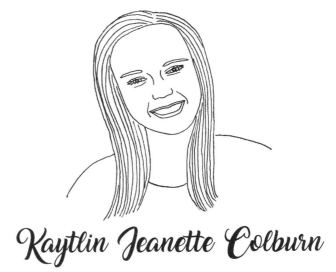

Kaytlin Jeanette Colburn

Geographic Information Systems Developer

Sweet Briar College , Class of 2011
Environmental Science Major

Madeline Shortt

Software Engineer

Mount Holyoke College, Class of 2015
Physics and Computer Science Major

Naomi A. Rose, Ph.D.

Marine Mammal Biologist/Advocate

Mount Holyoke College, Class of 1984
Biology and French Major

Rebecca Neiberg, M.S.

Senior Biostatistician

Salem College, Class of 1999
Biology and Mathematics Majors

Stacie Brenner, M.S.

DNA Forensic Scientist

Cedar Crest College, Class of 2008
Biology Major

Sylvia Gonsahn-Bollie, M.D.

Physician: Obesity Medicine

Wesleyan College, Class of 2006
Biology Major

Victoria Rosborough

Photonics Engineer

Mary Baldwin College for Women, Class of 2012
Physics Major

Alumnae Shout-Outs

Caitlyn Holland

Meredith College

Attending an all-women's college was probably the best decision I ever made. The atmosphere at a women's college is such an inspiring place to be, especially now. Going to Meredith College really shaped me into the person I am today. All the professors, faculty and staff truly believe in their students and in empowering women. They make it their mission to help students become stronger and to accomplish things that they might have thought impossible.

My faculty adviser, Dr. Hontz, is a prime example of a professor who goes out of her way to help her students. Dr. Hontz worked with me to plan out my academic career at Meredith and spent hours with me when I decided to add in a double major my junior year. She put me in contact with people who had internships open for the summer, and wrote every recommendation letter that I ever needed. My summer internship led to me getting a full-time job with the same company after I graduated. Dr. Hontz and I still have lunch together even after I graduated, just to catch up. She still gives me advice on career advancements and on life in general. I believe that the personal connection you develop with professors makes Meredith very unique and gives students the opportunity to learn more outside of the classroom as well.

Since the professors truly care about each student, they are really willing to work with you if you are having trouble in a class and need extra help, and this isn't just unique to the math department.

During my time at Meredith, I also had the opportunity to study abroad in Costa Rica and do my undergraduate research there. While studying abroad, I learned how to be more self-sufficient and independent. These life skills are not something you can learn in a classroom, but they are necessary in order to succeed in life. Meredith has numerous opportunities like this for students to grow as strong, independent women.

The final experience I would like to share about Meredith is the leadership development skills that I received there. When I attended Meredith, I was involved in a lot of organizations on campus early on. As my time at Meredith continued on, I developed more confidence in myself as a leader on campus, and decided to run for Student Government President. I won the election at the end of my junior year and I was the Student Government President my senior year. I accomplished a lot in this role and it felt rewarding to be able to give back to the school that had given me so much.

I could list countless reasons why Meredith is a great place for young women to grow, but I will leave you with these three points. Between the supportive faculty, the opportunities to become more independent and the leadership development opportunities, Meredith succeeds in its mission to empower women.

I will forever be grateful to Meredith for all the wonderful experiences I had there and for all the life skills that I learned. Since I love the college so much, I continue to serve on our young alumnae board to help raise money for the college and host events for alumnae to come back and visit campus.

Jenn Bonetti

Cedar Crest College

Cedar Crest College was so supportive of my STEM goals, and I truly do not feel that I would be where I am today without that support. It is well known for its science programs, and the school really invests in the futures of its students. From attending and presenting at professional conferences to performing undergraduate research, Cedar Crest went above and beyond in ensuring that its students were prepared for the field they would be entering. I personally presented several times at regional meetings and once at a national conference. These opportunities were integral in developing my public-speaking skills and my ability to effectively communicate scientific principles to a broader audience, capabilities whose utility in a professional scientific environment, particularly forensics, cannot be overstated.

Additionally, Cedar Crest placed a large emphasis on leadership. The small, all-women's college atmosphere made me very comfortable seeking out leadership positions in several science clubs, opportunities that I'm not sure I would have had or felt as comfortable with at a larger university. By serving on the executive boards of these organizations, I gained valuable experience in leadership, time and project management and teamwork that directly translated to skills required to be successful in my career. Our Forensic Science Student Organization consistently hosted fundraising events that enabled us to pay for students to attend conferences at no cost. These events required a great deal of planning and outreach to be successful. In addition, one of our large projects as the executive board of the Chemistry Club was working to start a chapter of a national Chemistry Honor Society at our college. This undertaking was more complicated than we initially expected, but we worked together to figure out the steps required and in the end, we were successful. In fact, the chapter is still active today!

Cedar Crest's program, small but mighty, is well known and has an excellent reputation in many forensic circles. Whenever I meet someone who has had any interaction with a Cedar Crest graduate in a professional setting, I am always told how impressed they are with the education that alumnae have received and the work ethic that comes along with it. I am very proud to be a Cedar Crest graduate and would make the same school choice in a heartbeat if given the option.

Marin Kress

Smith College

I decided upon Smith College because I liked the idea that, in addition to the traditional benefits of a small liberal arts college, it would be an environment totally supportive of women pursuing any academic subject they wanted.

There would also be no worries about "making boys look bad" in class because you knew the answer and they didn't; gender would be a nonissue. I had lots of guy friends in high school, but I thought it would be interesting to experience an environment where the classroom would be strictly women. I went to a large public middle school and a large public high school, and sometimes it seemed like people were just interested in being cool or goofing off in class, and the ones who were loudest about it were certain types of "cool guys." At Smith, that wasn't the case. Another benefit of Smith was that all the leadership roles were held by women, in student government, sports, activity groups, etc.

Also, and I remember this very clearly, I liked the cartoons they included in their mailings, and the fact that they extended their application deadline. After that deadline extension, I thought, "Hah, they understand people like me!"

Another selling point about Smith was that they had no required classes, unlike other schools which have "general education" or "distribution" requirements where you might spend one or two years taking classes that don't interest you. At Smith, you could take a variety of classes, but it was all up to you. It seemed very freeing to focus entirely on my interests. That freedom made me think that the students would be mature and interesting, and they were!

I noticed there is a different atmosphere when a classroom is all women. I can't quite define what the difference is, but it seemed to be more supportive, less about being the loudest or the funniest. I'm so glad I attended Smith College; I would not be the scientist I am today without it.

Sarah Schultz

Barnard College

My decision to attend Barnard for undergrad came as a stroke of luck. Hearing about their rigorous academics, I applied to Barnard on a whim, not sure if I wanted to go to a college attended solely by women. However, once I received the acceptance from Barnard, I decided to visit the campus to see if it was a good fit. To say I fell in love with Barnard when I visited would be an understatement. I found the campus location in New York City's Morningside Heights neighborhood and the opportunities, both academic and professional, available to me incredibly attractive. I remember sending in my deposit as soon as I got home.

I would not realize the value of attending a women's college until I arrived on campus to begin school. To be honest, I was still wary of attending in the months leading up to my first day. Barnard's unique status compared to other women's colleges helped to put my mind at ease. At Barnard, students are able to attend classes, join clubs, and even eat in the dining halls of Columbia University, located across Broadway. Barnard students take advantage of this opportunity as much or as little as they want. As someone who attended a co-ed high school, I appreciated the opportunity to choose the composition of the class I wanted to take. At first, I was intimidated at the prospect of taking classes with only female students. But after attending a seminar solely among Barnard students, I realized how different the dynamic was.

In my high school classes, I felt out of place. I always wanted to speak my mind, but my male peers talked over me or spoke down to me. In my Barnard seminar, my professor encouraged us to give our opinions about the material. It was the first time that I used my experiences to interpret the material and felt that my opinions were valid.

Vintage College Photographs of STEM Women

Cedar Crest College
Allentown, Pennsylvania

Photo Credit: Cedar Crest College

From its inception in 1867, science has been a part of the curriculum at Cedar Crest College. This photo shows students in the lab during the 1950s. Today, Cedar Crest offers a number of STEM degrees, from biology and forensic science to genetic engineering and nuclear medicine technology.

Mount Holyoke College
South Hadley, Massachusetts

Photo Credit: Mount Holyoke College Archives and Special Collections

This photo shows a zoology laboratory at Mount Holyoke College circa 1890. Renowned zoologist and instructor, Cornelia Clapp, far right, in her laboratory at Mount Holyoke College with students. At a time when few women pursued science at all, Clapp was devoted to it. She studied chick embryology at MIT and earthworms at Williams College. Clapp was one of the first women to earn a Ph.D. from an American university. In fact, she earned two: the first from Syracuse University in 1889, and her second from the University of Chicago in 1896. She was the first woman given a research position at the Woods Hole Marine Biological Laboratory and became its first female trustee. Clapp was instrumental in facilitating Mount Holyoke's transition from seminary to college. In 1923, Clapp Laboratory was named in her honor.

Wesleyan College
Macon, Georgia

Photo Credit: Wesleyan College

When Newtonian physics reigned supreme, photography was in its infancy and radio astronomy was decades in the future, Wesleyan students of 1890 studied the stars from the downtown campus. That year marked one of the most significant turning points in the history of astronomy with the publication of the Draper Catalogue of Stellar Spectra. This radical publication contained spectroscopic classifications for 10,351 stars and provided essential data for scientists and scholars well into the 20th century.

Index

Made in the USA
Columbia, SC
09 October 2018